D0540881

Transactions
of the
Royal
Historical
Society

SIXTH SERIES

XXVI

CAMBRIDGE
UNIVERSITY PRESS

Published by the Press Syndicate of the University of Cambridge
University Printing House, Shaftesbury Road, Cambridge CB2 8BS,
United Kingdom
1 Liberty Plaza, Floor 20, New York, NY 10006, USA
477 Williamstown Road, Port Melbourne, VIC 3207, Australia
C/Orense, 4, Planta 13, 28020 Madrid, Spain
Lower Ground Floor, Nautica Building, The Water Club,
Beach Road, Granger Bay, 8005 Cape Town, South Africa

First published 2016

A catalogue record for this book is available from the British Library

ISBN 9781107192478 hardback

SUBSCRIPTIONS. The serial publications of the Royal Historical Society, *Royal Historical Society Transactions* (ISSN 0080–4401) and Camden Fifth Series (ISSN 0960–1163) volumes, may be purchased together on annual subscription. The 2016 subscription price, which includes print and electronic access (but not VAT), is £176 (US $294 in the USA, Canada, and Mexico) and includes Camden Fifth Series, volumes 49, 50 and 51 and Transactions Sixth Series, volume 26 (published in December). The electronic-only price available to institutional subscribers is £148 (US $247 in the USA, Canada, and Mexico). Japanese prices are available from Kinokuniya Company Ltd, P.O. Box 55, Chitose, Tokyo 156, Japan. EU subscribers (outside the UK) who are not registered for VAT should add VAT at their country's rate. VAT registered subscribers should provide their VAT registration number. Prices include delivery by air.

Subscription orders, which must be accompanied by payment, may be sent to a bookseller, subscription agent, or direct to the publisher: Cambridge University Press, University Printing House, Shaftesbury Road, Cambridge CB2 8BS, UK; or in the USA, Canada, and Mexico: Cambridge University Press, Journals Fulfillment Department, 1 Liberty Plaza, Floor 20, New York, NY 10006, USA.

SINGLE VOLUMES AND BACK VOLUMES. A list of Royal Historical Society volumes available from Cambridge University Press may be obtained from the Humanities Marketing Department at the address above.

Printed in the UK by Bell & Bain Ltd, Glasgow

CONTENTS

Transactions of the RHS 26 (2016), pp. 1–23 © Royal Historical Society 2016
doi:10.1017/S0080440116000025

TRANSACTIONS OF THE

ROYAL HISTORICAL SOCIETY

PRESIDENTIAL ADDRESS

By Peter Mandler

EDUCATING THE NATION: III. SOCIAL MOBILITY*

READ 27 NOVEMBER 2015

ABSTRACT. This address asks how much has education contributed to social mobility in post-war Britain and considers other factors that may have contributed as much or more: labour-market opportunities, trends in income inequality, gender differences and 'compositional effects' deriving from the shape of the occupational hierarchy. Even where these other factors proved much more powerful – especially labour-market opportunities and compositional effects – democratic discourse both among politicians and among the electorate remained fixated on educational opportunities and outcomes, especially after the decline of the Croslandite critique of 'meritocracy'. That fixation has if anything been reinforced by the apparent end to a 'golden age' of absolute upward mobility for large sections of the population, not necessarily because education is an effective antidote but because the alternative political solutions are so unpalatable both to politicians and to voters.

In my first two addresses, I sought to explain the causes, extent and pace of expanding educational opportunity in Britain since the Second World War, in secondary and higher education.[1] I argued that expansion was powered not by expert opinion or technocratic demands or even by political calculation, but rather by the spread of a democratic political discourse which held that all citizens deserved 'the best' education much as they deserved the best health care in a welfare state based on universal (or the maximum possible) provision; and that the power of this discourse has

---

* I hope it will be clear that I could not have written this paper without drawing deeply on the work not only of historians, but also of sociologists and economists. For helping me tackle the social-science literature, I have to thank Alice Sullivan and especially Anna Vignoles, who needless to say bear no responsibility for my very partial understanding. I owe a continuing debt to Jon Lawrence, not least for a co-taught M.Phil. course on class and social mobility that has brought me more or less up-to-speed on the historical literature, and to Deborah Cohen, who gave this paper, as she did its predecessors, the benefit of her scrupulous and generous eye.

[1] 'Educating the Nation: I. Schools', *Transactions of the Royal Historical Society*, sixth series, 24 (2014), 5–28; 'Educating the Nation: II. Universities', *Transactions of the Royal Historical Society*, sixth series, 25 (2015), 1–26.

not yet diminished even as expectations of the welfare state have in other respects shrivelled. In this address, I turn from the causes of expansion to its effects, and in particular to the politically charged questions of who benefits from educational opportunity and what effect (if any) it has on social mobility, which has become one of the shibboleths that keeps popular (and political) faith in education alive.

There is a folk wisdom about the history of education and social mobility over the last fifty or sixty years that goes something like this. First, there was a 'golden age of social mobility' in the decades after the Second World War, in which the grammar school played the leading role, promoting through the practice of meritocracy great swathes of bright working-class boys (the folk wisdom assumes they were boys) into the salariat, and indeed into the elite. Then in the 1970s and 1980s something happened to bring this golden age to a close – it might have been the famous 'destruction of grammar schools' or it might have been stuttering economic growth or it might have been growing inequality (depending on your political views). But then expansion of higher education in the 1990s and noughties seemed to have opened up again avenues of opportunity. Finally, according to this folk wisdom, they may now be threatened again with closure, either by the over-supply of graduates or by the rising cost of education to the consumer. Poor Britain languishes at the bottom of the international league table for social mobility, where it will stay until some new educational panacea is devised to address its sorry state.

Now nearly every aspect of that fable is either demonstrably false or rests upon a conceptual confusion – particularly the assumption that education and social mobility are pretty nearly synonymous. To explain why this story is false and why people cling to it nonetheless will be the twin goals of my argument. In order to start telling an alternative story, however, I have to begin with some pretty forbidding technical issues, in order to clarify what social mobility means and what changes in economy, society and politics affect it.

I

The study of social mobility took off in a serious way in the 1950s and for a long time remained the province of sociologists, in this country led by a group at Oxford sometimes known as the Nuffield School.[2] The Nuffield School defined social mobility as movement between occupational categories across generations, using John Goldthorpe's famous seven-class schema as the basis for these occupational categories. Because movements

---

[2] A good summation of how the study of social mobility developed up to the Nuffield School is provided by a key text of that school, John H. Goldthorpe (with Catriona Llewellyn and Clive Payne), *Social Mobility and Class Structure in Modern Britain* (Oxford, 1980), esp. 17–29.

between contiguous classes have limited descriptive or explanatory value, sociologists tend to simplify the schema into three classes – a salariat (classes I and II), a working class (classes VI and VII, and sometimes V as well), and a rather mixed bag of intermediate classes in between. To measure movement between these three 'big' classes, sociologists employ a variety of datasets – large, representative samples they collect themselves (notably the 1949 survey led by David Glass and the 1972 Oxford Mobility Study led by A. H. Halsey); [3] representative samples from the 1946, 1958, 1970 and 2000 birth-cohort studies; and representative samples taken from other social surveys that were conducted for other purposes but which provide the requisite occupational and educational data, such as the British Election Surveys, the Labour Force Surveys and the British Household Panel Surveys and their successors. The grouping of specific occupations within these classes is regularly updated to ensure that new occupations are accommodated and changes in income and status registered. All in all, the sociologists hold that this seven-class (and the simplified three-class) hierarchy continues to work well as a proxy not only for the income hierarchy but also for the status hierarchy and for differences in autonomy and job security which neither income nor status can fully measure. Since the 1990s, however, the economists have challenged this sociological monopoly.[4] The economists prefer to measure social mobility instead by intergenerational movement between income deciles (or, using their own simplifications, quartiles or quintiles). On the whole, I will be using the sociologists' definitions and measures, because for most of the period they form the bulk of the evidence at hand; but for the most recent period, I will be comparing them to the different findings of the economists.

To make matters worse, sociologists make a clear distinction between two quite distinct types of social mobility – absolute and relative. Absolute social mobility is perhaps the common-sense understanding; it assesses raw movements up and down the social scale, how many and who are going up or down, from which class ('outflow') and into which class ('inflow'). In a post-war world characterised by greater affluence and generally progressive upskilling, absolute social mobility is dominated by upward mobility out of the working class and into the intermediate classes and the salariat. Relative social mobility is, in contrast, a measure of equality. It assesses deviations from 'perfect' equality of opportunity,

[3] *Social Mobility in Britain*, ed. D. V. Glass (1954); A. H. Halsey, A. F. Heath and J. M. Ridge, *Origins and Destinations: Family, Class, and Education in Modern Britain* (Oxford, 1980).

[4] On the 'entry of the economists', as seen by the Nuffield School, see John H. Goldthorpe, 'Understanding – and Misunderstanding – Social Mobility in Britain: The Entry of the Economists, the Confusion of Politicians and the Limits of Educational Policy', *Journal of Social Policy*, 42 (2013), 431–50.

in which every child born into any one class has an equal chance of ending up in any other class. Relative social mobility can tell you how unequal a society is and whether it is getting more or less equal. In these terms, downward mobility from the salariat is just as important as upward mobility from the working class – both are necessary to achieve 'equality of opportunity'. In what follows, I pay much more attention to absolute than to relative mobility, principally because it is what both people who experience mobility and politicians who sponsor it are most aware of and care most about. Not only do people in lower classes not notice so much when they are joined by downwardly mobile exiles from the upper classes, they do not care about them so much either – not as much as they care about their own opportunities for upward mobility. Politicians are surely right to regard those priorities. When people speak about 'equality of opportunity', they almost always mean equal chances to rise, not equal chances to fall. While sociologists frequently squeal that politicians are not paying attention to the sociologists' definition of social mobility, they might pay more attention themselves to the perfectly good reasons why politicians (and their constituents) prefer definitions of their own.

Finally, the sociologists are rightly concerned to fathom the extremely arcane interactions between education and social mobility, which are not nearly as straightforward as they appear. Schematically these interactions can be figured in terms of the OED triangle, a schema representing the relationship between class origins, education and class destinations. If social mobility were simply a function of education, as the folk wisdom so often has it, then the triangle would not be a triangle but a straight line, with E playing a straightforward mediating role between O and D. But it is not. At least three interactions have to be considered. First, how strong is the association between O and E? If strong, then education is simply reproducing social class, and inhibiting rather than promoting social mobility. Second, how strong is the association between E and D? If strong, then education may be performing a meritocratic function in guiding high educational achievers to the best jobs. But if OE and ED are both strong, then the independent role of education is reduced: only advantaged children are getting the educational qualifications that allow them to be guided into the best jobs, employers may only be using educational qualifications as proxies for class, and social mobility may not be promoted. For education to promote social mobility, you need weak OE association *and* strong ED association. But, to complicate matters further, even in cases of weak OE association and strong ED association, there is still plenty of room for a direct OD association that bypasses education altogether. That is, where you end up in the class structure may still have more to do with your class origins than your educational attainment – if, for example, employers use selection criteria that are more to do with your class than your education, or if your class gives you other benefits in job attainment regardless of education, or if educational qualifications just do not matter for the job at hand. As we will see – disappointingly, perhaps, for an educator such as myself – education rarely plays as much of a role in social mobility as we like to think.

As I did last time, I will slice the now seventy post-war years into three sections. First, the 'golden age of social mobility' from the late 1940s to the early 1970s; then the troubled period between the early 1970s and the early 1990s; and finally the last twenty years, not so troubled (at least to 2008) but plagued with conflicting verdicts from the sociologists and economists. For each period, I will both try to characterise the extent and nature of social mobility and the role education did or did not play, *and* try to say something about how far these different mobility regimes were actually appreciated in contemporary discourse: that is, what role they played in shaping the democratic discourse of education and the course of educational expansion.

II

First, the golden age of social mobility: there seems little question that the period from the late 1940s to the early 1970s *was* a golden age of social mobility, during which large proportions of the population experienced upward mobility from their class of birth, and the traditionally pyramid-shaped social structure began to turn into a diamond or an hourglass (itself a topic for debate).[5] In fact, despite its reputation as a particularly closed class society, even pre-war Britain had been more fluid than most other European countries, in large part because it had long before made its transition from an agricultural to an urban and industrial economy.[6] The true caste societies were those – which still included Germany, France and Italy in the early twentieth century – that retained a large peasantry, impervious to social mobility. In the post-war period, while these societies urbanised and became more mobile, Britain's long-urban society experienced a different kind of mobility, out of the working class and into the intermediate and salariat classes. Most strikingly, while fewer than 20 per cent of men entering the labour market just before the Second World War could be found in the salariat, by the 1970s over 40 per cent

[5] There is a vigorous debate principally among economists about 'hollowing out' or 'job polarisation' that might produce the hourglass shape; sociologists often still focus on the smallness of the elite and the diversity of the classes beneath them that models a diamond shape.
[6] D. V. Glass, 'Introduction', in *Social Mobility*, ed. Glass, 20–1; Jon O. Jonsson, Colin Mills and Walter Müller, 'A Half Century of Increasing Educational Openness? Social Class, Gender and Educational Attainment in Sweden, Germany and Britain', in *Can Education Be Equalized? The Swedish Case in Comparative Perspective*, ed. Robert Erikson and Jan O. Jonsson (Boulder, CO, 1996), 183–206.

of men could be found there, and by the 1970s men entering the labour market were equally likely to be found in the salariat and the working class. A similar trend applies to women, though with less movement into the salariat and more movement into the intermediate classes, reflecting women's over-representation in routine non-manual work in the retail and office sectors.[7] All in all, Britain is rapidly becoming in this period a less manual society and therefore a more upwardly mobile society – about half of all labour market entrants in the 1950s and 1960s end up in a higher class than their parents.[8]

This does not mean it is becoming a more equal or even a more meritocratic society. There is, as the sociologists put it nicely, more 'room at the top' – room for everyone. So salariat parents may be getting better at preserving their children's status – better at averting downward mobility – at the same time as working-class parents are getting better at promoting their children's status – better at promoting upward mobility. Relative mobility would remain static – which is exactly what the Nuffield School contends for this period.

Another effect of 'room at the top' is to limit the impact that education has on upward mobility. Although qualification for the salariat usually requires education, if the salariat is growing more rapidly than educational opportunity, then employers will simply recruit whomever they can, on grounds other than educational, to fill the vacant spaces. This could mean recruitment of working-class youths straight to the salariat or, more likely, it could mean staged mobility, with working-class youths entering intermediate jobs at school-leaving age, and then moving up to salariat jobs later in their careers. Again, this is exactly what the Nuffield School found. Only 4 per cent of working-class sons in this period were recruited directly to salariat jobs, but 20 per cent were recruited to intermediate jobs. By age 35, 17 per cent had reached the salariat and 34 per cent had reached intermediate classes. Over half the working class had left it, but by stages. The 4 per cent recruited to the salariat directly may have had an educational boost to get there, but almost everyone else did not need it and probably did not get it: after all, half of the working class were upwardly mobile, but only about a fifth had any experience of grammar school.[9]

In the age of the bipartite system, this stands to reason. Grammar school selection was palpably not growing rapidly enough to provide

[7] Anthony Heath and Clive Payne, 'Social Mobility', in *Twentieth-Century British Social Trends*, ed. A. H. Halsey and Josephine Webb (Basingstoke, 2000), 260–1.

[8] Lindsay Paterson and Cristina Iannelli, 'Patterns of Absolute and Relative Social Mobility: A Comparative Study of England, Wales and Scotland', *Sociological Research Online* (2007), www.socresonline.org.uk/12/6/15.html, Table 6.

[9] Goldthorpe, with Llewellyn and Payne, *Social Mobility*, 52; Halsey, Heath and Ridge, *Origins and Destinations*, 63.

sufficient new recruits. In fact, after the initial expansion in response to the Butler Act after 1944, it did not grow at all but shrank. Of those selected, a third were drawn from existing salariat families, so they could not by definition provide the new recruits. Although a growing proportion were recruited from intermediate families, this class fell far short on its own in supplying the necessary number of new salariat recruits.[10] And as we have seen, the form that upward mobility took tended to bypass educational qualifications altogether. Women went straight into the intermediate classes at school-leaving age, into clerical and retail jobs that did not require educational qualifications of any kind. Men similarly moved into the intermediate classes at school-leaving age, acquired new skills and aspirations on the job and were then available for recruitment into the salariat based on these life skills rather than their increasingly distant educational experience. As Paterson and Iannelli have shown, with the exception of the small numbers who had no secondary education at all, upward mobility in this period was experienced almost equally by people at all levels of educational attainment (Figure 1). Even a university degree did not really improve your chances of upward mobility very much, because if you got a university degree in this period you were likely to be from a salariat background already.[11] In terms of the OED triangle, the association between origin and education became less meritocratic; for this reason, the stronger association between education and destination benefited already advantaged classes more and so, on balance, was actually also less meritocratic; while the direct association between origin and destination, taking into account all mediating factors, was weaker and therefore *was* more meritocratic. In other words, 'decreasing merit selection in the education system' was offset by 'increasing merit selection in the labour market'.[12] The result – more upward mobility, but on balance no more equality of opportunity.

What relationship did this experience of social mobility bear to the prevailing political discourses of the period? As such, 'social mobility' hardly figured. It was entering the language of social scientists but not of politicians, still less of voters.[13] Before the Second World War, the social

[10] Halsey, Heath and Ridge, *Origins and Destinations*, 51, 63–4; Jean Floud and A. H. Halsey, 'English Secondary Schools and the Supply of Labour' (1956), in *Education, Economy, and Society*, ed. A. H. Halsey, Jean Floud and C. Arnold Anderson (New York, 1961), 85–7; A. H. Halsey, *Change in British Society*, 4th edn (Oxford, 1995), 157–8.

[11] Paterson and Iannelli, 'Patterns of Absolute and Relative Mobility', Table 8. Over half of all university students in this period came from salariat families: Halsey, Heath and Ridge, *Origins and Destinations*, 183.

[12] Fiona Devine and Yaojun Li, 'The Changing Relationship between Origins, Education and Destinations in the 1990s and 2000s', *British Journal of Sociology of Education*, 34 (2013), 768–9, referring to the Nuffield School findings for these earlier cohorts.

[13] The term appears sporadically in expert testimony to parliamentary committees in the 1950s but the first time it was ever uttered in parliament was in Lord Samuel's maiden speech

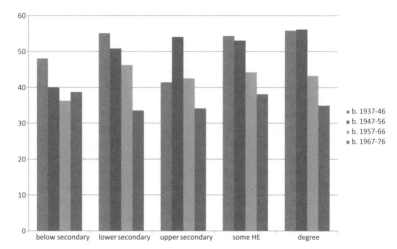

Figure 1 (Colour online) Proportions of birth cohorts who were upwardly mobile (by level of educational attainment): entry into labour market 1952–92
Source: Data from Paterson and Iannelli, 'Patterns of Absolute and Relative Mobility', Table 8.

imagination of most politicians was still surprisingly limited. There was some interest in social and political leadership – recruitment to a tiny elite – but Conservatives were happy with the existing elite and trade union leaders saw themselves as a counter-elite, if anything threatened by mobility out of the working class. Radical-liberal and revisionist-socialist intellectuals, lacking firm commitments to existing social strata, were an exception. R. H. Tawney and J. A. Hobson were unusual in advocating and setting out a practical plan for achieving 'a broad, easy stair' out of the working class.[14]

Even after the war, when 'social reconstruction' was an avowed aim of both parties, it remains striking how limited was the social imagination of the political leaderships of both main parties. Renewed attention was paid to education for economic efficiency, but much of this effort was

in the Lords in 1963, where he recognised 'This country is now a Welfare State and the gap between the classes is narrowing; there is social mobility upwards.' *Hansard (Lords)*, fifth series, 252 (1962–3), 24 July 1963. The next reference only came in 1967, employed by Edwin Brooks, a former geography lecturer. It appears occasionally in newspapers throughout the 1950s and 1960s but only with any frequency from the 1990s, for which see below, p. 14.

[14] Ben Jackson, *Equality and the British Left: A Study in Progressive Political Thought, 1900–64* (Manchester, 2007), 30–2.

still focused on an elite, though now a technocratic rather than a social or political elite. A discourse of 'equality of opportunity' became more fashionable across both major parties, based on the assumption that the goal of education ought to be the better use of 'wasted talent', both socially unfair and economically inefficient.[15] Depending on your political preferences, this could be achieved by greater investment in schools, with or without reorganisation, or better testing of ability, or more places in grammar schools and universities. It did not necessarily require or envisage more social mobility for most people.

It was only when Tony Crosland and his followers encountered the Nuffield School in the mid-1950s that social mobility began to move to the centre of some politicians' agenda, with a commitment to equality, not just of opportunity but to some extent of outcomes as well. In the initial stages, this first explicit acknowledgement of social mobility was framed almost entirely in terms of education, which was still seen as the sole route out of the working class. The sociologists Jean Floud, A. H. Halsey and their colleagues were able to convince Crosland that academic selection only reproduced existing inequalities in society. 'Equality of opportunity' at the very least required something more than equal opportunity to demonstrate intelligence – it also required equal opportunity to *acquire* intelligence. For Floud and Halsey, this approach dictated an end to academic selection at so early an age as 11 and the development of comprehensive schools that might to some degree level the playing field for children of different classes. Crosland certainly took up this cause and in government after 1964, with Halsey as a close adviser, he pursued comprehensivisation determinedly.[16] But there were other arguments in revisionist circles that placed less emphasis rather than more on education. Michael Young's *Rise of the Meritocracy* worried that equal opportunity to acquire intelligence might only cement further the rule of an educated elite, with privilege now given greater sanction as merit rather than inheritance.[17] As the sociologists put it, 'apparent justice may be more difficult to bear than injustice'.[18] One

[15] See, for example, Ellen Wilkinson in *Hansard*, fifth series, 424 (1945–6), 1813 [1 July 1945]; and see Carol Dyhouse, 'Family Patterns of Social Mobility through Higher Education in England in the 1930s', *Journal of Social History*, 34 (2000–1), 817–41, on the earlier history of 'wasted talent'.

[16] See the excellent discussion of revisionist thinking on education policy in Jackson, *Equality and the British Left*, 163–76, 196–202; and see Nicholas Ellison, *Egalitarian Thought and Labour Politics: Retreating Visions* (1994), 92–5, 143–5, on the revisionists' need to compromise with more conventional meritocratic views in their own party.

[17] In Young's satire, 'meritocracy' had been supported both by Conservatives and by 'practical socialists', though opposed by egalitarian socialists, a shrewd observation: Michael Young, *The Rise of the Meritocracy 1870–2033: An Essay on Education and Equality* (1958; 2nd edn, Harmondsworth, 1961), 36–48.

[18] Glass, 'Introduction', 25–6.

solution would be to change the value structure of education and society to shift aspiration away from traditional occupations in the salariat to more technological pursuits – which both Tories and Labour did attempt through promotion of technological education and manpower planning.[19] Another, which only Labour would pursue, would be to reduce the advantage of privileged origins through redistribution. Equality of outcome, achieved by redistribution, was just as important to the revisionists as to the traditional left. As Crosland himself confirmed, a just society could not have an aristocracy, not even an aristocracy of talent. Social mobility would be best achieved not by competition but by equality – 'an immensely high standard of universal provision'.[20] These new emphases on manpower planning and redistribution at least showed some awareness that social mobility was not all about education.[21]

As I argued in my first address, public opinion was in many respects actually ahead of political opinion. Aspirations to social mobility were already high in the interwar working class. The grammar school had rightly been identified as the best available avenue out of manual labour and into 'clean' jobs in the retail and office sectors. Before the growth of the non-manual classes took off in the post-war period, the more limited stock of such 'clean' jobs was indeed supplied by the grammar schools. One study of interwar grammar schools found that over half of their graduates became clerks and shop assistants, that is, intermediate rather than salariat occupations.[22] Unsurprisingly, this understanding of the labour-market role of grammar schools persisted into the post-war period, even though as we have seen upward mobility no longer required it. If anything, public opinion became more and more fixated on access to grammar schools, especially among those families most aspirational and most likely to be frustrated by selection. The association of education with the welfare state fortified people's determination to get a high universal standard of education just as they expected to get a high universal standard of health care. This pressure pushed politicians in both parties to advocate 'grammar schools for all', and gave the Croslandites their moment in the 1960s.

---

[19] This seems to have been encouraged by some of the sociologists: Olive Banks, *Parity and Prestige in English Secondary Education: A Study in Educational Sociology* (1955), 239–48; David V. Glass, 'Education and Social Change in Modern England' (1959), in *Education, Economy, and Society*, ed. Halsey, Floud and Anderson, 403–5; Floud and Halsey, 'English Secondary Schools and the Supply of Labour', 80–92.

[20] Jackson, *Equality and the British Left*, 198–200.

[21] For an unusually explicit understanding of the prevailing relationship between education and the labour market, see C. Arnold Anderson, 'A Skeptical Note on Education and Mobility' (1961), in *Education, Economy, and Society*, ed. Halsey, Floud and Anderson, 164–79.

[22] Michael Sanderson, 'Education and the Labour Market', in *Work and Pay in Twentieth-Century Britain*, ed. Nicholas Crafts, Ian Gazeley and Andrew Newell (Oxford, 2007), 273–5.

At the same time, however, most parents whose children had failed to secure grammar-school places did not remain frustrated for long. They did not blame their children for their failure to pass the 11+, especially when, soon enough, many more of those children achieved upward mobility than their parents had expected, and even those who did not experience upward mobility still reaped the rewards of affluence. So while there was general public support for comprehensivisation, there was also general public satisfaction with labour-market outcomes without comprehensivisation – as we might expect, given the buoyant state of the labour market through the early 1970s.[23]

III

This happy state of affairs – improving labour-market prospects for half the working class, even without educational reform – could not and did not last forever, as we find as we move into my second period, starting in the early 1970s. It may be useful to take the life-cycle experiences of the 1958 birth cohort as exemplary (it happens to be one of the best studied cohorts, and also mine). This cohort ended compulsory education in 1974, a boomtime for manual working-class employment (one reason, as I argued last year, why higher-education growth halted in the 1970s), though also a period of continuing growth in 'room at the top'. Those fortunate enough to enter the labour market then did well, whatever class they were joining. By 1981, 60 per cent of the cohort reported that they had already reached their career objectives, at 23 years of age.[24] Unfortunately, at just about that time the labour market collapsed. Unemployment levels were high throughout the 1980s, especially for younger people. A lot of people fell out of work, and those who stayed in work often had to accept downward mobility in order to do so. A relatively large proportion of this cohort entered the salariat early in their careers and then fell out of it.[25] When the labour market recovered in the 1990s, many of these people were on the move yet again – well into their 30s. So tracking experiences and expectations alike is very difficult for this turbulent generation. But taking the whole period through the early 1990s as a whole, for this period including but not limited to those born in 1958, we can safely say that there is still plenty of room at the top, ergo plenty of upward mobility,

[23] Mandler, 'Educating the Nation: I. Schools', 13–14 n. 23; see also Goldthorpe, with Llewellyn and Payne, *Social Mobility*, 231–2.

[24] Andreas Cebulla and Wojtek Tomaszewski, 'The Demise of Certainty: Shifts in Aspirations and Achievement at the Turn of the Century', *International Journal of Adolescence and Youth*, 18 (2013), 147.

[25] Gindo Tampubolon and Mike Savage, 'Intergenerational and Intragenerational Social Mobility in Britain', in *Social Stratification: Trends and Processes*, ed. Paul Lambert *et al.* (Farnham, 2012), 120–3.

though also more downward mobility, at unpredictable stages of the life cycle. Precarity starts to become a fact of life, and this will make an impact on the political discourse.

What role did education play in this generation? Again, there are many confusing factors, some of which I have considered in previous addresses. The school-leaving age was raised to 16 just in time to catch the 1958 cohort. Comprehensivisation was at its peak. Higher education was stagnating. Furthermore, this is the generation in which women began to move towards parity with men in labour-market participation and in educational attainment. The gap between men and women in the attainment of any tertiary education was quite wide for all classes in the 1946 cohort, but the gap had completely disappeared by the 1958 cohort, again for all classes.[26] This extraordinary change in gender roles and experiences makes all longitudinal comparisons more complicated: for earlier cohorts, sociologists were mostly content to track fathers' and sons' occupations, but for these cohorts they now found themselves puzzled as to how to identify class of origin (father's or mother's occupation?) and whether to track offspring separately by gender or together.

Nevertheless, oversimplifying grandly, we can try to make some comprehensible longitudinal comparisons. Though by definition upward mobility must in this period be diminishing – precisely because we start out with a larger proportion of the population already at the top – nevertheless, there is still considerable 'room at the top' for those below it: something like 38 per cent of this cohort is now in the salariat. Though less common for all, upward mobility is still a more or less equally common experience for people with all levels of education (Figure 1).[27] However, different effects are operating at each of these different levels of education. First of all, at the bottom, comprehensivisation seems to have made little difference one way or the other. Children of all abilities had about the same chance of achieving O-Levels in grammar and comprehensive schools. Working-class children of high ability did have a better chance of achieving A-Levels in grammar schools, but this temporary advantage is reversed by the time they achieve occupational maturity, and as a result 'selective-system schools considered as a whole appear to confer no significant absolute or relative class mobility advantage of any kind on anybody'. Of course, the corollary of this is that neither do comprehensive-system schools – another blow to those of us who want to

---

[26] Gerry Makepeace, Peter Dolton, Laura Woods, Heather Joshi and Fernando Galinda-Rueda, 'From School to the Labour Market', in *Changing Britain, Changing Lives: Three Generations at the Turn of the Century*, ed. Elsa Ferri, John Bynner and Michael Wadsworth (2003), 42–3.

[27] Paterson and Iannelli, 'Patterns of Absolute and Relative Mobility', Table 6.

think that social mobility has something (or even a great deal) to do with education.[28]

However, though school-type has little or nothing to do at this stage with social mobility, at the higher levels educational achievement probably does. Though people with a degree are not more likely to be upwardly mobile than people without, they *are* more likely to be mobile *because* of their degree. In other words, the education–destination association is stronger for people at the higher levels of attainment.[29] The salariat is still expanding and now a degree is your best guarantee of getting into it. About 90 per cent of all people of salariat origins with degrees remained in the salariat; but, extraordinarily, about 89 per cent of all people of working-class origins with degrees ended up in the salariat too. At this level, therefore, the ED association is strong – a degree gets you into the salariat, whatever your origins. At lower levels, however, the ED association is weaker. There are still far too few people with degrees to satisfy employers' demand for salariat positions. And when they dip down below degree-level to recruit, they are far more likely to recruit people of salariat background, whatever their qualifications – perhaps they like their clothes or their accent or just the cut of their jib. Even for people of salariat origins with almost no educational qualifications, their chance of staying in the salariat is up to 1 in 3. In contrast, for working-class people with almost no educational qualifications, the chance of getting into the salariat is not zero but still low – under 10 per cent.[30] Overall, parents of salariat origins are getting better at keeping their children in the salariat, whatever their educational qualifications; even if they started out lower, hit perhaps by high unemployment in the 1980s, they were still far more likely to end up in the salariat. In other words, despite continuing upward

---

[28]Two major studies came to this same conclusion: Vikki Boliver and Adam Swift, 'Do Comprehensive Schools Reduce Social Mobility?', *British Journal of Sociology*, 62 (2011), 89–110 (quote at 100), and Judith Glaesser and Barry Cooper, 'Educational Achievement in Selective and Comprehensive Local Education Authorities: A Configurational Analysis', *British Journal of Sociology of Education*, 33 (2012), 223–44. They both also found that high-ability working-class children selected for grammar schools were probably already at higher levels of ability at the point of selection than the high-ability working-class children in comprehensive schools to whom they are being compared, which may account for the apparent edge that grammar schools had in A-Level (but not O-Level) attainment.

[29]This tendency, for stronger ED association at higher levels of attainment, has been found for many countries: Richard Breen and Jan O. Jonsson, 'Inequality of Opportunity in Comparative Perspective: Recent Research on Educational Attainment and Social Mobility', *Annual Review of Sociology*, 31 (2005), 234.

[30]Goldthorpe, 'Understanding – and Misunderstanding – Social Mobility', 444; Erzsebet Bukodi and John H. Goldthorpe, 'Social Class Returns to Higher Education: Chances of Access to the Professional and Managerial Salariat for Men in Three British Birth Cohorts', *Longitudinal and Life Course Studies*, 2 (2011), 189–91; Erzsebet Bukodi and John H. Goldthorpe, 'Class Origins, Education and Occupational Attainment in Britain', *European Societies*, 13 (2011), 358, 360–1.

mobility, there are no improvements in equality of opportunity – and education, unless you are one of the lucky few with a degree, is no help.[31]

The economic ups-and-downs of this period from the early 1970s to the early 1990s further obscured what was already pretty obscure to contemporary policymakers, the extent and causes of social mobility. Attention remained fixed instead – if anything, more fixed – on economic performance. Thatcherism, it is true, introduced a new language of aspiration, but it did not connect aspiration to public policy – rather the contrary. It adopted a practically Social-Darwinist approach to social mobility which encouraged competition between individuals and families for social position, based on hard work and other forms of self-help.[32] At its most Social-Darwinist, for example in Keith Joseph's 1979 book on equality, it accepted in-born or inherited social position as a just basis for inequality.[33] Joseph praised state education not for any contribution it made to social mobility but simply for defusing class tensions. But this stance proved unpopular with Thatcherism's core constituency, as I argued in my second address. Attempts to scale back investment in education or to introduce fees or to reintroduce selection were firmly rebuffed by public opinion and by backbench Tory MPs. Thatcher turned to the more emollient Kenneth Baker, who sought instead to expand educational opportunity, both as a strategy for economic growth and also to some extent as a response to anxiety about downward mobility, now a growing risk.[34] This shift to a closer association between education and social mobility in the Conservative mentality became even clearer under John Major, who emphasised his own upward mobility more than Heath and Thatcher had done, and although he had little education was happy to play up the contribution that education might make. The language of social mobility, both explicit and implicit, undoubtedly begins to rise in prominence in political discourse in the early 1990s, as opportunities for upward mobility evidently begin to slow, and anxieties about downward mobility sharpen.[35]

IV

This brings me to my final phase, the period since the early 1990s. Recent experiences notwithstanding, the past twenty years have been a period of more stable labour markets and, mostly, continued economic

[31] Heath and Payne, 'Social Mobility', 263–4.

[32] Florence Sutcliffe-Braithwaite, 'Neo-Liberalism and Morality in the Making of Thatcherite Social Policy', *Historical Journal*, 55 (2012), 497–520.

[33] Keith Joseph and Jonathan Sumption, *Equality* (1979), 14–15, 29–34, 86–97.

[34] Mandler, 'Educating the Nation: II. Universities', 19–22.

[35] The use of the term 'social mobility' begins to make a more than sporadic appearance in *The Times* around 1990, though levels remain far below what they would reach in the 2000s. In the *Guardian*, more attuned to contemporary sociology, the pace picks up earlier, in the late 1970s.

growth and upskilling. As a result, there continues to be 'room at the top'. However, the rate of growth at the top has slowed, and who gets there has changed. Upward mobility into the salariat has decelerated for men but accelerated for women, benefiting from new educational *and* labour-market opportunities.[36] Parents in the salariat continue to be good at keeping their children in the salariat, though this tends to mean keeping men in the higher salariat (class I) and women in the lower salariat (class II). Still, there is sufficient room at the top to keep upward mobility into the salariat flowing from below. This despite the fact that more parents are now competing with their children for these salariat positions – such large proportions of the population are now in or near the salariat that competition for these positions becomes increasingly fierce. And this changing composition of the entire labour market necessarily implies that, while upward mobility continues, the risks of downward mobility are growing too. Just on the probabilities, a society with lots of people at the bottom – say, the society we began with, immediately after the war – is less exposed to downward mobility than the society we are ending up with, with lots of people at the top. Statistically, these are known as composition effects. And sure enough, for men at least downward mobility *is* increasing.[37] The most recent finding – still by a team that includes Goldthorpe! – takes us up to the birth cohort of the early 1980s, who have not yet reached occupational maturity today, but for whom it is suggested that men are now equally likely to fall as to rise (whereas during the 'golden age' they were two or three times more likely to have risen); that is, the authors observe, 'the balance of men's upward and downward mobility is now tending to move *in quite the opposite direction* to that which prevailed in what has become known as the "Golden Age" of mobility in which social advancement predominated'. Note that in a top-heavy labour market, more downward mobility is not only likely but also indicates more rather than less equality of opportunity – if you are at the top and your origins and your destinations are only loosely connected, then you should be more likely to move down.[38] Not that that is any consolation to those moving down – a point to which I will return.

[36] Yaojun Li and Fiona Devine, 'Is Social Mobility Really Declining? Intergenerational Class Mobility in Britain in the 1990s and the 2000s', *Sociological Research Online* (2011), www.socresonline.org.uk/16/3/4.html; cf. the earlier, gloomier, view taken by Geoff Payne and Judy Roberts, 'Opening and Closing the Gates: Recent Developments in Male Social Mobility in Britain', *Sociological Research Online* (2002), www.socresonline.org.uk/6/4/payne.html, which predicted a contraction of the salariat.

[37] Li and Devine, 'Is Social Mobility Really Declining?'; Paterson and Iannelli, 'Patterns of Absolute and Relative Social Mobility'.

[38] Erzsebet Bukodi, John H. Goldthorpe, Lorraine Waller and Jouni Kuha, 'The Mobility Problem in Britain: New Findings from the Analysis of Birth Cohort Data', *British Journal of Sociology*, 66 (2015), 104, 111.

In this period, education still does not appear to play a more prominent role in determining social mobility. As we track the cohorts into the labour market of the 1990s, we see that the tendency to upward mobility has dropped, but that level of education is still not a great determinant of your likelihood of upward mobility (Figure 1).[39] This does not mean that education is irrelevant. The trend towards a stronger association between education and destination at the higher levels of education may be continuing, now especially among women. It may be their much better access to higher education that allows the upper salariat to keep their offspring in the upper salariat. They are not upwardly mobile, but their access to higher education protects them from downward mobility. And yet if you control for education, men from upper salariat backgrounds still have twice the chance of reaching an upper salariat position as men from working-class backgrounds with the *same* levels of education.[40] Even those diminishing numbers of men from salariat backgrounds with few educational qualifications were finding their way into the salariat, with a little help from their social and cultural capital, entering positions in sales and personal services that did not require much formal education but for which 'soft skills' and *savoir-faire* were quite potent.[41]

At this point, with about half the population in the salariat, logic suggests that this 'big class' schema is of diminishing utility in measuring social mobility. Even if the sociologists continue to calibrate occupation accurately, and even if occupation is easier to characterise and track, it seems less useful to use these categories when so many people are at the top, and when compositional effects suggest that 'upward' and 'downward' mobility have become mere artefacts of our categories. Why not develop a different measure that assesses better differences within the 50 per cent of the population now in the salariat?

Enter the economists. They began to play more of a role in debates over social mobility in the early 1990s, in part because of their increasingly imperial drive to colonise all areas of social policy, but in part, too, because the data for income were improving, because income inequality was

---

[39] Paterson and Iannelli, 'Patterns of Absolute and Relative Mobility', Table 6.

[40] Devine and Li, 'Changing Relationship', 783–4. For a finding that the expansion of higher education has tended generally to increase inequality, see Francesco Vona, 'Does the Expansion of Higher Education Reduce Educational Inequality? Evidence from 12 European Countries', OFCE – Centre de recherche en economie de Sciences Po, No. 2011–12 (June 2011). But cf. Goldthorpe, 'Understanding – and Misunderstanding – Social Mobility', 441; John H. Goldthorpe, 'The Role of Education in Intergenerational Social Mobility: Problems from Empirical Research in Sociology and Some Theoretical Pointers from Economics', *Rationality and Society*, 26 (2014), 265–89; E. Bukodi and J. H. Goldthorpe, 'Educational Attainment – Relative or Absolute – as a Mediator of Intergenerational Class Mobility in Britain', *Research in Social Stratification and Mobility*, in press, 9, which does accept growth in class returns to education at least between the 1958 and 1970 cohorts.

[41] Goldthorpe, 'Understanding – and Misunderstanding – Social Mobility', 443–5.

obviously growing, and so it seemed both desirable and possible to assess social mobility in terms of income rather than occupation. Among the advantages were the ability to create income deciles or quartiles which divide the population up evenly and therefore eliminate some (though not all) of the compositional effects, and also to make distinctions within the 50 per cent of the population that had reached the salariat. Among the disadvantages were the continuing inadequacy of the data – actually not as easy to adjust for changes in the gendering of the workforce as occupational data – and, as the sociologists insisted, the inability of income to tell you much about job autonomy or status.[42]

Nevertheless, the economists did start generating distinct conclusions about social mobility from the early 1990s, and in 2005 they burst into the public debate in a most spectacular way. A report for the Sutton Trust by economists Jo Blanden, Paul Gregg and Stephen Machin, which achieved wide public currency, argued that intergenerational mobility based on income quartiles gave a much grimmer picture of social mobility in Britain than did occupational data, and in fact put Britain near the bottom of the international mobility tables. Furthermore, they argued, much of the advantage enjoyed by top-quartile families in Britain derived from their better access to educational qualifications – in other words, the origin–education association was too strong. Although they echoed the sociologists in acknowledging that non-educational factors (such as the widening gaps between income deciles) were also important, they drew particular attention to the widening gap at higher levels of education as a factor in worsening the prospects of upward mobility, consistent with the interests of their sponsors, the Sutton Trust, which itself certainly focused attention on the education gap.[43]

I will come to the impact these findings had on public debate in a moment, but for now I will confine my comment to the ensuing to-and-fro between the economists and the sociologists over whether social mobility was actually declining or not and what role education might play. The sociologists held quite firmly that while upward mobility was in decline, that was a reflection of compositional effects, not equality of

[42] For an emollient reconciliation of these problems and differences, see Jo Blanden, Paul Gregg and Lindsey Macmillan, 'Intergenerational Persistence in Income and Social Class: The Effect of Within-Group Inequality', *Journal of the Royal Statistical Society*, series A, 176 (2013), 541–63.

[43] Jo Blanden, Paul Gregg and Stephen Machin, *Intergenerational Mobility in Europe and North America: A Report Supported by the Sutton Trust* (Centre for Economic Performance, LSE, Apr. 2005). This study relied heavily on contrasts between the 1958 and 1970 cohorts, whose educational experience was by then already some way in the past; but cf. Jo Blanden and Stephen Machin, 'Educational Inequality and the Expansion of UK Higher Education', *Scottish Journal of Political Economy*, 51 (2004), 230–49, which creates semi-cohorts for a more recent period, when inequality in degree attainment was then declining.

opportunity, and that since downward mobility was increasing, equality of opportunity might even be improving. Overall, they thought, relative mobility in Britain was pretty stable and not much different from other developed nations. And while the association between education and destination may have become stronger at the higher levels, they did not believe there was a strengthening association between origin and education, so that overall educational change had not affected upward mobility much one way or the other. Ill-tempered exchanges ensued – which had perhaps as much to do with the attention the economists were getting in public-policy circles as with anything else. But in fact the economists began to back off from their claims. A follow-up study for the Sutton Trust, which got very little publicity, found that the increasingly unequal access to higher education previously detected for the period of the late 1980s and early 1990s had not persisted into the later 1990s. As higher education expanded very rapidly in the 1990s, access equalised somewhat, and, Blanden and Machin concluded in December 2007, 'It seems that the oft-cited finding of a fall in intergenerational mobility between the 1958 and 1970 cohorts appears to have been an episode caused by the particular circumstances of the time.'[44] They still held, however, that income inequality was making it more difficult to clamber up income deciles, thus introducing a composition effect of their own to explain declining upward mobility.[45] Other researchers, however, have found better income mobility in Britain, closer to the Nordics than to the United States.[46]

The historian will find it very difficult to choose between the claims of the economists and the sociologists, but here I want to conclude with some reflections on why this debate became so politically significant, after years when social mobility as discussed by sociologists was largely ignored both by policymakers and public opinion. As we have seen, social mobility was already becoming a matter of palpable public concern in the

---

[44] Jo Blanden and Stephen Machin, *Recent Changes in Intergenerational Mobility in Britain*, Report for Sutton Trust (Dec. 2007), 18–19. It is striking that the 2009 White Paper 'New Opportunities: Fair Chances for the Future', Cm. 7533 (2009), 17–20, is still citing the 2005 report as evidence for declining relative mobility on the basis that 'the latest data on relative mobility relate to people born in 1970'.

[45] Blanden, Gregg and Macmillan, 'Intergenerational Persistence', 561–2.

[46] Markus Jäntti *et al.*, 'American Exceptionalism in a New Light: A Comparison of Intergenerational Earnings Mobility in the Nordic Countries, the United Kingdom and the United States', IZA Discussion Paper No. 1938 (Jan. 2006), 14–15, 17; Stephen Gorard, 'A Re-Consideration of Rates of "Social Mobility" in Britain: Or Why Research Impact is Not Always a Good Thing', *British Journal of Sociology of Education*, 29 (2008), 321–3; John Jerrim, 'The Link between Family Background and Later Lifetime Income: How Does the UK Compare to Other Countries?', Working Paper No. 14–02, Department of Quantitative Social Science, Institute of Education (Feb. 2014), which moderates the claims that Britain's income mobility compares badly with other developed economies.

early 1990s, as upward mobility began to slow and downward mobility threatened. The advent of New Labour in the later 1990s dramatically raised the stakes, partly for political and partly for sociological reasons. Sociologically, all classes were finding that they had a social mobility problem. Mobility into the salariat was slowing. Downward mobility from the intermediate classes and from the lower salariat was growing. The upper salariat was maintaining its position but only with difficulty, using all the educational and non-educational tools at its disposal. New Labour saw here a political opportunity, one that fitted neatly with its 'One Nation' orientation. Upward mobility for all was the new mantra. This meant addressing problems of 'social exclusion' for the working class, but also emphasising new educational opportunities – through higher standards in schools and widening participation in higher education – for the intermediate classes and the salariat.

It is important to note that these policies were not necessarily aimed at greater equality of opportunity. Upward mobility for all, even if achieved, would not necessarily address the disparities between classes – it might simply upscale the whole labour market, as we have seen happened during the post-war 'golden age'. This might restore the growth of absolute mobility – more 'room at the top' – but, as the sociologists pointed out with increasing irritation, to achieve improvements in relative mobility – that is, true 'equality of opportunity' – would mean inciting downward mobility from the salariat as well as upward mobility from lower classes.[47] While an intellectually coherent position, the requirement for more downward mobility seems to ask of politicians more than they can conceivably deliver, and more than their constituents would have asked of them. Even the revisionists, who believed in equality of outcome, had made their biggest impact through educational reform, which extended opportunity to lower groups without, as it turns out, reducing the privileges of higher ones. New Labour did believe in some limited redistribution, but the purpose of higher taxation was not principally to incite downward mobility among the wealthy, rather it was to invest in childcare, education and community services that would enhance upward mobility among the poor – 'predistribution' as it has recently been called.[48]

---

[47] Goldthorpe, 'Understanding – and Misunderstanding – Social Mobility', 436–7; Geoff Payne, 'A New Social Mobility? The Political Redefinition of a Sociological Problem', *Contemporary Social Science*, 7 (2012), 56–7, 67–9; Phillip Brown, 'Education, Opportunity and the Prospects for Social Mobility', *British Journal of the Sociology of Education*, 34 (2013), 680–2; but Li and Devine, 'Is Social Mobility Really Declining?', are more realistic about the political possibilities. For an unusual sociological critique from the right, see Peter Saunders, *Social Mobility Delusions* (2012).

[48] 'Predistribution' was introduced into public debate in 2012, when Ed Miliband (who got it from the American political scientist Jacob Hacker) took it up, but it refers to a suite of policies that New Labour had already gone a long way towards adopting when in office.

It was into this febrile environment of hope (for renewed upward mobility) and anxiety (about growing downward mobility) that the economists entered and made their formidable impact. As late as 2001, a government report that had used the sociologists' findings to warn about possible future declines in 'room at the top' had gained little traction in public opinion. But the Sutton Trust report of 2005, by alleging an already established trend in declining social mobility, dating back to the 1980s, comparing Britain badly to other nations, and drawing attention to possible educational explanations, struck a media chord.[49] For some Conservatives, it was a stick with which to beat the comprehensives and call for a return to grammar schools – though Blanden, Gregg and Machin had not mentioned grammar schools, and had focused their recommendations on universities.[50] For the Sutton Trust, it *was* all about widening access to higher education. For New Labour, it was a rallying cry to redouble their efforts at 'predistribution', with an ever-widening gamut of policies from early years investment to community-building to standards in schools to vocational training to widening participation in higher education.

'Social mobility' entered the language of all parties. There has been a succession of 'social mobility' czars appointed by governments of all three main parties over the past ten years, more or less intoning the same mantra, of upward mobility without downward mobility, and of education and training as the route upwards, while, understandably, skipping over those factors (which may in fact be the most important) which social policy cannot easily fix: rising income inequality, the ability of privileged groups to retain their privilege even controlling for education, the export of high-skilled jobs due to globalisation, the polarisation of the labour market between a large high-skill salariat and a large (though smaller) low-skill working class, and the need for as much downward as upward mobility if true equality of opportunity is to be attained.[51]

[49] References to 'social mobility' in *The Times* had been edging up from single figures per annum in the late 1980s to dozens in the early 2000s, and then mushroomed to 156 in 2005, 313 in 2007 and 504 in 2010. My calculations from Lexis/Nexis. Payne, 'A New Social Mobility?', 58, observes a similar chronology but for some reason at much lower levels; and see also Geoff Payne, 'Labouring under a Misapprehension: Politicians' Perceptions and the Realities of Structural Social Mobility in Britain, 1995–2010', in *Social Stratification*, ed. Lambert *et al.*, 224–42.

[50] Boliver and Swift, 'Do Comprehensive Schools Reduce Social Mobility?', 90–1; cf. Gorard, 'Re-consideration of Rates', 318.

[51] A rare and brief exception was the rhetoric of the Liberal Democrats in the Coalition Government, around 2011, when 'relative mobility' was mentioned specifically, although even they had a tendency to define it as 'an equal chance of getting the job they want or reaching a higher income bracket': cf. Claire Crawford, Paul Johnson, Steve Machin and Anna Vignoles, 'Social Mobility: A Literature Review', Department for Business, Innovation and Skills, Mar. 2011, 6; *Opening Doors, Breaking Barriers: A Strategy for Social Mobility* (Apr.

V

Taking the long view, finally, what can we as historians conclude about the history of social mobility over the last half century or more that might shed light on the present predicament? First, it is important to be clear how modest an effect educational policy has had on social mobility, both in the periods when it was high and in the present period when it may be in decline. After the war, Britain led a standard trajectory which shrank the working class and grew the salariat, based on the requirements of all developed twentieth-century economies, which has resulted in considerable convergence between all these developed economies in the present day. Though British politicians felt they were stimulating this development – whether by extending grammar schools, or comprehensivising them, or by seeking to channel young people into science and engineering careers – in fact none of these initiatives was very decisive; neither grammars nor comprehensives changed the course of social mobility very much, and as I argued last year young people refused to follow instructions to take up science and engineering careers, with no evident impact either on economic growth or on social mobility. Public opinion wanted social mobility, and most people got it, but educational policy does not deserve the credit. Nor, before the 1990s, did politicians really even conceptualise their initiatives in terms of social mobility – their focus was on economic growth, and rising levels of consumption for all, rather than any reengineering of the social structure. So, although social mobility was spoken of in terms of equality of opportunity (when it was spoken of at all), there was in fact no improvement in equality of opportunity – and no real pressure for it, as people were satisfied with upward mobility and affluence.

As upward mobility slowed, and downward mobility loomed, social mobility did rise up the political agenda. But what, realistically, could public policy do to make a difference? Thatcherism at least had an anti-interventionist ideology that justified inaction, while endorsing the struggle of individuals and families to improve their own lives. But anti-interventionism could not be sustained in the 1990s and after, even among Conservatives. Frustrations and anxieties in all classes were mounting. Self-help was clearly not enough. And there were other, novel considerations to take into account. Rampant income inequality and globalisation, possibly connected, posed problems that politicians could not easily address. Social mobility for all seemed a more realistic proposition, especially after the entry of the economists and the suggestion

2011), 15; Vince Cable, 'Supporting Social Mobility and Lifelong Learning', 17 Oct. 2012, www.gov.uk/government/speeches/supporting-social-mobility-and-lifelong-learning, accessed 4 July 2016.

in the Sutton Trust report that education after all did make a difference. For all the inadequacies of 'predistribution', it has to be said that the joined-up effort made by New Labour came closer to a realistic public policy programme for social mobility than any of its predecessors even attempted. 'Sure Start', 'Excellence in Cities' and other community-building programmes at least understood that educational reform alone could not overcome the social and cultural capital deficits of less advantaged families. And New Labour's educational reforms, notably the introduction of the educational maintenance allowance (EMA), had some modest sociological impact that went beyond the mantra of 'standards' in weakening the association between origins and educational attainment, although even here it is salutary to recall the verdict of a recent sociological assessment of New Labour's educational reforms: 'the biggest story is really the over-claiming from both sides'.[52] Nevertheless, it seems in retrospect like quite a political achievement to yoke a whole series of programmes aimed at only about 15 per cent of the population to the interests of a majority of the population under the banner of 'social mobility for all' – especially in light of the war of all against all into which we appear to have lapsed since.[53]

What is the alternative? The obvious answer, the one the revisionists supplied in the 1950s, is redistribution, which would not only enforce some downward mobility for privileged groups (at least as measured by income), but by bringing the income deciles closer together ought to facilitate upward mobility for the less privileged. Redistribution of income does not directly redistribute social and cultural capital, which will still be used by privileged groups to game the labour market, but it probably facilitates the acquisition of social and cultural capital by those to whom income is distributed. The countries in Europe that have been most successful in using social policy to build equality of opportunity have been the Nordics, with both a relatively egalitarian education system and a relatively flat income hierarchy.[54] The problem is that it is more difficult

---

[52] Anthony Heath, Alice Sullivan, Vikki Boliver and Anna Zimdars, 'Education under New Labour, 1997–2010', *Oxford Review of Economic Policy*, 29 (2013), 227–47, quotation at 242; see also Geoff Whitty and Jake Anders, '(How) Did New Labour Narrow the Achievement and Participation Gap?', LLAKES Research Paper 46, Institute of Education, Centre for Learning and Life Chances in Knowledge Economies and Societies (2014).

[53] Payne, 'Labouring Under a Misapprehension', 237–9. Cf. Jäntti *et al.*, 'American Exceptionalism in a New Light', 28, which recommends just such a focus on 'interventions designed to increase the mobility of the very poorest'.

[54] Richard Breen and John H. Goldthorpe, 'Explaining Educational Differentials: Towards a Formal Rational Action Theory', *Rationality and Society*, 9 (1997), 294–6; Breen and Jonsson, 'Inequality of Opportunity', 226–7, 234; Richard Breen, Ruud Liujkx, Walter Müller and Reinhard Pollak, 'Non-Persistent Inequality in Educational Attainment: Evidence from Eight European Countries', *American Journal of Sociology*, 114 (2008–9), esp. 1478–80; Sandra E. Black and Paul J. Devereux, 'Recent Developments in Intergenerational

to sell politically a redistributive policy than it was in the 1950s, for the same reason that downward mobility is more of a threat today – there are too many people in the middle. The Nordics were able to sell equality of opportunity when very few people had opportunity, and very few people were threatened with its loss. Today, in Britain, after three generations of upward mobility, most people have experienced it already and are understandably reluctant to abandon it. In that sense, Britain is already a more equal society. It is true that there is more income inequality. But that income inequality is very unusually distributed. Most of it sits in the top few percentiles.

Redistribution that focused on those top few percentiles would not go very far in fostering social mobility.[55] (It might have other advantages.) Redistribution that went much further again asks too many people to give up privileges that they may rightly feel have been hard won by themselves and their parents. The golden age of social mobility was almost certainly a one-off. We cannot go there again. Perhaps we ought to return to the idea that the purpose of education is not so much to foster equality of opportunity as to educate.[56]

Mobility', IZA Discussion Paper 4866 (Apr. 2010), 16, 19, 24, 30–1; Jo Blanden, 'Cross-Country Rankings in Intergenerational Mobility: A Comparison of Approaches from Economics and Sociology', *Journal of Economic Surveys*, 27 (2013), 61–2; Goldthorpe, 'Understanding – and Misunderstanding – Social Mobility', 445.

[55] Jäntti *et al.*, 'American Exceptionalism in a New Light', 19; Jerrim, 'Link between Family Background', 21–2.

[56] A conclusion shared by Goldthorpe, 'Understanding – and Misunderstanding – Social Mobility', 446–7.

Transactions of the RHS 26 (2016), pp. 25–41 © Royal Historical Society 2016. This is an Open Access article, distributed under the terms of the Creative Commons Attribution licence (http://creativecommons.org/licenses/by/4.0/), which permits unrestricted re-use, distribution, and reproduction in any medium, provided the original work is properly cited. doi:10.1017/S0080440116000037

'BETTER OFF DEAD THAN DISFIGURED'? THE CHALLENGES OF FACIAL INJURY IN THE PRE-MODERN PAST

By Patricia Skinner

READ 8 MAY 2015

ABSTRACT. This paper argues that facial disfigurement has been neglected in the historiography of medieval Europe, and suggests some reasons for this oversight before examining the evidence from legal and narrative texts. One reason for this may be the lack of first-person accounts of being disfigured, preventing historians from accessing the experience of being disfigured. By situating the medieval examples within a wider frame of modern responses to disfigurement, it becomes apparent that whilst medical advances have assisted in restoring the damaged face, social responses to facial difference remain largely negative.

When architect Louis Kahn, responsible for some of the most iconic buildings of the mid-twentieth century, especially in the Indian subcontinent, was badly burnt on his face and hands as a child, his father expressed the sentiment that he was 'better off dead than disfigured'. Kahn's mother, fortunately for him, took a different view, arguing that Kahn would 'live and become a great man some day'. As recounted by Kahn's daughter, this almost hagiographical episode epitomises triumph over adversity, and this early experience is even credited with shaping Kahn's later practice as an architect. Ravi Kalia attributes Kahn's later sensitivity to the play of light and shadow in his monumental public buildings to the fact that he would wear a soft hat pulled low to disguise and shade his scarred face from the sun. Both his father's reaction and Louis's own attempt at disguise, though, express the strength of feeling that seeing a disfigured face could elicit.[1]

The subject of this paper touches upon some sensitive issues of perceived and actual facial difference. Many of the examples I will be discussing, medieval and modern, are of catastrophic, acquired

---

[1] Quotation from Alexandra Tyng, *Beginnings: Louis I. Kahn's Philosophy of Architecture* (Chichester, 1984), 3; Ravi Kalia, *Gandhinagar: Building National Identity in Postcolonial India* (Columbia, SC, 2004), 77.

facial injuries, uncomfortable at best to look at and often portrayed in highly emotive terms by the authors reporting them. Part of the shock in the reports is generated by the circumstances of the acquisition: unlike congenital conditions, or visible birthmarks, or difference in skin colour, a disfigurement acquired through violence or accident is a sudden, often traumatic life change. The real trauma inherent in acquired facial disfigurement arises from its suddenness, the switch from one face to another, rather than a gradual transition. I have not, therefore, foregrounded diseases as causes of acquired disfigurement in this discussion. Leprosy, for example, for all that its more severe, lepromatous form could destroy the facial features, is not a subject for enquiry here, not least because it has formed the subject of numerous, recent studies and continues to attract attention as new archaeological discoveries expand and revise our knowledge of this disease and responses to it in the early and central Middle Ages.[2] The process of adaptation, I suggest, is entirely different.

The fact that the medieval examples lived centuries ago might be thought to provide something of an insulating barrier between 'us' and 'them', but it should not. Facial disfigurement challenges basic, encoded human responses, which value symmetry and wholeness, and accounts of violence done to the face signal that something extreme is going on. Whilst the medical technologies to repair the damaged and diseased face have become ever more sophisticated, societal attitudes towards people with acquired disfigurements have remained largely static. Why should this issue concern historians? Primarily because people living *with* disfigurement, as modern campaigners for facial equality prefer to describe it, just like other minority groups, have been overlooked by history. Like E. P. Thompson's 'poor stockinger', or Sheila Rowbotham's 'hidden' women, or Anne Borsay's 'excluded' people with disabilities, people with disfigurements have been left out of historical narratives because their faces, quite literally, do not fit.[3] They might even work quite hard to remain out of sight. This paper, and an associated monograph, aim to restore a historical voice to this invisible group – they are invisible

---

[2] Elma Brenner, 'Recent Perspectives on Leprosy in Medieval Western Europe', *History Compass*, 8 (2010), 388–406; Elma Brenner, *Leprosy and Charity in Medieval Rouen* (Woodbridge, 2015); Luke Demaitre, *Leprosy in Premodern Medicine* (Baltimore, 2007); Carole Rawcliffe, *Leprosy in Medieval England* (Woodbridge, 2006); Guenter P. Risse, *Mending Bodies, Saving Souls: A History of Hospitals* (Oxford, 1999), 167–230; Simon Roffey and Katie Tucker, 'A Contextual Study of the Medieval Hospital and Cemetery of St Mary Magdalen, Winchester, England', *International Journal of Paleopathology*, 2 (2012), 170–80.

[3] That these texts have become 'classics' of history signals how important looking for excluded and marginalised groups has become in the discipline: E. P. Thompson, *The Making of the English Working Class* (1963, rev. 1968); Sheila Rowbotham, *Hidden from History: 300 Years of Women's Oppression and the Fight against It* (1973); Anne Borsay, *Disability and Social Policy in Britain since 1750: A History of Exclusion* (Basingstoke, 2004).

because no one had thought to look for them, but if you start looking, there they are.[4] Their experiences deserve our attention.

The 'triumphing over adversity' model is still a popular approach when engaging with disfigured faces in modern media: in the Anglophone world, we have only to think of the autobiographical accounts of Falklands veteran Simon Weston, or Changing Faces charity founder James Partridge, or the depressing number of female victims of facial attack by their partners (Katie Piper, Carmen Tarleton and Tina Nash), to see that the individual story can be used as a vehicle to raise awareness, understanding and, often, hard cash for the multiplicity of charities that support victims of congenital or acquired facial disfigurement.[5] Such accounts often start with a low point similar to Louis Kahn's: Tina Nash, whose violent partner gouged out her eyes, recalls that 'I asked my family to finish me off because I didn't want to be here any more.'[6] Part of the road to recovery and rehabilitation in these stories revolves around the repeated and often long-term surgical interventions to try to repair or, in Carmen's case, actually replace, the damaged face. Tina will soon be getting matching glass eyes, not because she will be able to see her restored face, but because those around her, particularly her children, will. Afghan woman Aisha Mohammadzai, just one of many women abused and disfigured by violent family members in that part of the world, made highly politicised headlines when a photograph of her mutilated face, missing its nose, was featured on the cover of *Time* magazine in 2010, and she was swiftly flown to the USA, where she now lives, for treatment.[7] The increasing sophistication of maxillofacial surgery, including the production of incredibly lifelike prostheses to replace facial elements destroyed by accident or disease, is seen as a major advance in twentieth- and twenty-first-century medicine.[8] Another charity, Saving Faces, is headed up by surgeon Professor Iain Hutchison, who commissioned a

---

[4] Patricia Skinner, *Living with Disfigurement in the Early Middle Ages* (New York, in press). The research was supported by Wellcome Trust Grant no. 097469, and I am grateful to the Trust for its continuing support.

[5] Simon Weston (burns), *Going Back: Return to the Falklands* (1992); James Partridge (burns), *Changing Faces: The Challenge of Facial Disfigurement* (1990); Katie Piper (attacked with acid), *Beautiful* (2011); Carmen Blandin Tarleton (attacked with caustic alkali), *Overcome: Burned, Blinded and Blessed* (n.p., 2013); Tina Nash (partner gouged out her eyes), *Out of the Darkness* (2012).

[6] Quoted in the *Guardian*, 4 Dec 2012, online at www.theguardian.com/society/2012/dec/04/blinded-woman-wanted-to-die (accessed 12 Apr. 2015).

[7] I have explored her case in more detail in Patricia Skinner, 'The Gendered Nose and its Lack: "Medieval" Nose-cutting and its Modern Manifestations', *Journal of Women's History*, 26 (2014), 45–67.

[8] Sander Gilman, *Making the Body Beautiful: A Cultural History of Aesthetic Surgery* (Princeton and Oxford, 1999); D. Reisberg and S. Habakuk, 'A History of Facial and Ocular Prosthetics', *Advances in Ophthalmic Plastic Reconstructive Surgery*, 8 (1990), 11–24.

series of stunning before-, during- and after-surgery portraits of some of his patients to assist them in coming to terms with their new faces, and to help the broader public to understand the human stories underlying the pictures.[9] Interest in historical accounts of disfigurement, too, has increased in recent years. In the wake of centenary commemorations for the First World War, those who survived the war but with terrible facial and other injuries have been the focus of both major academic projects and broader, public-facing media.[10] The BBC has a site called 'How do you fix a face that's been blown off by shrapnel?',[11] and colleagues at Exeter University have been engaged in a project with the Institut Faire Faces in France to explore the cultural significance of facial injury and broader meanings of the face in early twentieth-century Europe.[12]

What links all of these accounts and investigations, however, is the fact that we hear something of the voices of those who experienced and still experience living with disfigurement. What happens if the focus of enquiry shifts to 915 or 1015 rather than 1915 or 2015? What changes, I think, is the fact that religious observance and models of patient forbearance assisted in explaining and living with medieval disfigurement, whilst modern secular society blames the perpetrator or tries hard to fix the damage with technological wizardry. But the ongoing use of deliberate disfigurement as a sign of moral lack or the abuse of power has a visible and persistent continuity across centuries.

Drawing upon a wide range of medieval source material from Western Europe and Byzantium, including narratives from chronicles and (to a lesser extent) hagiography, letters, legal codes, archaeological remains and iconography, it is possible to explore how acquired facial disfigurement was documented, represented, analysed and commented upon by authors, and ask whether it was possible to gain access to the experience of the disfigured person themselves. It is fair to say that the sheer prevalence of facial injury in the material was a surprise, but the absence of voices of the disfigured themselves was not: the voices of disadvantaged groups rarely make it into the medieval record (except, sometimes, through ventriloquy). In the period under review, from *c.*

---

[9] Portraits by Mark Gilbert, of patients before, during and after surgeries, were most recently exhibited in *Saving Faces* at the University of Exeter, 25 Feb. to 25 Mar. 2015. Rosemarie Garland-Thomson, *Staring: How We Look* (Oxford, 2009), 6–7, features Gilbert's portrait of the late Henry de Lotbiniere, barrister. The project is featured on the Saving Faces website: http://savingfaces.co.uk/news-media/art-project/35-news-media/art/15-art-exhibition (accessed 12 Apr. 2015).

[10] Susannah Biernoff, 'The Rhetoric of Disfigurement in First World War Britain', *Social History of Medicine*, 24 (2011), 666–85; Susannah Biernoff, *Portraits of Violence: War and the Aesthetics of Disfigurement* (Ann Arbor, forthcoming).

[11] http://www.bbc.co.uk/guides/zxw42hv (accessed 12 Apr. 2015).

[12] http://blogs.exeter.ac.uk/1914faces2014/ (accessed 12 Apr. 2015).

600 to *c*. 1200, just two accounts are of first-person experience of facial difference, one at the less serious end of the spectrum (broken nose and increasing swelling in the jaw), and the other more catastrophic (on the receiving end of a deliberate blinding). Thietmar, bishop of Merseberg, describes his own face in the first example, whilst the second account is embedded within a hagiographic account of the mission of St Bruno to the Rus, where Wipert, one of the accompanying priests and the only survivor when the saint and his party are murdered, is deliberately blinded.[13] The spectrum of disfigurement is itself important, for if some of the facial injuries it covers might literally seem 'superficial' – the word itself is telling here – their meaning for medieval writers was anything but. Within the category of disfigurement, therefore, can be included anything from temporary facial scratches (from thorns and fingernails, the former used to identify a cattle-thief in Anglo-Saxon England)[14] and shaving of hair or eyebrows or beard, to scalping, deliberate facial burning, branding, blinding, severe head wounds and cutting off of noses, ears, lips and tongues, most of which would have led to permanent impairment.

The lack of 'patient perspective', as it might be termed in modern medical parlance, may go some way to explaining why disfigurement has been such a neglected topic in medieval studies. Another reason lies in the very specificity of facial injury: the mass disfigurement and rehabilitation of cohorts in modern warfare enables group studies, but most experience of disfigurement is at an individual level, resisting generalisation. That is not to say that group disfigurement did not exist in the Middle Ages: there are plenty of examples, particularly in the thirteenth century, of disfigurement and mutilation used as weapons of war, for example the atrocities of the Albigensian crusade reported by Peter of Les-Vaux-de-Cernay, or Frederick II's deliberate mutilation and blinding of the

---

[13] Thietmar of Merseberg, writing in the early eleventh century, reflects on his nose and jaw: *Thietmar Mersebergensis Episcopi Chronica*, Bk IV.75, ed. Robert Holtzmann, *Monumenta Germaniae Historica, Scriptores Rerum Germanicarum* (*MGH SSRG*), n.s. IX (Berlin, 1935), 51: 'videbis in me parvum homuncionem, maxillum deformem leva et latere eodem, quia hinc olim erupit semper turgescens fistula. Nasus in puericia fractus de me ridiculum facit. Idque totum nil questus essem, si interius aliquid splendescerem'. English translation in *Ottonian Germany: The Chronicon of Thietmar of Merseburg*, trans. David A. Warner (Manchester, 2001), 203–4. The cleric Wipert's account of his eyes being taken out on a mission to the East: 'Meos oculos eruere fecit . . . Ex illo tempore pro Deo peregrinando circuivi plurimas provincias, invocans sanctos sanctasque in christianorum auxilia . . . Omnium christianorum in karitate Dei deposco auxilium, quod mee vite fiat patrocinium, vestrorum peccatorum eternum remedium': Wipert's account is reproduced in the preliminary matter to the *Vita S. Adalberti Episcopi*, in *Monumenta Germaniae Historica, Scriptores* (*MGH SS*), IV, ed. G. H. Pertz (Hannover, 1841), 579–80.

[14] Documented in the so-called Fonthill Letter, dating to the late ninth/early tenth century: Mechtild Gretsch, 'The Language of the "Fonthill Letter"', *Anglo-Saxon England*, 23 (1994), 57–102, at 99.

Genoese archers defending Milan in 1245, or the actions of Ezzelino da Romano after his capture of Friuli in 1259, when he is reported to have mutilated and disfigured nearly the whole population of that city.[15] Even if some of these reports invite mistrust of their credibility, they are deployed strategically to criticise each of the perpetrators in turn.

'The disfigured' as a group, however, do not appear in medieval sources alongside 'the poor' and 'the weak' or 'lepers' or 'widows and orphans' among the vulnerable groups in our texts (nor, come to that, do 'the impaired or disabled', presumably classed as 'weak' instead). Indeed, it is even difficult to find any commonly used term in the medieval Latin and Greek sources for 'disfigurement' at all, either as a process – becoming disfigured, inflicting disfigurement – or a condition – being disfigured. Writers certainly focus on the ways in which the face was injured, and/or describe the scar/s left by the wounds, but they do so using verbs for wounding, cutting, branding and burning. Search for 'disfigured' people electronically in online resources for medieval Europe, then, and you will not find them. (Modern translators, by contrast, often employ 'disfigured' to translate some of these verbs.)

A further impediment might lie in the ways in which history has fragmented into so many sub-disciplines: ironically, the post-modern 'democratisation' of the subject, opening out into many hitherto neglected areas of human experience, has led to an increased specialisation that itself leaves gaps. This has meant that the history of disfigurement has fallen into a space between histories of medicine and studies of pre-modern disability. For most medieval victims of disfigurement, there was apparently little hope of medical intervention, meaning that medical historians have tended to ignore the medieval evidence for surgical procedures on the face, and focused largely on practical texts emerging in the early modern period, such as those of Heinrich von Pfolspeundt and his German contemporaries from the fifteenth century, or of Ambroise Paré and Gasparre Tagliacozzi in the sixteenth.[16] Studies of disability in the medieval period, on the other hand, focus on sensory or motor impairments, which are much better documented and have formed the

---

[15] *The History of the Albigensian Crusade: Peter of Les-Vaux-de-Cernay's Historia Albigensis*, trans. W. A. Sibly and M. D. Sibly (Woodbridge, 1998), I.142; *Bartholomaei Scribae Annales*, s.a. 1245, in *MGH SS*, XVIII, ed. G. H. Pertz (Hannover, 1863), 219; *Rolandini Patavini Chronica*, XI.17, ed. P. Jaffé, in *MGH SS*, XIX, ed. G. H. Pertz (Hannover, 1866), 136.

[16] Leo Zimmermann and Ilza Vaith, *Great Ideas in the History of Surgery* (Baltimore, 1961), 203–17 (Germans), 179–92 (Paré) and 261–7 (Tagliacozzi). Recent work on the latter has been done by Emily Cock, '"Leading 'em by the nose into publick shame and derision": Gaspare Tagliacozzi, Alexander Read and the Lost History of Plastic Surgery, 1600–1800', *Social History of Medicine*, 28 (2015), 1–21.

basis of a number of recent, rich surveys.[17] For disfigurement to appear in the latter, however, it needs to be accompanied by a physical impairment, otherwise it is at best tangential and at worst irrelevant to the concerns both of medieval authors and modern commentators. The social disability inherent in a damaged face is hardly considered.

Surely, though, the history of a damaged face has featured in work on the medieval body, whether whole or fragmented, whose physical and metaphorical meanings have been dissected for nearly half a century by cultural historians and literary scholars alike?[18] In fact this turns out not to be the case: much work on the body has focused on the female body, medical theories including one- and two-sex models,[19] or reproductive health,[20] or the fleshly implications of women's affective piety and self-mortification,[21] or, as we have seen already, the impaired body. The diversity of the field, with no central argument, was commented upon as early as 1995 by Caroline Walker Bynum, and Sarah Coakley in 1997 suggested that 'It is as if we are clear about an agreed cultural obsession – the "body" – but far from assured about its referent.'[22] Disembodied heads have recently been the subject of study, and the fascination of genitalia (and their lack) continues to loom large in such analysis, but the major

---

[17] E.g. Irina Metzler, *Disability in Medieval Europe: Thinking about Physical Impairment during the High Middle Ages* (2006), and her *A Social History of Disability in the Middle Ages: Cultural Considerations of Physical Impairment* (2013); *The Treatment of Disabled Persons in Medieval Europe*, ed. Wendy J. Turner and Tory Vandeventer Pearman (Lewiston, 2010); *Disability in the Middle Ages: Reconsiderations and Reverberations*, ed. Joshua Eyler (Aldershot, 2010); Edward Wheatley, *Stumbling Blocks before the Blind: Medieval Constructions of a Disability* (Ann Arbor, 2010).

[18] *Framing Medieval Bodies*, ed. Sarah Kay and Miri Rubin (Manchester, 1994); Caroline Bynum, 'Why All the Fuss about the Body? A Medievalist's Perspective', *Critical Inquiry*, 22 (1995), 1–33; *The Body in Late Medieval and Early Modern Culture*, ed. Darryl Grantley and Nina Taunton (Aldershot, 2000); *Fleshly Things and Spiritual Matters: Studies on the Medieval Body in Honor of Margaret Bridges*, ed. Nicole Nyffenegger and Katrin Rupp (Newcastle, 2011).

[19] Thomas Laqueur, *Making Sex: Body and Gender from the Greeks to Freud* (Cambridge, MA, 1992), stimulated much subsequent discussion: Joan Cadden, *The Meanings of Sex Difference in the Middle Ages* (Cambridge, 1995); *Third Sex, Third Gender: Beyond Sexual Dimorphism in Culture and History*, ed. Gilbert Herdt (New York, 1996); *The Body in Balance: Humoral Medicines in Practice*, ed. Peregrine Horden and Elizabeth Hsu (Oxford and New York, 2013); Helen King, *The One-Sex Body on Trial: Classical and Early Modern Evidences* (Aldershot, 2013).

[20] E.g. Monica Green, *Making Women's Medicine Masculine* (Oxford, 2008); Elisheva Baumgarten, *Mothers and Children: Jewish Family Life in Medieval Europe* (Princeton, 2004); Jennifer Wynne Hellwarth, *The Reproductive Unconscious in Medieval and Early Modern England* (2003).

[21] Discussed by Liz Herbert McAvoy, 'Writing the Self: Sex, Body and Soul', in *A Companion to British Literature*, I: *Medieval Literatures 700–1450*, ed. Roberto DeMaria, Heesok Chang and Samantha Zacher (Chichester, 2014), 114–29; Claire Marshall, 'The Politics of Self-mutilation: Forms of Female Devotion in the Late Middle Ages', in *The Body in Late Medieval and Early Modern Culture*, ed. Grantley and Taunton, 11–22.

[22] Caroline Bynum, 'Why All the Fuss about the Body?'; Sarah Coakley, 'Introduction', in *Religion and the Body*, ed. S. Coakley (Cambridge, 1997), 2.

vehicle of interpersonal communication, the face, has been curiously omitted.[23] This despite the fact, as Ruth Mazo Karras has pointed out, that female beauty has long been blamed for the inappropriate behaviours of men.[24] And whilst anger has featured as the subject of study within the burgeoning field of the medieval emotional landscape, it has not generated much consideration of how connected facial mutilation is with outbursts of extreme rage in the sources.[25]

Disfigurement itself, however, is a gendered phenomenon in the medieval evidence. Deliberate disfigurement is, at its core, a power play, a show of dominance over the victim, whether authorised through judicial channels, or totally illicit and intended to challenge that authority. Male on female acts not only reinforce a hierarchy of physical strength, but also demonstrate masculinity (whether articulated as hardness or familial discipline) to other men. Deliberate acts of disfigurement dominate in medieval accounts, in early law codes, in narratives and in archaeological reports: accidental facial injury is in fact relatively rare in the material explored, although two possible examples will be discussed a little later in this paper. Those who disfigured deliberately, with just a handful of exceptions, were men, but those whom they disfigured were almost all other men, at least in the records (domestic violence against women, however, was and remains a largely hidden or ignored phenomenon).[26] It is striking that male aggression towards women, where it is documented at all, is thought to have gone too far if it reaches the woman's head or face, signalling a lack of self-control on the part of the husband.[27]

And whilst some forms of disfigurement, mainly those on the severe end of the spectrum, might be fatal, they were not intended to be. Byzantine authors report that political and judicial blindings were often carried out by the executioner, but he had to be good at his job and in this case keep his victims alive. (A particularly lengthy, possibly eye-witness, account in Michael Psellos, for example, has the executioner tie one of his victims down to prevent him moving at the point of impact, and being told by

---

[23] The essays in *Disembodied Heads in Medieval and Early Modern Culture*, ed. Catrien G. Santing, Barbara Baert and Anita Traninger (Leiden, 2013), include only one on the face (in early modern portraiture); *Castration and Culture in the Middle Ages*, ed. Larissa Tracy (Cambridge, 2013). At the time of writing, I have not as yet had access to Przemysław Tyszka, *The Human Body in Barbarian Laws, c. 500–c. 800: Corpus Hominis as a Cultural Category* (Frankfurt, 2014), which promises consideration of 'body parts' in one of its chapters.

[24] Ruth Mazo Karras, *Sexuality in Medieval Europe: Doing unto Others* (New York, 2005), 39.

[25] *Anger's Past: The Social Uses of an Emotion in the Middle Ages*, ed. Barbara H. Rosenwein (Ithaca, NY, 1998).

[26] Hannah Skoda, *Medieval Violence: Physical Brutality in Northern France, 1270–1330* (Oxford, 2013), 193–230, highlights this issue of under-recording with some stark examples.

[27] E.g. if a wife uttered a 'shameful word' to her husband in medieval Wales, he could claim monetary compensation or strike her three times with a rod, but not on the head: *Laws of Hywel Dda (The Book of Blegywryd)*, trans. Melville Richards (Liverpool, 1954), 67.

another, in an act of bravado, that if he moves the executioner should nail him down.[28]) Disfiguring injuries and blindings were designed to disable, to humiliate, to cause pain and suffering, and above all to demonstrate the power of the person injuring.[29] Whether that was intended to bring approval – the just punishment of recidivist criminals in Cnut's laws for England, for example – or showed the perpetrator up as the worst kind of tyrant – Cnut in his younger days can take a bow here too, as the mutilator of Anglo-Saxon hostages – was beside the point.[30] Both sides of the coin demonstrated dominance, however it was written up.

Social class also mattered to reports of disfigurement: it hardly ever seems to occur across class boundaries (except in a few isolated cases of oppression in saints' lives), but is carried out within the peer group to which both the perpetrator and victim belong. When servants became involved in the disputes of their lords, they attacked each other.[31] Attacking someone else's servants or subjects, however, was a powerful mutilation-by-proxy of the lord or king himself, and in the words of sociologist Erving Goffman, a 'face-threatening act'.[32] (Not that a 'face-threatening act' needed to target the physical face of course, but the latter presented a very obvious and visible target.) Medieval honour culture – injuries between equals, and the focus of much historical enquiry – existed alongside and has not been sufficiently distinguished from medieval 'face' culture, where the injuries, physical or verbal, were inflicted between people of different social status.[33] This is what gives Cnut's actions such resonance as a challenge to Aethelred's 'face' as king in 1014. It is also why an attack by pirates on the Saxon coast in 994, in which Thietmar of Merseberg nearly

---

[28]Michael Psellos, *Chronographia*, v.40–50, translated as *Fourteen Byzantine Rulers: The Chronographia of Michael Psellos*, trans. E. R. A. Sewter (1979), 145–51.

[29]William Ian Miller, *Eye for an Eye* (Cambridge, 2006), 151–9, writing about revenge, explores the dilemma of 'Killing him or keeping him alive for scoffing': deliberate disfigurement was always intended to fulfil the latter function. See also Mitchell Merback, *The Thief, the Cross and the Wheel: Pain and the Spectacle of Punishment in Medieval and Renaissance Europe* (1999); Klaus van Eickels, 'Gendered Violence: Castration and Blinding as Punishment for Treason in Normandy and Anglo-Norman England', *Gender and History*, 16 (2004), 588–602.

[30]II Cnut: Secular Laws, 53 and 53.1, trans. D. Whitelock, *English Historical Documents*, I: *500–1042* (rev. edn, 1979), 463; *The Anglo-Saxon Chronicle: A Revised Translation*, C (D, E) for 1013 and 1014, ed. Dorothy Whitelock (1961), 92–3.

[31]With a little supernatural help: see the case of Heldolf reported in the chronicle of St Peter's abbey near Halle, Germany, in the early twelfth century: *Chronicon Montis Sereni*, ed. E. Ehrenfeuchter, *s.a.* 1126, in *MGH SS*, XXIII, ed. G. Waitz (Hannover, 1874), 140.

[32]Erving Goffman, *Interaction Ritual: Essays on Face-to-Face Behaviour* (1967), 5–46.

[33]Full discussion of this contention in Skinner, *Living with Disfigurement*, ch. 1. On the distinction between 'honour' and 'face' cultures, Angela K.-Y. Leung and Dov Cohen, 'Within- and Between- Culture Variation: Individual Differences and the Cultural Logics of Honor, Face and Dignity Cultures', *Journal of Personality and Social Psychology*, 100 (2011), 507–26.

ended up being given as a hostage, remained a focal point of discussion nearly a century after it happened, since it included the maiming of noble hostages who 'lived a long time after, a reproach to the Empire and a pitiful spectacle for all the people', according to Adam of Bremen.[34] Neither king nor emperor was able to prevent the atrocities, and were themselves written up as weakened as a result.

The writing-up process, though, introduces a problem of its own. Generations of scholars of early medieval laws, for example, have pointed out that these were directly affected by the process of conversion to Christianity across Europe, and shaped by clerical ideas of ideal kingship. Nearly all of the narrative sources, too, emanate from the pens of male, clerical writers, and all but one or two of the texts are produced within a Christian frame of reference. And it shows. Medieval violence, in particular violence against the face, is often presented with biblical *exempla* in mind, most drawn from the Old Testament. The mutilation of clerics' or rulers' faces or heads called to mind the Levitical ban on men with deformities serving as priests (particularly in Byzantium, where political depositions might include cutting off noses and lips, blinding or simply tonsuring and exile);[35] the judicial mutilation of adulteresses, pimps and the incestuous with nose-cutting reflected the fate of the prostitute Oholibah in Ezekiel;[36] and any ruler who went beyond the boundaries of acceptable use of mutilation as judicial punishment was likely to be compared, explicitly or not, with the 'tyrant' Herod (Ezzelino's atrocity against the Friulians, mentioned earlier, included attacking innocent babies, for example). The model of Malchus's mutilation by Peter in the Garden of Gethsemane was almost certainly in writers' minds when they described and discussed the loss of ears.[37] Absent from this panoply

---

[34] *Magistri Adam Bremensis Gesta Hammaburgensis Ecclesiae Pontificum*, II.xxxi, ed. Bernhard Schmeidler, *MGH SSRG*, II (Hannover and Leipzig, 1917), 29: 'pyratae mox in furorem versi, omnes, quos in vinculis tenuerunt, meliores ad ludibrium habentes, manus eis pedesque truncarunt ac nare precisa deformantes ad terram semianimes proiciebant. Ex quibus erant aliqui nobiles viri, qui postea supervixerunt longo tempore, obprobrium imperio et miserabile spectaculum omni populo.' English translation: *Adam of Bremen, History of the Archbishops of Hamburg-Bremen*, trans. Francis J. Tschan with introduction and notes by Timothy Reuter (New York, 2002), 75–6. Cf. Thietmar's account: Thietmar, *Chronicon*, IV.23–5.

[35] And this was a motif available to Jewish authors too: see Josephus's account of the mutilation of Hyrcanus, the High Priest: *Jewish War*, I.13.9 (1.276), and *Antiquities*, XIV.13.10, cited in Miller, *Eye for an Eye*, 139.

[36] Such prescriptions appear in Byzantine law in the eighth century, Cnut's laws for England in the eleventh and Norman law in the kingdom of Sicily in the twelfth, preserved in Frederick II's codification a century later, and are discussed in Skinner, 'The Gendered Nose and its Lack'.

[37] Malchus's loss of his ear (subsequently restored by Christ) is one of the few iconographical depictions of a disfigurement, as preserved in the Winchester Psalter, British Library, Cotton MC Nero C IV, fo. 21r.

of biblical figures is any reference to the mark of Cain the murderer, but since the Bible is totally opaque on what that 'mark' may have been, this is unsurprising. The influence of the *idea* of a mark, though, may be seen in the practice of literally marking a criminal if he or she was *not* to be put to death, mirroring God's intention as set out in the Bible.[38]

The net effect of this biblical framework, it seems, is to close down discussion of any incidence of facial disfigurement that could not easily be related to biblical models, Old or New Testament. Many accounts, after all, were written up with an explicitly moral lesson about self-restraint and its lack, or the power of God through the saints, or the control of sexuality. A failure to grant mercy, for example, underpins the story of King Henry I of England's order to blind two knights (against the advice of his companions) and a minstrel, Luke of La Barre, as reported by Orderic Vitalis. Luke, in fact, prefers to kill himself rather than be blinded ('better off dead' again?), and Orderic's mournful comment on his death makes it clear that Henry had got it very wrong here.[39] Strikingly, the few women being disfigured in the sample are presented (and punished) as whores, whether their punishment is for sexual crimes or not. For example, in his sixth-century *History of the Franks*, Gregory of Tours reports the treason of the royal nursemaid, Septimina, but is as much concerned, possibly even more concerned, with the fact that her accomplice was her lover, Droctulf, to whom she had gone 'like a whore' after killing her husband. She is punished with burning to the face ('cauteriis accensis in faciae vulnerata') unlike Droctulf's loss of his ears.[40] And almost without exception, the individuals (and some groups) whose disfigurement is reported are either socially prominent, such as Charles the Bald's son Young Charles, who was grievously injured in the face during a bout of swordplay with his peers, and/or have a specific story that *brings* them to prominence and justifies their case being reported, such as that of the priest Walchelin, again in Orderic.

As has already been emphasised, stories of disfigurement tend to be stories of individuals, and two particular cases, Charles and Walchelin, bring out the contrasting approaches of medieval authors when recounting such tales. Charles's injury is carefully described in the Annals of St Bertin record for the year 864:

> Young Charles ... returning from the hunt in the Cottian woods, while he only meant to enjoy some horseplay with other young men of his own age ... by the work of the devil

[38] Genesis 4.15.

[39] *Ecclesiastical History of Orderic Vitalis*, XII.39, ed. Marjorie Chibnall (6 vols., Oxford, 1969–80), VI, 352–6.

[40] *Gregorii Episcopi Turoniensis Libri Historiarum X*, ed. B. Krusch and W. Levison, *Monumenta Germaniae Historica, Scriptores Rerum Merovingicarum*, I (Hannover, 1951), Book IX.38.

was struck in the head with a sword by a youth named Albuin. The blow penetrated almost as far as the brain, reaching from his left temple to his right cheekbone and jaw.[41]

There is always the lurking suspicion, with any accidental injury to a royal figure, that this was no accident, but the annalist leaves it as 'the work of the devil' and allows the reader to make up his or her own mind. The major injury Charles received is described in detail, and indeed the diagonal sword-slash to the face is a relatively common injury visible in osteoarchaeological remains – Albuin was clearly right-handed.[42] But there was no hint in the source that his assailant intended to injure Charles, no reference in the annals to compensation by, or punishment of, Albuin being demanded. (If this had been Iceland, as William Miller has illustrated, things might have been rather different.[43]) Charles apparently suffered epileptic fits thereafter, and it is doubtful whether he escaped other impairments given the severity of the injury, but he did remain as sub-king of Aquitaine (albeit a largely inactive one) for the remaining two years of his life. Because Charles *was* so prominent, however, we have more than one account of the injury: Ado of Vienne (d. 870) reports that Charles was 'molestatus et dehonestatus' by the incident and his injury.[44] Later, Regino of Prum (d. 915) tells a rather different story of the incident, saying that Charles provoked Albuin's attack 'out of the levity of youth' and that his assailant struck him on the head with his sword, leaving him half-dead with a 'vultu deformatus'.[45] For Regino, therefore, writing at a safe chronological distance, the disfigurement was Charles's own fault, a condition that his irresponsible behaviour had brought upon himself. That is, the story of an accident could be written up and recast as a moral example of the folly of young men swinging swords at each other, almost asking to be injured. The more the moral frame intrudes, the

[41] *Annales Bertiniani*, s.a. 864, ed. G. Waitz, *MGH SSRG*, v (Hannover, 1883), 67: 'Carolus iuvenis . . . noctu rediens de venatione in silva Cotia iocari cum aliis iuvenibus et coaevis suis putans, operante diabolo ab Albuino iuvene in capite spatha percutitur pene usque ad cerebrum; quae plaga a timore sinistro usque ad malam dextrae maxillae pervenit.' English translation: *The Annals of St Bertin: Ninth-Century Histories*, I, trans. J. L. Nelson (Manchester, 1991), 111–12.

[42] T. Anderson, 'Cranial weapon injuries from Anglo-Saxon Dover', *International Journal of Osteoarchaeology*, 6 (1998), 10–14; Piers D. Mitchell, 'Trauma in the Crusader Period City of Caesarea: A Major Port in the Medieval Eastern Mediterranean', *International Journal of Osteoarchaeology*, 16 (2006), 493–505; Piers D. Mitchell, Y. Nagar and R. Ellenbaum, 'Weapon Injuries in the Twelfth-Century Crusader Garrison of Vadum Iacob Castle, Galilee', *International Journal of Osteoarchaeology*, 16 (2006), 145–55.

[43] William Ian Miller, *Bloodtaking and Peacemaking: Feud, Law and Society in Saga Iceland* (Chicago, 1990), 51–76, on 'the politics of accident'.

[44] *Ex Adonis Archiepiscopi Viennensis Chronico*, ed. I. de Arx, *MGH SS*, II (Hannover, 1829), 323.

[45] *Reginonis Abbatis Prumiensis Chronicon*, s.a.870, ed. F. Kurze, *MGH SSRG*, L (Hannover, 1890), 101.

more negatively Charles's disfigured face is viewed. He is, after all, a king, and so there is clearly some disquiet being expressed about his continuing fitness to be king. Here, the power of his family maintained him, but it could not silence the critics.

Was there any way to 'change face' then? Could victims of disfigurement manage others' responses to them, and be seen as the person behind the injury? Open to clerical commentators, of course, was the contrast between fleshly and spiritual health, and certainly Thietmar laments his sinful soul more than his misshapen face. As has been alluded to earlier, these writers might have recourse to religious explanations and comfort. The scars on the surface of the skin mattered little when integrity of the soul was what counted. Wipert, blinded on his mission with Bruno, in fact emphasises that his subsequent life as a blind, wandering beggar was spiritually beneficial to him and to those who gave him alms.

The same message seems to emerge from an extended account in Orderic Vitalis of the visions of a priest named Walchelin. Extending over several pages in the modern edition, the heart of the story has Walchelin recounting a vision he had had fifteen years earlier, in which he had seen the walking dead, and been attacked and dragged along the ground by an evil knight with burning hands. Fifteen years later, he recounted his tale to Orderic, who believed his informant on the basis that 'I saw the scar on his face caused by the touch of the terrible knight.'[46] The story is a striking one, and Orderic's belief in its authenticity rests upon the only material proof remaining, Walchelin's still-scarred face. By recording the priest's tale in writing, Orderic adds another layer of authority and in effect tells us: 'This is Walchelin, just wait till you hear how he got those burns on his face.' The tale of the terrible knight, fifteen years ago in a vision, is a compelling story. By re-telling it, Walchelin gains social capital and validation – 'My vision was so real it has left scars' – deflecting enquiry as to the mundane reason for his facial difference, which in all probability was a childhood accident with boiling water or a fire.

Children – and accidents – are in fact totally under-represented in the written material explored, and this partly reflects a reality that in most law codes accidents were not actionable, and children rarely appear as a separate group. The *Damweiniau* or 'Eventualities', an appendix of case law added to the legal codes of Wales, for example, explicitly said that 'there is no damage done by a person's fire to another person's flesh, without the person's act associated with it, for which compensation is paid'. That is, the fire had to be deliberately wielded or applied for the

[46]'... faciem eius horrendi militis tactu lesam perspexi': *Ecclesiastical History of Orderic Vitalis*, VIII.17, ed. Chibnall, IV, 248–9.

injury to become actionable.[47] But such evidence of accidents is quite rare.

Moving on to consider children and congenital impairment, it seems that this was an acquired disfigurement for the *parents*. A child born with a birthmark might arouse some attention; a cleft lip or palate (even assuming that the surgical treatment outlined in the Anglo-Saxon leechbooks was ever attempted) could present more challenging problems.[48] *Pace* Ariès and his detractors, the focus here is not whether parents felt an emotional bond towards impaired children, but in evidence from archaeology showing if a child had a congenital impairment and died young, it was either treated entirely neutrally in the burial rite, undifferentiated from able-bodied children, or might be made special with bespoke items.[49] Not having reached social adulthood was a protection of sorts. But what if he or she grew up? A thirteenth-century account in the chronicle of Salimbene features a monk named Aldevrandus, described as having a deformed head in the shape of a helmet, and copious hair on his forehead (excessive hairiness was almost always written up negatively, whether in historical or fictional works). When his turn came to start off the responses (antiphon) and, presumably, with all eyes upon him, the other monks would laugh, causing him to be upset and blush.[50] Salimbene, of course, turns this harassment into an edifying tale of Aldevrandus's Christ-like humility in the face of his persecutors, but it is worth speculating how he had come to be in a monastic community at all. Perhaps he was a child oblate, offered to the church perhaps to protect him from wider attention, but condemned to a life of pain from his so-called brothers.

If the stories of Wipert and Walchelin are perhaps medieval examples of triumph over adversity, Aldevrandus's gives us pause before we become too optimistic about the status of people with disfigurements in medieval society. We have to remember that Walchelin – or indeed Orderic – felt the need to construct a more exciting story to explain his appearance (which, we should note, is never fully described). Why? Modern psychological studies about facial difference have included a consideration of its capacity to elicit a disgust response, which Miller has also investigated from a historical perspective. According to him, medieval people felt no shame

[47] *The Laws of Hywel Dda: Law Texts from Medieval Wales*, ed. and trans. D. Jenkins (Llandysul, 1986), 171.

[48] Leechbook I, in *Leechdoms, Wortcunning and Starcraft of Early England*, ed. O. Cockayne (3 vols., 1864–6), II, 59.

[49] Undifferentiated: E. Craig and G. Craig, 'The Diagnosis and Context of a Facial Deformity from an Anglo-Saxon Cemetery at Spofforth, North Yorkshire', *International Journal of Osteoarchaeology*, 23 (2013), 631–9; special cup for child with cleft palate: Sally Crawford, *Childhood in Anglo-Saxon England* (Stroud, 1999), 95.

[50] *Chronica Fratris Salimbene Ordinis Minorum. Liber de Praelatio*, ed. O. Holder-Egger, in *MGH SS*, XXXII, ed. G. H. Pertz (Hannover, 1913), 137.

at pointing, staring and being repelled by scenes of violence, or cruelty, or the mutilation of others and its aftermath; this, he says, is what distinguishes medieval people from us 'moderns', who would be too ashamed or embarrassed to behave in the same way.[51] Certainly, there are accounts of political enemies or criminals being publicly paraded and publicly mutilated, suggesting that the so-called 'medieval theatre of cruelty' was not simply the product of medieval dramatists.[52] But whilst there are explicit examples of difference in appearance being ridiculed, the disgust that Miller posits is notably absent from the language of the sources.

If we go to the other end of the scale, Jacques Le Goff long ago suggested that medieval Europe teemed with the disease-ridden, impaired and mutilated, implying that a disfigured face would not have been seen as all that exceptional.[53] Not surprisingly, I disagree with this view as well, because having a different face clearly *did* involve stigmatisation of some kind. Why else did legislators from Ireland to Byzantium penalise apparently trivial injuries to the face and teeth, and at the same time utilise such measures to express their own authority against wrongdoers? A visibly beaten-up Lombard male in Italy, according to the laws, suffered ridicule and shame for his state;[54] Gregory of Tours recounts that a group of conspirators against King Childebert II were deprived of their ears and noses then 'let out as a subject of ridicule';[55] in the early Irish law code Bretha Dein Checht, the shame of the public scar on the face exposed its victim to public ridicule – hence, the law states, a fine has to be paid for every public assembly the victim has to endure with facial disfigurement;[56] and Thietmar of Merseberg, even as he dismisses the importance of his 'ridiculous' face, still goes to the trouble of using that term. It is no coincidence that these are all men, and the danger to their reputations was not that people would find them repulsive or disgusting, but that they would *laugh* at them. Ridicule, as Irish poets knew well, was a devastating weapon, and perhaps Henry's anger at Luke of La Barre might not have been so terrible had not that poet circulated scurrilous

[51] K. Shanmugarajah, S. Gaind, A. Clarke and P. E. M. Butler, 'The Role of Disgust Emotions in the Observer Response to Facial Disfigurement', *Body Image*, 9 (2012), 455–61; William Ian Miller, *The Anatomy of Disgust* (Cambridge, MA, 1997), 19.

[52] Jody Enders, *The Medieval Theater of Cruelty: Rhetoric, Memory, Violence* (Ithaca, NY, 2002).

[53] J. Le Goff, *Medieval Civilization, 400–1500*, trans. J. Barrow (Oxford, 1988), 240.

[54] *Leges Langobardorum, Edictus* 41, ed. F. Bluhme, *Monumenta Historica Germaniae, Leges*, IV, ed. G. H. Pertz (Hannover, 1868), 20.

[55] *Gregorii Episcopi Turoniensis*, VIII.29 (c. 585 CE) and X.18 ('ad ridiculum laxaverunt'), ed. Krusch, 393 and 509.

[56] Bretha Dein Crecht, clause 31, cited in Fergus Kelly, *A Guide to Early Irish Law* (Dublin, 1988), 132.

(and presumably amusing) rhymes at the king's expense. Humour, as early medievalists have highlighted, can be highly dangerous.[57]

This brief survey has sought to demonstrate that disfigurement is a constant of human history, whether congenital or acquired, but what counts as a 'normal' appearance fluctuates over time and place. Medical historians have privileged interventions, looking at ways in which faces have been fixed or 'saved', and thus have overlooked the social history of people with disfigurements, except in very prominent cases where, for example, that person became an exhibit.[58] This reinforces the objectification of those with disfigurements as passive recipients of treatment. Of course, almost all accounts of people with facial difference before the age of surgical intervention are equally objectifying – we get little sense of what it felt like to become and be disfigured, and have to rely upon the assumptions of legislators and chroniclers that it *was* humiliating and shameful. Clerics were able to draw lessons and, even, some comfort from their faith about their facial difference, but for most medieval elite men, the bulk of our sample of some 400 separate references to disfigurement, humility and patient acceptance was not part of the honour package.

What, though, about our own practice as historians? What assumptions do we bring to this subject matter? It is all too easy to equate the face, the surface, with the person and, if we have not personally experienced disfigurement, to think of it in entirely negative terms. Valentin Groebner's book *Defaced* and his preceding article, 'Losing Face, Saving Face', express this sense of loss and lack.[59] Reading modern accounts, the journey to a restored sense of selfhood comes through a combination of good surgeons, effective cosmetics, supportive families and, in most cases, access to resources. This is not so different from our medieval cases, but here the combination might omit the first, have limited access to the second and rely far more on the third and fourth, and add 'supportive community or priest' as a fifth element. In both periods, however, a good back-story matters, however horrific it might be. People with disfigurements who make it into the medieval record, however, are often *already prominent*, whether through their office, rank, birth or actions. Military men, bishops and clergy, courtiers and royalty

---

[57] See the essays in *Humour, History and Politics in Late Antiquity and the Early Middle Ages*, ed. G. Halsall (Cambridge, 2010).

[58] Rosemarie Garland-Thomson, 'Introduction: From Wonder to Error – A Genealogy of Freak Discourse in Modernity', in her edited volume *Freakery: Cultural Spectacles of the Extraordinary Body* (New York, 1996), 1–22.

[59] Valentin Groebner, *Defaced: The Visual Culture of Violence in the Late Middle Ages* (New York, 2008); Valentin Groebner, 'Losing Face, Saving Face? Noses and Honour in the Late Medieval Town', *History Workshop Journal*, 40 (1995), 1–15. Groebner, as can be seen, conflates 'face' and 'honour' in his analysis.

are all represented. Wealthy merchants are held hostage and mutilated in order that they ransom their remaining digits or facial features, not so very different from medieval judicial systems that mutilate those who cannot pay compensation. By contrast, many of the biographies identified at the start of this paper are of people who *became* prominent because of their disfigurement. Does this represent the cultural shift that Miller recognised? Has surgical 'progress' heightened expectations that everyone can – even *should* – look more 'normal', and thus marginalised those who are judged not to? Is the atomised, individualistic nature of modern society such that individuals with impaired faces are more isolated than they might have been in medieval society? This does not assume a cosy, comforting view of medieval village or monastic communities looking after their own (a small community, after all, turned into something of a living hell for Aldevrandus), but simply access to support and acceptance if the person was well known. By contrast, as Luke Demaitre has argued, the sharp rise in urban dwellers in the thirteenth and fourteenth centuries, often strangers to each other but living in close proximity, heightened awareness of facial difference so much that we have far more records of doctors being consulted for often trivial conditions (sunburn, spots, hair loss), suggesting that first impressions – based on the human reflex of facial scrutiny – mattered more in this context.[60] By continuing to study how different communities viewed disfiguring conditions and injuries, and analysing, insofar as we can, how those with different faces responded to their change in appearance, we can perhaps make connections not only with their experiences in the past, but provide a firmer platform for arguing for social justice and equality in the present.

[60]Luke Demaitre, 'Skin and the City: Cosmetic Medicine as an Urban Concern', in *Between Text and Patient: The Medical Enterprise in Medieval and Early Modern Europe*, ed. Florence Eliza Glaze and Brian K. Nance (Florence, 2011), 97–120.

Transactions of the RHS 26 (2016), pp. 43–58 © Royal Historical Society 2016
doi:10.1017/S0080440116000049

WHO WAS SIMON DE MONTFORT, EARL OF LEICESTER?*

By John Maddicott

READ 12 MARCH 2015

AT DE MONTFORT UNIVERSITY, LEICESTER

ABSTRACT. This paper surveys the political career and personal life of Simon de Montfort. Derived largely from the author's biography of Montfort, it lays stress on his initial position as an outsider in English politics whose military abilities, diplomatic usefulness and personal charisma fostered his rise to power at the court of Henry III, but who subsequently fell out with the king and eventually became his fiercest opponent. It describes his position as lord of the honour of Leicester, from which town he expelled the Jews, and it goes on to assess the paradoxical and contrasting elements in Montfort's character, which combined deep piety and religious fervour with avarice and a self-seeking desire for his own and his family's advancement. It argues that personal differences, based largely on a strong sense of grievance and reflecting some of these character traits, rather than constitutional principles, lay behind his opposition to Henry III. It concludes by reviewing Montfort's role in the period of baronial reform and rebellion, 1258–65, and by describing his legacy, both to Henry III in his later years and to Edward I.

A short answer to the above question is this. Simon de Montfort was by origin a minor French noble who went on to become one of the leading English magnates of the thirteenth century and the brother-in-law of King Henry III. He was first the close friend of the king and later his bitter enemy. He was a devout Christian, a crusader and a kindred spirit to scholars and bishops; but he was also a grasping landlord and an unscrupulous politician. Many people saw him as hero and a holy man, many others as a tyrant and a troublemaker. He played a leading role in the movement of baronial opposition to the crown which began in 1258 and which took over the country's government in a revolutionary way. He died in battle, fighting (as he would have said) for the same cause, at Evesham in Worcestershire on 4 August 1265. Those are some of the features of his life and career, of what he was and did. What he was not,

---

* This lecture followed the opening of the De Montfort University Heritage Centre by the Royal Historical Society's president and formed part of the university's parliamentary and Magna Carta commemorations.

contrary to popular historical folklore, was the founder of the English parliament.[1]

We could reasonably ask whether Montfort was a good man or a bad man, a saint or a sinner. We are justified in asking these judgemental questions, of a sort which historians usually try to avoid, not only because they are questions which contemporaries also raised, but also because in Montfort's case they face us in a particularly obtrusive way. Their starkness is to be explained by our ability to know more about Montfort's character and temperament than about those of any other medieval nobleman. Historians can rarely assess medieval character except in the case of kings and churchmen: kings because they were the focus of public attention and the interests of chroniclers, churchmen because they often expressed themselves through their writings. But with almost all members of the medieval nobility, character and personality are very largely obscure. When historians try to construe character, they usually have to fall back on bland generalities. Because character is so difficult to elucidate, the listing of attributes has to do duty instead: nobles are 'powerful', 'wealthy', 'chivalric', 'influential' and so on. But whether these men were good humoured or bad tempered, kind or callous, clever or stupid, devoted or detached husbands and fathers, we can hardly ever know. Montfort's example is different, however, and we can speak about him with a degree of psychological penetration equally possible, among his contemporaries, only in the case of King Henry and of one or two of his bishops. This is partly because he was at the centre of public affairs for much of his life, and therefore closely observed by some very observant chroniclers, notably Matthew Paris; but also because a large part of his family archive survives, including some very informal documents which provide us with a good deal of intimate detail – some of it actually in dialogue form, like the parts of a play.[2] In addition, his intimacy with a group of highly intelligent reforming churchmen reveals much about his personality through their letters, in some cases letters of rebuke as well as praise. This leaves the historian well placed at least to ask whether Montfort was a saint or a sinner (though not necessarily to provide an answer).

A survey of Montfort's career in England may help us to disentangle some of the contradictions which his character presents. Nothing about that career was predictable from his origins, which lay wholly in France. He was born about 1208, the second son of a leading French noble, another Simon de Montfort, whose family lands lay near Paris. Much of his childhood was spent in the south of France, where his father was fighting the Albigensians, the heretical enemies of the church. As a

---

[1] A full account of Montfort's career will be found in J. R. Maddicott, *Simon de Montfort* (Cambridge, 1994), which provides comprehensive references to the sources.

[2] C. Bémont, *Simon de Montfort* (Paris, 1884), 343–53.

younger son, he had no particular prospects, and as a Frenchman he had no particular interest in England. What took him across the Channel was a family claim to the English lands of the honour of Leicester, centred on the midland town which was the location for this lecture. Robert de Beaumont, earl of Leicester, the last of the Beaumont earls of Leicester, died childless in 1204. His heirs were his two sisters: Amicia, the widow of another Simon de Montfort, our Montfort's grandfather, and a second sister, Margaret, wife of Saer de Quincy, earl of Winchester. In 1207, the Beaumont lands were divided between the two sisters. Amicia's share descended first to Simon de Montfort, Amicia's son and our Montfort's father, and then to our Montfort's elder brother, Amaury de Montfort. In 1229–30, Simon bought out his brother's claim to the lands and the title, at some considerable expense, and in 1231, he arrived in England to claim in inheritance the Montfort half of the old earldom of Leicester. Rather surprisingly, Henry III allowed the claim of this unknown Frenchman, so giving Montfort a first footing in his new country.[3]

During Montfort's early years in England, his landed holdings were confined to the honour of Leicester. Although the honour spread into southern England, its core lay in Leicester itself and in the nearby demesne manors of Hinckley, Shilton, Bagworth, Thornton and Desford. Kenilworth and its castle in neighbouring Warwickshire, which he acquired from the king in 1244, later extended his interest in this part of the world. One of his earliest actions in what was now his home town has made him notorious: in 1231 or 1232, he expelled the Jews from Leicester. This act of zealotry, presented as one for the salvation of Montfort's soul and for the relief of the Leicester townspeople from the burden of Jewish usury, was very much in line with contemporary values. Even enlightened churchmen saw the Jews as collectively guilty of the murder of Christ, men who were a threat to Christendom and who lived by the usury condemned both in the Bible and by Aristotle. It is significant that Robert Grosseteste, then archdeacon of Leicester and later the moral leader of the English bishops, approved of Montfort's action. It was one which had no particularly horrific consequences, since the Jews merely moved to Leicester's eastern suburbs, held not by Montfort but by his great aunt Margaret de Quincy, coheiress at the time of the earldom's partition in 1207. To condemn Montfort as a rabid anti-Semite, as some would today, is to judge him by standards very different from those of his own age.[4]

---

[3] Maddicott, *Montfort*, 1–7.

[4] J. Nichols, *The History and Antiquities of the County of Leicester* (4 vols. in 8, 1795–1815), I. i. appendix, 38; *The Letters of Robert Grosseteste, Bishop of Lincoln*, trans. F. A. C. Mantello and J. Goering (Toronto, 2010), 65–9; Maddicott, *Montfort*, 15–17.

In the 1230s, Montfort rose rapidly at Henry's court and began to enjoy the fruits of royal patronage. He was a foreign favourite of just the sort whom he himself was later to oppose. The reasons for his rise probably lay both in his French connections and in his personal qualities. Until 1258, the whole aim of Henry's diplomacy and foreign policy was to regain Normandy, Anjou and Poitou, the French lands held by his Angevin ancestors and lost by King John and during Henry's own minority. Montfort's ancestral roots near the borders of Normandy might facilitate the king's ambitions, and his service and possible manpower resources might have a useful part to play in future campaigns. Perhaps blooded in the renewed crusades of 1226–9 against the Albigensians, even as a young man Montfort may have been in the process of acquiring the powerful military reputation which was to culminate in his later years of warring against the king. If he was not yet 'the most sagacious of warriors' which he was to become,[5] the general and field commander may already have been in the making. Combined with a persuasive way of speaking and a winning manner, these assets do much to explain Henry's high regard for him.[6]

The culmination of Montfort's rise to power came with his marriage in 1238 to the king's sister Eleanor, the greatest prize which the king had to bestow. As Henry's brother-in-law, Montfort was now one of the family, and, thanks partly to his marriage, a very wealthy one at that. Aged only twenty-three at time of her marriage, Eleanor was already the widow of another great noble: William Marshal, earl of Pembroke, son of the even greater William Marshal who had helped to save Henry's throne and kingdom in the civil war which followed Magna Carta in 1215. The younger William had died in 1231. As his widow, Eleanor was allowed by custom a third of her dead husband's lands as dower: in this case, a particularly valuable asset. Her dower lands in England alone, effectively in Montfort's control after the marriage, were worth about £550 a year, and there were claims to other Marshal lands in Wales and Ireland. Since the Leicester lands were worth only about £500 a year, the result of the marriage was thus to more than double Montfort's income. But here Montfort faced an uncertain future. The dower lands were held by Eleanor and her husband only for Eleanor's life and could not be alienated. At her death, they would revert to the Marshal heirs of her first husband. This prospect was a disturbing one, since it meant that the couple's large family – they had five sons by 1258 – were dependent for their future support on an endowment whose integrity would not last

[5] *Flores Historiarum*, ed. H. R. Luard, Rolls Series (3 vols., 1890), II, 504; Maddicott, *Montfort*, 109, 308.

[6] *The Chronicle of William de Rishanger of the Barons' Wars*, ed. J. O. Halliwell, Camden Society (1840), 6; Maddicott, *Montfort*, 9, 350–1.

beyond Eleanor's death. The temporary nature of a substantial slice of his family's wealth is likely to have created the pervasive sense of insecurity which provides us with a key to many of Montfort's actions.[7]

Both Montfort's rise in general and his marriage in particular were opposed by the English baronage. They saw him as a favoured royal intimate, a foreigner who had no natural standing in the country. In marrying Eleanor, he had not only achieved a position of supremacy at court but also removed from the board a valuable diplomatic counter who could have been used to advance the nation's interests through a different marriage and a possible foreign alliance. In the interests of an alien, Henry had fecklessly wasted an important asset. Yet baronial opposition did nothing to obstruct the road to fame and fortune on which Montfort's marriage seemed to have set him. In 1239, he was formally created earl of Leicester, with English lands, an English wife, and now an English title.[8] Then, unexpectedly and from the same source as Montfort's elevation, came disaster. A few months after Montfort's acquisition of his title, he and Henry quarrelled bitterly. Henry accused Montfort of seducing Eleanor before her marriage and even hinted that she had been pregnant at the time of their wedding. But more serious, and more certainly rooted in reality, was the financial basis of the quarrel. In the 1230s, Montfort had contracted a number of onerous financial obligations, caused in part by his buying out his brother Amaury's claims to the Leicester inheritance. These obligations were beyond his ability to meet, and in 1239, presuming on his position at court, he had named Henry as security for the repayment of a loan, apparently without Henry's knowledge. Already intending to crusade, Montfort had by now taken the cross, and the febrile atmosphere at court, the product of the grand falling out between the new earl and his patron, now precipitated his departure for the Holy Land.[9]

After achieving little in the east except the establishment of his good name as a crusader, Montfort returned to England in 1242. But the old friendly relationship with Henry was never fully revived. Henry could not do without Montfort. Not only was he one of the family, but his range of contacts in France, and particularly at the French court, where by the 1250s (and perhaps earlier) he was on good terms with Louis IX, continued to be important for Henry's diplomacy. On the other hand, Montfort was never again quite trusted by his brother-in-law. He was more intelligent than Henry, and a far more effective and charismatic military

---

[7] Maddicott, *Montfort*, 49–52. For Eleanor's life, see now L. J. Wilkinson, *Eleanor de Montfort: A Rebel Countess in Medieval England* (2010).

[8] L. W. V. Harcourt, *His Grace the Steward and Trial of Peers* (1907), 112–14; Maddicott, *Montfort*, 23.

[9] Maddicott, *Montfort*, 24–8.

leader, but also a man notably less mild tempered and more inclined to violent extremes. In 1248, Henry sought to make use of these qualities by sending him to Gascony, with a commission to impose order on what was a particularly disturbed and disorderly province. But the result was a steep deterioration in an already tense relationship. Once in Gascony, Montfort spent Henry's money freely and lavishly on building castles and raising troops. At the same time, he antagonised the Gascons by using the strong-arm tactics which he claimed were necessary to put down what amounted to terrorist banditry. When the Gascons complained to Henry behind Montfort's back, Henry undermined Montfort's position by entertaining their complaints and then putting him on trial at Westminster in 1252. The sense of injustice which his trial engendered was compounded by his persistent claims that his service in Gascony had left him out of pocket. Although it was inconclusive, with most of the English nobles backing Montfort, the trial left a residue of bitterness between the two men sharper even than that resulting from their first great quarrel of 1239.[10]

Montfort's misgovernment of Gascony (as Henry saw it) marked a distinct stage in their association. What followed in the next few years took them further along the path to conflict. Their worsening relationship has to be seen against the wider political background of the 1250s: a time of increasing discontent with Henry's regime and of rising magnate and clerical opposition to his policies. The exercise of royal patronage was perhaps the primary cause of contention. Henry's promotion of his four Lusignan half-brothers, the sons of his mother Isabella of Angouleme by her second marriage to Hugh of Lusignan, count of La Marche in western France, was especially resented. Coming to England in 1247, the Lusignans had benefited enormously from Henry's favour, particularly in respect of the English lands which came the way of their leading member, William de Valence. As a result, popular and baronial hatred of aliens, and a concomitant rise in English national feeling, both of them factors in English politics since the reign of Richard I, now became increasingly marked, costing the king who was the Lusignans' patron prestige and respect.[11] A parallel and socially more broadly based source of discontent lay in the fiscal pressure which Henry was applying to his subjects, particularly to the gentry and peasantry of provincial England. Henry's personal rule from the mid-1230s onwards had been characterised by personal extravagance, heavy spending on building (the vastly expensive rebuilding of Westminster Abbey began in 1245) and

---

[10] *Ibid.*, 106–24. For the trial, see Matthew Paris, *Chronica Majora*, ed. H. R. Luard, Rolls Series (7 vols., 1872–83), V, 287–96, and *The Letters of Adam Marsh*, ed. and trans. C. H. Lawrence (2 vols, Oxford, 2006–10), II, 78–91.

[11] Maddicott, *Montfort*, 127–8.

by grandiose plans for the recovery of his lost French lands. The result was a relentless drive for money, making for oppressive and extortionate government in the localities exercised chiefly through the agency of the king's ministers, his provincial sheriffs and the justices of his courts.[12] One final and crucial flashpoint lay in the question of Sicily. In 1254, Henry had accepted Pope Innocent IV's offer of the throne of Sicily on behalf of his second son, Edmund. Innocent's object was to induce Henry to drive the Hohenstaufen opponents of the papacy from their entrenched position as the rulers of Sicily. But as a consequence of his acceptance of the Sicilian throne, Henry became obliged both to send an army to reconquer the island and also to meet the papal debts already incurred in the war for Sicily. This piece of royal folly, directed towards an end which Henry stood no chance of achieving, left Henry's kingdom saddled with a huge financial burden, which fell largely on the church. The Sicilian Business, as it has come to be known, was one of the immediate causes of the revolution which began in 1258.[13]

Montfort shared in some but not all of the accumulating grievances which Henry's government provoked. In particular, he detested Henry's Lusignan half-brothers. Not only were they his successful rivals in the competition for royal patronage, but William de Valence, their leader, had acquired through marriage the lordship of Pembroke in Wales, which Eleanor de Montfort claimed as part of her Marshal dower. Montfort's rivalry with the Lusignans exemplifies a broader truth: that until 1258 his antagonism towards Henry was more personal than political or constitutional. This was still more true of the financial issues which were the main cause of his growing resentment at Henry's rule. By 1258, when the government of the country was taken out of the king's hands, Montfort claimed that Henry owed him thousands of pounds. His debts had resulted partly from Montfort's service in Gascony but more especially from the intractable problems arising from Eleanor's dower. Besides her first husband's English lands, one third of which had been effectively settled on her, she also had similar claims on William Marshal's lands in Ireland and Wales, which had not been met. By a complicated process Eleanor had accepted an annual payment of £400 from the Marshal heirs in lieu of the actual land, and, at a second stage, in 1244, Henry had become the guarantor for the payment of this sum. By the 1250s, the king appears to have been defaulting on these annual payments.[14] In addition, the

[12] J. R. Maddicott, 'Magna Carta and the Local Community', *Past and Present*, 102 (1984), 44–8; D. Carpenter, *The Struggle for Mastery: Britain, 1066–1284* (Oxford, 2003), 350–1; Maddicott, *Montfort*, 126.

[13] B. K. U. Weiler, *Henry III of England and the Staufen Empire, 1216–1272* (Woodbridge, 2006), 147–70; Maddicott, *Montfort*, 128–9.

[14] Maddicott, *Montfort*, 50, 129–33.

Montforts were claiming that the £400 payment was entirely inadequate as a true valuation of the widow's dower third in Ireland and Wales and that the sum had been inequitably fixed when Eleanor was under age and in the king's power. They went on to demand arrears of payment stretching back over twenty-six years and amounting, outrageously, to more than £24,000.[15] A related grievance lay in another of Henry's undertakings. In 1253, he had promised Montfort an annual fee of £400 a year, with the further promise that the fee would later be replaced by lands of an equivalent value. But in the mid-1250s Henry had little land to give and what there was went to the Lusignans, so providing Montfort with still fiercer grounds for resentment at the Lusignans' position at court and at Henry's apparent untrustworthiness. If the Lusignans could benefit from Henry's generosity, why should the Montforts be excluded?[16]

By 1258, therefore, the Montforts reckoned that they had been very badly done by and that Henry owed them a great deal, mainly in money but also in land. This culminating but protracted episode in the history of Montfort's personal relationship with Henry might lead us to suppose that the claims and grievances of both men lay at the heart of that relationship and that Montfort was little more than a self-interested party who used his near indispensability to the king to extract what he could from a monarch who needed his service and loyalty. Such a verdict would be to diminish both Montfort's status and the contradictions which his career embodied. On the positive side, it is clear that Montfort was a man of great abilities, powers of leadership and practical intelligence. The best evidence of these qualities comes in part from the regard in which he was held by others. In 1241, the crusader barons, knights and citizens of the kingdom of Jerusalem wanted to have him as their governor, while in 1253, the French nobles offered him the stewardship of France, in effect the regency, during Louis IX's absence on crusade. These were very high honours, coming independently from two different directions. Neither bore fruit, but each shows the wide range of Montfort's international connections and value set on his leadership outside England.[17] His special ability, and one which, as we have seen, commended him to Henry III, was military. One small example of his varied skills here comes from his rebuilding of his great midland castle at Kenilworth. So well fortified and stocked was the castle that in 1266, after Montfort's death, it was able to withstand a six-month siege, the longest in English medieval history. He was in all ways a man of weight, the Cromwell of his day. Yet his original

---

[15] *Treaty Rolls*, I: *1234–1325*, ed. P. Chaplais (1955), 48; Maddicott, *Montfort*, 183.

[16] Maddicott, *Montfort*, 135–7.

[17] *Manners and Household Expenses of England in the Thirteenth and Fourteenth Centuries*, ed. T. H. Turner, Roxburghe Club (1841), xviii–xix; Paris, *Chronica Majora*, V, 366, 371–2; Maddicott, *Montfort*, 30, 76, 121.

position as an outsider in England, never completely forgotten, to some extent qualified his standing. Despite his putting down roots north of the Channel, his family home had been in France, and he maintained multiple contacts there, both with Louis IX, with the nobles of the French court and with his own relatives.[18] He was a cosmopolitan figure, with a range of experience in Gascony, France and the Holy Land which extended well beyond his English estates and which set him apart from the increasingly insular English nobility.

Montfort's weight was partly moral. He was in many ways a particularly devout Christian and a true son of the church, though he did not always behave like either. Medieval nobles are often described as 'conventionally religious' in their beliefs and practices, but Montfort's religion was more profound and heartfelt than this bland phrase implies. We know an unusual amount about his personal religious habits, since these were closely observed by his friends and servants and set down in the chronicles. He wore a hair shirt, the traditional underwear of the medieval holy man, and he dressed simply, normally wearing russet, the cheapest, coarsest cloth. Even in the company of magnates, he rarely wore scarlet, the most prestigious and most expensive cloth. He knew by heart the psalter and primer, spending part of each night in prayer and vigil, rising at midnight to pray, and using a candle clock to tell the hours.[19] Equally striking is Montfort's friendship circle. He was on close terms with a group of reforming bishops who formed the moral heart of the contemporary church. He was especially close to Robert Grosseteste, bishop of Lincoln, and Walter de Cantilupe, bishop of Worcester, both of them deeply conscientious pastors, and Grosseteste in addition one of the greatest scholars of the age. He had other close friends among the Franciscan friars, especially those of Oxford, the church's leaders in scholarship and moral example, and particularly renowned for their pastoral work among the urban poor.[20] Practice and experience, habit and association, all aligned Montfort with what contemporaries would have regarded as the most progressive elements in the thirteenth-century church: the crusade, the universities, pastorally minded bishops and *dévot* friars. Probably set on course by his early upbringing amid his father's wars against the Albigensians in the febrile crusading atmosphere of southern France, his piety may have been in part derived from the religious zealotry which characterised the lives of both his parents.[21] Like his claim to the Leicester lands, it was an aspect of his inheritance.

---

[18] Maddicott, *Montfort*, 90–2, 101–2, 205–6, 243–4.
[19] *Chronica de Mailros*, ed. J. Stevenson, Bannantyne Club (Edinburgh, 1835), 207–16; *Chronicle of William de Rishanger*, ed. Halliwell, 6–7; Maddicott, *Montfort*, 87–90.
[20] Maddicott, *Montfort*, 79–84, 91–5.
[21] *Ibid.*, 4–6.

But it is at this point that the contradictions in Montfort's character become most evident. In his relations with others, Montfort was often rapacious and covetous, and the aggressive pursuer of his own interests. Here, we see the 'saint or sinner' paradox in its sharpest form. His sense of injustice at the debts which Henry owed to him was avaricious in its intensity, and in his relations with his tenants, and with at least one of the citizens of Leicester, his lordship proved to be unrelenting and sometimes extortionate.[22] He showed a good deal of self-knowledge when, according to a contemporary account, he prayed to be delivered from the sin of avarice.[23] He was sometimes rebuked by his high-minded friends among the bishops and friars for his harshness to others. Consistent with all these traits was his apparent lack of generosity and openhandedness. One striking omission from the contemporary accounts of his personal religion is their failure to say anything about the gifts to the poor which would have been expected of any noble. Nor was he particularly generous to monastic houses, often the main beneficiaries of charitable giving by the aristocracy.[24] Both acquisitive and tightfisted, he may have felt financially threatened by his partial dependence on his wife's dower, by the need to endow his large family and by his inability to secure from Henry the repayment of the money which he reckoned that the king owed him. But with an annual income which had risen to about £2,500 by 1258,[25] placing him among the richest half dozen of the earls, he could hardly claim poverty as an excuse for avarice.

We need to keep in mind these contrasting facets of Montfort's character as we move towards the last phase of his life: the period of baronial reform and rebellion lasting from 1258 to 1265. In 1258, baronial discontent with Henry III's government reached a climax and the mounting grievances of the previous years gave birth to a new political order. The promotion of Henry's half-brothers, the Lusignans, the oppressive government of the localities, the king's financial mismanagement and the extravagant stupidity of his acceptance of the Sicilian throne produced a movement of near unified opposition to Henry's regime. In combination with new divisions at Henry's court, leading former courtiers to desert the king, these grievances gave rise to a great baronial coalition which came together to demand a general reform of the kingdom. Montfort was a prominent member of that coalition, though he was by no means its sole leader. The government of the country was taken out of the king's hands and handed over to a baronial council of

<hr />

[22] *Letters of Grosseteste*, trans. Mantello and Goering, 171–2; Maddicott, *Montfort*, 99–100, 176.

[23] *Chronicle of William de Rishanger*, ed. Halliwell, 6–7.

[24] Maddicott, *Montfort*, 100–1.

[25] *Ibid.*, 47, 149.

fifteen. Of this council, Montfort was again a member. A series of reforms, the Provisions of Oxford, were drawn up at the Oxford parliament of June 1258, which the leading barons and the king himself swore to maintain. These were later augmented by other reforms of law and administration, culminating in the Provisions of Westminster of October 1259, the whole programme being known collectively (and confusingly) as the Provisions of Oxford. The oath to the Provisions was to be central to the future history of the movement.[26]

These measures constituted something like a revolution. With the transfer to the new council of powers central to Henry's kingship, most notably perhaps the power to appoint ministers,[27] the crown had effectively been put into commission. This was a quasi-republican constitution, even going beyond what had been attempted by King John's opponents in 1215. In essence, the new movement aimed to curb the king's powers of decision making, to reform the law and to institute a more just and equitable system of local government. Beyond these objectives, the movement had certain characteristics which served to define it. In the first place, it embodied popular as well as baronial aspirations. Promising better government for the localities, it was widely supported by the knights and country gentry and even by the peasantry. The social breadth both of political awareness and of political discontent in the country and the countryside was a factor on the barons' side. But the movement was also seen as a moral crusade: one which had justice for its watchword and which sought for fair dealings between government and subjects. This moral dimension does much to explain the support given to the movement by some of the English bishops. It was demonstrated by one of the most unusual features of the reform movement: the attempt to apply reforming principles not only to relations between the king and his subjects but also to those between the barons and their tenants. In its early stages at least, this was not just a political rising against the king but an attempt to deliver justice on a much broader front.[28]

What happened in the next few years is a complicated story. The baronial council survived until the last days of 1260 and for most of that time it governed the country. It gradually disintegrated, and with it the great coalition of 1258, because of the unwillingness of most barons to apply reform to their own estates, because of the bidding power of royal patronage, and because of an underlying conservative

[26] *Ibid.*, 150–72, 178–9, 184–5; P. Brand, *King, Barons and Justices: The Making and Enforcement of Legislation in Thirteenth-Century England* (Cambridge, 2003), 15–41.

[27] *Documents of the Baronial Movement of Reform and Rebellion, 1258–1267*, ed. R. F. Treharne and I. J. Sanders (Oxford, 1973), 222–3; Maddicott, *Montfort*, 158, 261, 361.

[28] Maddicott, *Montfort*, 166–9, 353–4.

loyalty to the monarchy which had always been one of Henry's strengths. Montfort's course, however, was different from that of his timeserving fellow magnates. His guiding star throughout these years was his oath to the Provisions of Oxford: an oath which he could not deny without perjuring himself and risking his soul. A major factor which came into play here was Montfort's conscience. On moral matters, Montfort had a particularly tender conscience. Its operation can be seen particularly clearly in relation to his marriage. That his wife Eleanor had taken a vow of chastity after being widowed made him very uneasy, and his marriage was entered into, says one of the chronicles, 'not without harm to his conscience'. This was the force which was now brought to bear on the politics of reform.[29]

Yet Montfort's conscience was a selective instrument, one which did nothing to inhibit his pressing his private claims against the crown and which used reform to private ends. All through the early years of the reform movement he continued to pursue Henry for the payment of Eleanor's dower. The dower and the Provisions interlocked in complicated ways. In 1259, Montfort deliberately obstructed an Anglo-French settlement in an attempt to secure the settlement of his and Eleanor's financial claims, giving little attention to the enforcement of the reforming programme which occupied his fellow councillors; while in 1262, he published in England a papal bull confirming the Provisions only after negotiations at Louis IX's court for a settlement of his private claims had broken down.[30] Oath-bound to the Provisions he may have been, but the reforms also gave him a lever which could be used to private advantage. There were times when what was expedient and what was moral helpfully coincided.

The disintegration of the baronial opposition from 1261 onwards combined with Montfort's virtuous but judicious adherence to the Provisions to give him the leadership of what remained of the reforming cause. In 1262, Henry had obtained papal absolution from his oath to the Provisions, a coup which seemed to confirm his restoration to power and the overthrow of reform. The only way in which reform could now be maintained was through force. By 1263, Montfort and his followers, mainly members of the minor baronage, the local knights and his own retinue, were openly pitted against the king in what became a civil war. In May 1264, during the course of that war, Montfort won a great victory over the royalists at Lewes in Sussex. It delivered the king and his eldest son, the Lord Edward, into his hands and left him effectively in command of the country. Although there remained a dangerous periphery of continuing

[29] Flores Historiarum, ed. Luard, II, 227; Maddicott, Montfort, 84–7, 161–2, 170, 363.
[30] Maddicott, Montfort, 183–8, 218–19, 358–60.

royalist resistance from the barons of the Welsh marches, this was the high point of his power.[31]

In some ways, he used that power very effectively. In June 1264 and January 1265, he held two famous parliaments, summoning elected knight from the counties to both and burgesses from the towns to the second. What was new here was not so much their presence, for knights at least had appeared in earlier parliaments, but their acceptance as an integral part of the political community and their participation in political discussion.[32] Montfort's backing by a broadly based parliament was seen as a way of legitimising what was otherwise a thoroughly illegitimate regime, its power based on little more than victory in battle. In the autumn of 1264, Montfort's forces, supported by some prominent bishops, held off for some months a threatened French invasion and successfully challenged a papal legate who threatened the country with an interdict. Nor were the Provisions forgotten. They were published throughout the shires in December 1264 and enforced in the ensuing January parliament.[33] These events made Montfort something of a national hero – his country's leader against an alien power, the scourge of an oppressive monarch and the vindicator of reform.

In retrospect, however, we can see that Montfort was heading for disaster. He had replaced the king as the country's ruler, and although orders still went out in Henry's name he was effectively a captive. Montfort's novel access to the whole machinery of government and patronage now allowed full play to the acquisitiveness which had always been a central feature of his character. He used power to pile up a fortune for himself and his family. Many of the lands confiscated from the losers at Lewes were given to his sons. Guy, the fourth son, was given vast lands in Devon and Cornwall which had belonged to Richard of Cornwall, the king's brother, and another of the Lewes captives. Amaury, the clerical third son, was made treasurer of York, one of the richest positions in the church.[34] Victory had given him the means to endow his sons which his marriage alone could not have given him. His wealth brought him a huge following, seen in the 140 paid knights who kept company with him when he spent Christmas 1264 at his great castle of Kenilworth.[35] His obvious relish for power, its trappings and the opportunities for self-advancement which it provided in the end cost him much support. Yet what is more remarkable is that throughout this period so many of his

[31] *Ibid.*, 270–8.

[32] *Ibid.*, 284–9, 314–17; J. R. Maddicott, *The Origins of the English Parliament, 924–1327* (Oxford, 2010), 254–61.

[33] Maddicott, *Montfort*, 314–15.

[34] *Ibid.*, 322–7.

[35] *Flores Historiarum*, ed. Luard, II, 504; Maddicott, *Montfort*, 310.

followers, including those among the bishops, still stood by him. His rule was not entirely a one-man enterprise and he was evidently still seen to offer a better prospect of justice and good government than was likely to come from a restored monarchy.

Despite his apparent supremacy, in the late winter of 1265 Montfort's position began to deteriorate. The crucial step in his downward path was his desertion by Gilbert de Clare, earl of Gloucester. The only member of the higher nobility whose support Montfort had secured, Clare had become antagonised by Montfort's aggrandisement, by his failure to give Clare an adequate share of the spoils after Lewes, and by his treatment of Henry and Edward. In addition, he apparently raised the question of Montfort's alien origins, thus bringing into the open one of the ambiguities always latent in Montfort's position as an English magnate.[36] In combination with the continuing danger posed by the Welsh marcher barons (of whom Clare himself was one), Clare's desertion threatened to undermine Montfort's whole position. In April 1265, Montfort attempted to take military action against Clare and the marchers by launching a campaign on the south-eastern borders of Wales, but with an inadequate army. In the following month, the Lord Edward escaped from custody in Hereford and moved north to join forces with the marchers at Wigmore. The loss of Edward, whose military skills rivalled Montfort's, was the beginning of the end. In July, Montfort moved eastwards, crossing the Severn and hoping to link up with his son, Simon, whom he expected to advance to join him with an army from Kenilworth. But this tactic failed. Simon's army was surprised and scattered in a dawn raid on Kenilworth by Edward's forces. They then advanced on Evesham, where Montfort's little army was trapped in the great bend of the Avon which winds around the town. In the battle which followed, Montfort and his eldest son Henry were both killed, Montfort's body dismembered, the king released and the altar of the abbey at Evesham left running with the blood of those Montfortians who had vainly thought to find sanctuary there.[37] The whole experiment of baronial reform seemed to be over.

But here, appearances were partly deceptive. It is true that after Evesham Henry's monarchy seemed to have been liberated. The baronial council had gone, and with it all formal constitutional restraints on the monarchy, save those embodied in Magna Carta. Royal authority was restored. Although until 1267 there was continuing resistance to

---

[36] William Rishanger, *Chronica et Annales*, ed. H. T. Riley, Rolls Series (1865), 32; Maddicott, *Montfort*, 327–9.

[37] Maddicott, *Montfort*, 331–42. For the slaughter in the abbey, see O. de Laborderie, J. R. Maddicott and D. A. Carpenter, 'The Last Hours of Simon de Montfort: A New Account', *English Historical Review*, 115 (2000), 411–12.

the restored monarch, in London, at Kenilworth and in parts of the countryside, peace gradually returned. Yet much had changed. Until his death in 1272, Henry ruled in a generally acceptable way. There were no in-groups of alien favourites; parliament was consulted about taxation and policymaking; the knights of the countryside acquired a larger place in politics; and the Montfortians were gradually brought back into public life after the débâcle of Evesham. Most significant of all perhaps, the bulk of the legal and administrative reforms introduced by the baronial council were given permanent legal force in the Statute of Marlborough of 1267. Montfort and the reformers had taught Henry the importance of consensus in politics and of ruling through a broadly based oligarchy of magnates and ministers rather than through a narrow clique of friends and courtiers. The same policies were followed by Edward I, the princely victor of Evesham, who, in the first part of his reign from 1272 to 1294, restored the legitimate authority of the crown in a period of brilliantly successful kingship. The posthumous Montfort was thus more successful than his bloody end at Evesham might have led any of his friends or enemies to expect.[38] He himself became the focus of a popular cult. Miracles were said to be worked at his shrine on the Evesham battlefield, and the sick and the lame travelled across England to seek cures there. So in the eyes of at least some contemporaries Montfort, though no doubt a sinner, was certainly a saint as well.[39]

A final verdict on Montfort is difficult to reach. In many ways, he stands out as an adventurer. In his younger days, he had been very much a man on the make: a younger son, a foreigner with no background in England, driven by ambition, whose marriage to the king's sister gave him the richest prize imaginable. Both before and after the great political divide of 1258, he showed the same personal qualities of self-promotion and self-seeking. The internal tendencies evident in his rise to power in England in the early 1230s were equally evident when he ruled the country in the 1260s. Yet the idealist is almost as conspicuous as the go-getter, visible not only in Montfort's devoutness, his austere practices and his circle of high-minded friends in the church, but more especially in his defence of the Provisions of Oxford, the core measures of baronial reform. When almost all the magnates had dropped away from the reforming cause, Montfort stood fast, bound hand and foot in conscience by his oath to maintain the Provisions. In 1262, when the king was in the ascendant and almost all the barons had submitted, Montfort left for France, saying that

[38] Maddicott, *Montfort*, 366–7; Brand, *Kings, Barons and Justices*, 185–6.

[39] For the cult, see 'Miracula Simonis de Montfort', in *Chronicle of William de Rishanger*, ed. Halliwell, 67–110, and C. Valente, 'Simon de Montfort, Earl of Leicester, and the Utility of Sanctity in Thirteenth-Century England', *Journal of Medieval History*, 21 (1995), 27–49.

he would rather die landless than abandon the truth as a perjured man.[40] He did not have to act thus. He could at any time have settled with Henry, submitted, abandoned the Provisions and enjoyed a quiet life in England. But this his conscience would not allow him to do.

We cannot therefore simply say that Montfort was a hypocrite. He was genuinely and deeply committed to political reform, which he saw as a sort of moral crusade and a matter of conscience. Nor, certainly, can he be acquitted of the charge of unscrupulously and consistently pursuing his own interests. There is no entirely satisfactory answer to the conundrum posed by Montfort's character, but part of an answer may lie in his capacity for self-deception. We might see him as the victim of what Dr Johnson called, in a memorable and moving phrase, 'the treachery of the human heart':[41] that is to say, the infinite ability which we all possess to some extent to delude ourselves about our real motives and by this kind of self-deception to confuse what we are doing for ourselves with a more selfless and abstract good. His pursuit of Eleanor's dower claims against Henry came at a time of ongoing political crisis in 1258–9; but was he not also seeking for himself the justice which the reformers intended to make freely available to all? The point is made still explicitly by one of the chronicles writing about the events of 1264–5 after the battle of Lewes. Montfort, he says, took personal control of the lands, castles and possessions of the defeated royalists because he foresaw that only in this way could he maintain his dominance until the Provisions had been finally secured.[42] The interests of Montfort, in other words, were the interests of reform. We may be sceptical about this interpretation of his actions. Yet it may well be the case that Montfort really did see his advancement in these terms and that he really had persuaded himself that reform was best served by his own promotion.

In the end, we should perhaps see Montfort as a classical tragic hero: a man of high abilities and intelligence, a master of men and a figure of weight and moral worth, who in the end overreached himself and was brought down by his own ambitions and personal failings. It would be foolish to pretend that such a depiction is in all ways psychologically convincing. But it is one mark of Montfort's unique position that there is no other medieval noble whose mind we can hold up to the light in quite so subtle a way.

[40] 'Annales de Dunstaplia', in *Annales Monastici*, ed. H. R. Luard, Rolls Series (5 vols., 1864–9), III, 217; Maddicott, *Montfort*, 214.

[41] See Johnson, *The Rambler*, No. 93, Tuesday, 5 Feb. 1751.

[42] *Chronicle of William de Rishanger*, ed. Halliwell, 41–2; Maddicott, *Montfort*, 317–18.

Transactions of the RHS 26 (2016), pp. 59–77 © Royal Historical Society 2016
doi:10.1017/S0080440116000050

'PROTESTANTISM' AS A HISTORICAL CATEGORY

By Alec Ryrie

READ 6 FEBRUARY 2016

ABSTRACT. The term 'Protestant' itself is a historical accident, but the category of western Christians who have separated from Rome since 1517 remains a useful one. The confessionalisation thesis, which has dominated recent Reformation historiography, instead posits the two major Protestant confessions and Tridentine Catholicism as its categories, but this can produce a false parallelism in which the nature of the relationship between the confessions is oversimplified. Instead, this paper proposes we think of a Protestant ecosystem consisting of self-consciously confessional Lutheranism, a broad Calvinism which imagined itself as normative, and a collection of radical currents much more intimately connected to the 'magisterial' confessions than any of the participants wished to acknowledge. The magisterial / radical division was maintained only with constant vigilance and exemplary violence, with Calvinism in particular constantly threatening to bleed into radicalism. What gives this quarrelsome family of 'Protestants' analytical coherence is neither simple genealogy nor, as has been suggested, mere adherence to the Bible: since in practice both 'radical' and 'magisterial' Protestants have been more flexible and 'spiritual' in their use of Scripture than is generally allowed. It is, rather, the devotional experience underpinning that 'spiritual' use of the Bible, of an unmediated encounter with grace.

How should we speak about the Christians in the Latin tradition who have separated themselves from communion with Rome over the past five centuries? On one level this is a trivial, semantic question, but there are deep and murky waters below it. Religious labels are very often problematic, not only because they tend to originate either as terms of abuse or as contested claims which groups make about themselves, but also because they imply the coherence or even existence of a particular group when that may not be obvious. So it is with 'Protestantism'.

When Luther's movement first erupted in Germany in the years around 1520, the labels first associated with it were immediately split into self-serving definitions such as Gospel preachers or evangelicals, and hostile terms which implied heresy – either existing heretical labels such as Hussite, or the neologism 'Lutheran' which Luther himself so disliked.[1] As well as being terminologically unstable, this made defining who was

---

[1] Martin Luther, *Luther's Works*, XLV: *The Christian in Society II*, ed. Walther I. Brandt (Philadelphia, 1962), 70.

in the movement and who was not very difficult. So when, in April 1529, six German princes lodged a formal 'protestation' against the Second Diet of Speyer's reinstatement of the Edict of Worms, they set in train the creation not only of a well-defined anti-papal party, but of a genuinely useful label. *Protestant* quickly became as much a political as a religious label, meaning, simply, a member of or sympathiser with the Schmalkaldic League. As such, it might have been expected to disappear after the destruction of the League in 1547, or at least after the Peace of Augsburg in 1555 rendered the 1529 Protestation moot. And indeed, since the world of anti-papal Latin Christianity, for want of a better term, was by then becoming sharply divided between two mutually antagonistic factions of Lutherans and a self-styled Reformed Christianity which was already being labelled Calvinist, to say nothing of the small but high-profile radical communities whom those two main factions both anathematised, the term 'Protestant' did not seem to be of that much use any more.

It eventually became useful again for polemical reasons. First, Catholic polemicists were keen to turn *Protestant* from a political to a religious term, and to apply it more widely to the constellation of heresies they faced. As Peter Marshall has pointed out, it fitted with the core accusation that Luther and his fellow-travellers taught newfangled human inventions rather than the faith once revealed to the Apostles. A name which implied that the movement only began in 1529 was grist to this mill. So the now-routine division of western Christendom into 'Catholic' and 'Protestant' first emerged as a polemical gambit, in which the ancient, true and universal church was opposed to a quarrelling farrago of heretical innovators. Naturally, this use did not carry with it any claim that 'Protestantism' existed as any kind of coherent doctrine: the very opposite. The English Jesuit Lawrence Anderton made the point succinctly enough with the title of his 1633 tract *The Non-Entity of Protestancy: Or, A Discourse, Wherein Is Demonstrated, that Protestancy Is . . . a Meere Nothing.*[2]

Marshall has traced the process by which the word slowly insinuated itself at least into English usage by sheer utility, for want of any better umbrella term to describe non-papal Christians. Even so, for a long time it retained two negative connotations: first, for a generation or more it still seemed foreign, and second, its inclusiveness was derogatory. If members of England's Reformed establishment used it, they did so contemptuously, to refer to the widest possible group of their countrymen who had gone along with the Reformation as a cultural phenomenon, many of them without having embraced the Gospel in any way that a preacher would find acceptable. The adjective most readily attached to

---

[2] Peter Marshall, 'The Naming of Protestant England', *Past and Present*, 214 (2012), 87–128, esp. 112.

the noun 'Protestant' was 'carnal'. Yet while this inclusivity was potentially embarrassing, it was also an opportunity. For those who wanted to deny Catholics' claim that their opponents were a sackful of ferrets, 'Protestant' was a useful word, potentially allowing a united front to be formed against them – if, that is, enough common denominators could be found to prove that Protestantism was *not* a nonentity. The most enduring, and slippery, attempt to do this was another English tract of the 1630s, William Chillingworth's *The Religion of Protestants A Safe Way to Salvation*, which famously declared that the Bible alone was the religion of Protestants, a banner behind which all could unite against Rome.[3] As that example implies, the use of the word 'Protestant' as a self-description over the following centuries is usually an index of the ambition to build a broad anti-Catholic coalition. In post-Restoration England, a religiously plural society united by anti-Catholic paranoia, 'Protestant' became a sufficiently useful glue-word that it was written into the Coronation Oath in 1689. In Ireland, 'Protestant' became and remains a way of welding together Anglicans, Presbyterians and others against popery. In Bismarck's Germany, following the forced mergers of Lutheran and Reformed churches earlier in the century, Protestantism was opposed to Catholicism as a hallmark of German identity. In the United States, even when confessional tensions were easing in the mid-twentieth century, the tripartite division of the country into three acceptable religions – Protestants, Catholics, Jews – remained proverbial.[4]

This is, then, an accidental word, drafted into service by polemicists on both sides who found an umbrella term of this sort indispensable. That process cut any real connection to the events of 1529, so that the modern term 'Protestant' is almost empty of intrinsic meaning. The Chinese terms equivalent to 'Catholic' and 'Protestant' – respectively *tianzhujiao*, 'the religion of the Lord of Heaven', and *jidujiao*, 'the religion of Jesus' – may have very different literal meanings, but they differentiate between the two groups at least as effectively as the western labels.[5] This paper's aim is not to parse the implications of the word 'Protestant', or indeed *jidujiao*, but to argue that the category which both describe is a historically useful one: that the non-papal Christianities which emerged from the

---

[3] William Chillingworth, *The Religion of Protestants: A Safe Way to Salvation* (RSTC 5138.2, Oxford, 1638); 'Chillingworth, William (1602–1644)', Warren Chernaik in *Oxford Dictionary of National Biography*, ed. H. C. G. Matthew and Brian Harrison (Oxford, 2004); online edn, ed. David Cannadine, Jan. 2010, www.oxforddnb.com. oxfordbrookes.idm.oclc.org/view/article/5308 (accessed 26 June 2016).

[4] Kevin M. Shultz, *Tri-Faith America* (Oxford, 2011).

[5] Jean-Pierre Charbonnier, *Christians in China: AD 600 to 2000*, trans. M. N. L. Couve de Murville (San Francisco, 2007; cf. French edn 2002), 352. There is no common Chinese equivalent to the generic term 'Christianity'.

Reformation era retain enough common features that analysing them as a group is meaningful. It will also argue, however, that if we look at 'Protestantism' (for want of a better word) historically rather than theologically, its definition becomes unstable. That is, if we look at what Protestants have actually done, believed, experienced and felt, rather than at what their theologians and apologists have argued they ought to have believed, we end up somewhere different from where any of the polemicists would have sent us.

After confessionalisation

It needs to be said that this suggestion runs against the main current of (in particular) German Reformation scholarship for the past generation. The so-called confessionalisation thesis developed by Wolfgang Reinhard and Heinz Schilling appears to render the term 'Protestant' redundant for the study of the Reformation era, by suggesting that the category of all non-papal western Christians is simply not useful. Reinhard and Schilling have from the 1970s onwards challenged us to see the Catholic and Protestant Reformations as parallel rather than opposed forces, and in particular as instruments of state-building.[6] Religious reformations of all kinds allowed early modern states and princes to deepen their authority over their territories, using sharply and antagonistically defined religious identities as a means of social control. The work of definition was done at a formal level by confessions of faith which large sections of some populations were required to profess, and which were increasingly drafted, redrafted and refined with the aim of unambiguously excluding outsiders. On this view, there are two sensible scales on which to examine the religion of the period: the scale of the individual confession, which means, predominantly, the trio of Orthodox Lutheranism, Reformed Calvinism and Tridentine Catholicism; or comparatively across all the confessions. A category such as Protestant, which attempts to yoke together two of these groupings while excluding the third, courts the accusation not simply of arbitrariness but of special pleading.

The confessionalisation thesis has been an enormously helpful tool of historical analysis. It has forced us to think, not only of the parallels

---

[6] H. Schilling, *Konfessionskonflict und Staatsbildung* (Gütersloh, 1981); H. Schilling, *Religion, Political Culture and the Emergence of Early Modern Society* (Leiden, 1992); W. Reinhard, 'Reformation, Counter-Reformation and the Early Modern State: A Reassessment', *Catholic Historical Review*, 75 (1989), 385–403; *Die Katholische Konfessionalisieung*, ed. W. Reinhard and H. Schilling (Gütersloh and Münster, 1995). The literature on the confessionalisation thesis is vast. Amongst the most useful in English is *Confessionalization in Europe, 1555–1700*, ed. J. M. Headley, H. J. Hillerbrand and A. J. Papadas (Aldershot and Burlington, 2004); and Ute Lotz-Heumann, 'The Concept of "Confessionalization": A Historiographical Paradigm in Dispute', *Memoria y Civilización*, 4 (2001), 93–114.

between the confessions, but of the dynamics that tied them together, such as the arms races which forced very different entities to adopt parallel strategies in order to counter one another. The thesis' explanatory power is that this competition itself becomes one of the engines driving modernity. The model has also managed at least partly to outgrow its inbuilt limitations. Although its focus is on state-building, it has been plausibly extended to explore the way some populations without state backing in effect self-confessionalised, such as Mennonites in Denmark or, indeed, Catholics in Ireland.[7] Although it was designed for the German lands, where it closely reflects the legal status granted to the two or three confessions by the imperial treaties of 1555 and 1648, there have been useful attempts to apply its insights beyond the empire.[8]

For all this explanatory power, however, the confessionalisation thesis was a child of its times, that is, the latter part of the Cold War. In what could have been a model of 1970s détente, it emerged from the collaboration of a Catholic scholar, Reinhard, trying to shake off the negativity of the term 'Counter-Reformation', and a Protestant scholar, Schilling, who had worked on both Lutheran and Calvinist confessional states. Hence the self-consciously comparative nature of their work from the beginning, and the attempt to move away from the direct religious confrontations. This work was conceived during a period when most thinking people honestly expected the stalemate between eastern and western blocs to endure indefinitely, unless of course it ended in mutual annihilation. In those circumstances, it was both natural and analytically useful to think of opposing forces as mirror-images and even as unwilling collaborators, carving a continent up between them. What was not at all plain at the time was that the apparent similarity between those opposing forces was an illusion. That only became clear when the Soviet bloc went from superpower to virtual collapse within six years, almost entirely due to its own internal dynamics. The decades since have given us a very different paradigm of conflict: asymmetric warfare, in which entities that are in no sense parallel to one another fight at cross-purposes, with weapons, tactics, strategies, logistics and motivations which may have virtually no contact with those of their opponents.

The analogy should not be pushed too far. However, if the Cold War revealed one face of early modern religious conflict to us, so the period since can help reveal another. The Reformation period's various religious

---

[7] Michael D. Driedger, *Obedient Heretics: Mennonite Identities in Lutheran Hamburg and Altona during the Confessional Age* (Aldershot, 2002).

[8] See, for example, Peter Marshall, 'Confessionalization, Confessionalism and Confusion in the English Reformation', in *Reforming Reformation*, ed. Thomas F. Mayer (Farnham, 2012), 43–64.

groupings were not simply providing different answers to the same question. As Thomas Kaufmann and other critics of confessionalisation have emphasised, the thesis tends to flatten out the different confessions' individuality, and efface the extent to which they did not share a common theological or devotional language. In interconfessional 'debates', the parties mostly talked past one another, and more regularly mocked or caricatured than seriously engaged each others' views: they were living in different mental worlds, with different concerns, priorities, patterns of reasoning and emotional substructures.[9] Comparable asymmetries can be seen in the confessional conflicts themselves. In the struggle for Europeans' souls, the Catholic establishments held enormous strategic advances: inertia, collective memory, loyalty, ceremonial richness and, not least, money. The Protestant insurgencies had a very different set of advantages: no awkward track record to defend; a willingness to invite whole populations to participate in theological argument; and a much lighter material footprint, which not only made Protestantism cheap but made the destruction of Catholicism's expensive material complexity such an effective ploy.

   These are not new critiques, and Reinhard and Schilling have given interestingly different responses to them. Schilling's liberal-Protestant response is to integrate the differences between confessional actors into the thesis without fundamentally changing it. Reinhard, by contrast, has argued that that examination of the confessions' distinct cultures is another subject and should be kept separate. My suggestion, likewise, is that confessionalisation's attempt to slice post-Reformation religion into parallels has done its work. The thesis has blurred distinctions which we need to understand. The thesis has broken Reformation history's long habit of crass partisanship, but we now risk falling into the opposite error, of treating all religious parties with scrupulous even-handedness. The risk is a kind of BBC impartiality, in which conscious balance leads us to conjure matching parties into existence when the reality may be much messier; and in which we feel unable, for example, to say something which could be construed as praise or criticism of one set of early modern religious actors without a nod to the other side too. We need to recognise that the confessions were not only different from each other, but different in different ways.

The Protestant ecosystem

By arguing for the utility of 'Protestant' as a category, I am not, therefore, trying to downplay the differences between the different Protestant

---

[9] Thomas Kaufmann, 'Die Konfessionalisierung von Kirche und Gesellschaft', *Theologische Literaturzeitung*, 121 (1996), 1008–25, at 1112–21.

confessions. On the contrary, I am arguing that the confessionalisation thesis has underplayed Protestantism's plurality and diversity in two key respects: first, in its treatment of the two magisterial confessions, Lutheranism and Calvinism, as parallel cases, and second, in its inadequate account of radicalism.

Anyone who has tried to teach the Reformation to undergraduates knows how difficult it is to explain the distinction between Lutheranism and Reformed Protestantism. We tend naturally to dwell on the litmus-test issues such as, above all, the Eucharistic presence, but those issues are in the end simply symptoms of deeper, subtler differences of mood, flavour and intellectual tramlines. The manner in which the Eucharistic arguments were conducted is as revealing as their substance. Luther's outrage at the intolerable blasphemy of Zwingli's doctrine, which not only robbed Christians of the comfort of the sacrament but implicitly denied the Incarnation itself, was badly mismatched by the condescension of Zwingli and his successors, who saw their doctrine as self-evidently reasonable, and who believed that Luther was still half-sodden in the dregs of popery and implied that he simply had not thought it through. While the canonical account of this dispute focuses on the Marburg colloquy, the further rounds of the battle over the decades that follow are equally revealing. And in this context, it makes sense to use the somewhat anachronistic term *Calvinists* for the Reformed Protestant party: since Calvin was more directly responsible than anyone else for bringing and keeping together the disparate spectrum of magisterial reformers which stretched from Bullinger to Bucer, and forging them into something that could reasonably be called a single confession, above all in the Zurich Consensus of 1549.[10]

Calvin's intention was that the Consensus should be only a step on the way. A vital part of the purpose of his *Institutio*, from its first, 1536, edition, was to unify the Reformation, chiefly by persuading Lutherans and Zwinglians that in their sacramental argument both sides were missing the point. He never met either Luther or Zwingli, though he did treasure reports that Luther had spoken kindly of him.[11] He did meet Philip Melanchthon, several times, and maintained an intermittent correspondence with him which was almost equally frustrating to both men. What made it so was Calvin's conviction that he and Melanchthon were essentially in agreement. Repeatedly, he challenged Melanchthon to admit that they shared similar doctrines of predestination, of *adiaphora* and above all of the Eucharist. Melanchthon, as Timothy Wengert has

[10] Bruce Gordon, *Calvin* (New Haven, 2009), esp. 161–80.
[11] Timothy George, 'John Calvin and the Agreement of Zurich (1549)', in his *John Calvin and the Church: A Prism of Reform* (Louisville, 1990).

shown, usually responded to these appeals by falling silent: he reportedly tore up one of the letters in frustration.[12]

Calvin, and the Reformed in general, found Melanchthon's reticence mystifying and infuriating. That itself shows the gulf that already separated Calvinism from Lutheranism. Reformed Protestantism understood itself as a broad, centrist reformism drawing on the best humanist and evangelical scholarship. It was, in its own eyes, self-evidently reasonable. Its international reach, its lack of a single overweening theological voice, its self-consciously formidable learning: all of this contributed to a patrician sense of itself as the natural intellectual centre of gravity, and to a sense of its doctrines as the faith which has been believed everywhere, at all times and by all people. It was the theological consensus of the best minds of the age, excepting only those who were enslaved to the popish Antichrist. Or it would have been if only Melanchthon and the Lutherans had admitted that in truth they belonged to it too.

Which is to say, Calvin and the Reformed in general failed to take Lutheranism seriously. They may have been at least partly right about Melanchthon and Philippist Lutheranism in general, and for that very reason it would have been politically lethal for Melanchthon to admit to common ground with Calvin. The so-called Gnesio-Lutheran party, however, looked at Calvinism's broad, complacent consensus, and saw themselves as prophets crying in the wilderness. It was bomb-throwing idealism versus soothing pragmatism. Flacius Illyricus and his allies went beyond simply despising Melanchthon's compromises. They deeply distrusted the humanist, Erasmian principles which so thoroughly infused Calvinism, and which risked selling Protestantism's *sola fide* birthright for a mess of civic virtues and pragmatic ethics, and contaminating Gospel purity with a brackish rationalism. The distinct attitudes to the two groupings' respective confessions of faith are instructive. There was never a single Reformed confession of faith. The Heidelberg and the Second Helvetic confessions came close, but repeated attempts to produce a single, harmonised version failed. Yet it did not seem to matter very much, and it certainly did not prevent the Reformed family from recognising one another as brethren. Their confessions were understood to be limited, provisional documents, subject to revision and improvement. No Reformed Protestant came close to claiming what Georg Spalatin claimed for Lutheranism's grounding document, the Augsburg Confession: that the presentation of the Confession back in

[12] Timothy Wengert, '"We Will Feast Together in Heaven Forever": The Epistolary Friendship of John Calvin and Philip Melanchthon', in *Melanchthon in Europe: His Work and Influence Beyond Wittenberg*, ed. Karin Maag (Grand Rapids, 1999), 19–44.

1530 was 'the most significant act which has ever taken place on earth'.[13] Spalatin was perhaps over-excited. Johannes Mathesius, more soberly, merely reckoned the Confession as the most important event since the time of the Apostles. It was certainly routine for Lutherans to class it alongside the ancient Creeds, and the Book of Concord explicitly did so.[14]

Lutheranism in the age of orthodoxy was, then, precisely, a Confession, with its spiritual parameters defined at Augsburg in 1530 and its legal parameters at the same city in 1555. As such, it confessed. It bore witness constantly to the truth once revealed, a truth it burnished lovingly, guarded jealously and defended fiercely, a truth in which it trained its population and beyond whose doctrinal or geographical boundaries it showed little desire to venture. It was orthodox Lutherans, not predestinarian Calvinists, who taught that Christ's command to make disciples of all nations had expired with the Apostles' own generation.[15] This persisted until Pietism seeped into the joints. Calvinism was something completely different, except where the political pressures of the age of Orthodoxy forced it into a Lutheran-shaped mould. It was open-ended, discursive and profoundly unstable, yet convinced even as it argued with itself that the world revolved around it. The surest sign of that difference was that many Calvinists continued to cherish an unrequited love for Lutheranism, or at least for what they imagined Lutheranism to be. They dreamed schemes for reunion, usually beginning with an intra-Reformed agreement into which the Lutherans could then be invited. These schemes are reminiscent of a child's plan to dig a hole to the other side of the world: that is, very easy to begin. They always and quickly foundered on Calvinists' effortlessly generous assumption that everyone should be invited to join their loose, quarrelsome family of faith, and to do so strictly on their hosts' terms.[16] Calvinism, then, should be seen not as a unified 'confession' in any strict sense, but as an ecumenical movement for Protestant unity. Yet it never properly understood the Lutherans' different worldview, and as such (and perhaps in any case inevitably) the project failed.

---

[13] Robert Kolb, 'Luther, Augsburg, and the Concept of Authority in the Late Reformation: Ursinus vs. the Lutherans', in *Controversy and Conciliation: The Reformation and the Palatinate, 1559–1583*, ed. Derk Visser (Allison Park, PA, 1986), 36.

[14] Kolb, 'Luther, Augsburg, and the Concept of Authority', 36, 38.

[15] James A. Scherer, *Gospel, Church and Kingdom: Comparative Studies in World Mission Theology* (Minneapolis, 1987), 66–9; James Tanis, 'Reformed Pietism and Protestant Missions', *Harvard Theological Review*, 67 (1974), 65–73.

[16] Alec Ryrie, 'The Afterlife of Lutheran England', in *Sister Reformations: The Reformation in Germany and England*, ed. Dorothea Wendebourg (Tübingen, 2011), 213–34; W. B. Patterson, *James VI and I and the Reunion of Christendom* (Cambridge, 1997), 165–80; J. Minton Batten, *John Dury: Advocate of Christian Reunion* (Chicago, 1944).

The attempt had some significant consequences, however. The most notorious took place in Geneva in 1553. The execution of the anti-Trinitarian Michael Servetus should not be over-read: no territory in Europe would have openly tolerated Servetus's ideas. Yet Calvin's determination to pursue a trial and execution, as opposed to the easy option of banishment, must be understood in the context of his wider ecumenical project, which that autumn was at a critical stage. It was strategically vital for Calvin to demonstrate his essential orthodoxy both to Lutheran and to Catholic Europe, and therefore to draw a line against the wild excesses which Servetus, perhaps more than anyone else then alive, embodied. What clearer way to draw a line than in someone else's blood?

In this sense, at least, we are compelled to recognise that Servetus's execution succeeded. It helped to inscribe a fundamental distinction to which most scholars still faithfully subscribe, between magisterial and radical reformers. Hence, my second quarrel with the confessionalisation thesis. By focusing on the relationships between religion and state power, it has perpetuated the magisterial reformers' artificially sharp and ultimately self-serving distinction between themselves, the 'mainstream' of Protestantism, and the Anabaptists and other radicals whose status as Protestant is sometimes denied altogether. Recent research is making clear, however, quite how many reformers pitched their tents astride this supposed gulf. Susan Royal has demonstrated how no less mainstream and respectable a magisterial reformer than John Foxe, the English martyrologist, had a distinct whiff of radicalism hanging around him, giving houseroom to some very radical-sounding views on issues like pacifism, the use of oaths and the validity of tithes. In this context, Foxe's well-known opposition to the use of the death penalty for religious crimes begins to look less like an isolated quirk.[17] Similarly, Foxe's mentor, John Bale, a man who was amongst other things surprisingly polite about the Anabaptist Balthasar Hubmaier, did not actually prohibit juridical oaths like Anabaptists did, but was sufficiently affected by the Gospel warnings against swearing to classify oaths as morally equivalent to homicide, that is, damnable unless explicitly required by a magistrate.[18] A contemporary of Bale's, Katharina Schütz Zell, the most distinguished female Protestant theologian of the early Reformation, put considerable effort in the early 1540s into bringing Caspar Schwenkfeld, whom we conventionally class as a 'radical', into conversation with the Lutheran Johannes Brenz and

---

[17] Susan Royal, 'John Foxe's "Acts and Monuments" and the Lollard Legacy in the Long English Reformation' (Ph.D. thesis, Durham University, 2014).

[18] John Bale, *Yet a Course at the Romyshe Foxe. A Dysclosynge or Openynge of the Manne of Synne* (RSTC 1309, Antwerp, 1543), fo. 51v; [John Bale], *A Christen Exhortacion vnto Customable Swearers* (RSTC 1280, Antwerp, 1543), fo. 6v.

the Zwinglian Conrad Pellican on the basis of a common adherence to Scripture.[19]

Those efforts were never going to succeed, not because of any unbridgeable theological gulf, but because, after the bloody disaster of the kingdom of Münster in 1534–5, the label Anabaptist was politically toxic. Even so, the newly drawn boundary between radical and magisterial reformers was still subject to cross-border raiding. Before Münster, there had been some genuinely debatable land. Some Anabaptists had embarked on ventures that look decidedly magisterial, that is, territorial, comprehensive and coercive. As well as the Münster kingdom itself, there is the tantalising example of Balthasar Hubmaier's state Anabaptism in Nikolsburg in Moravia in 1526–7, which hinged on the conversion of the town's nobleman and its evangelical pastors. It only lasted three months before the Habsburgs crushed it. However, Hubmaier's expressed intention to create 'a Christian government at whose side God hung the Sword' sounds very like a magisterial Reformation.[20] Later Anabaptists were embarrassed about it, but if they had had other opportunities to enact territorial Reformations with the aid of princes, are we really to imagine that they would have forgone them?

Traffic went in the other direction, too. Martin Bucer had openly wondered whether infant baptism was Scriptural in 1524, back when such thoughts were still thinkable. He concluded that it was prudent and expedient to retain infant baptism, but not, apparently, necessary.[21] Indeed, Bucer, with his commitment to congregational discipline and his willingness to separate that from magisterial oversight, continued to have a whiff of radicalism about him. Separatism, indeed, would become a consistent feature of underground Reformed congregations in France, England, Scotland, the Netherlands and elsewhere across the mid-sixteenth century, congregations which Luther reviled as 'the work of rats and sects'. Indeed, in social terms, how different is a self-policing underground Calvinist congregation from a Mennonite one? Reformed theologians might tell their people that Catholic baptisms remained valid, but in practice many believers refused to submit their children to popish baptismal rites, even at the risk of their lives.[22] In mid-seventeenth-century England, the radical–magisterial distinction broke down altogether. English Independents; New England Congregationalists; the antinomian

[19] Elsie Anne, 'A Lay Voice in Sixteenth-Century "Ecumenics": Katharina Schütz Zell in Dioalogue with Johannes Brenz, Conrad Pellican, and Caspar Schwenckfeld', in *Adaptions of Calvinism in Reformation Europe*, ed. Mack P. Holt (Aldershot, 2007), 81–110.

[20] James M. Stayer, *Anabaptists and the Sword* (Lawrence, KS, 1976), 141–3.

[21] Hughes Oliphant Old, *The Shaping of the Reformed Baptismal Rite in the Sixteenth Century* (Grand Rapids, 1992), 52, 54–6.

[22] See, for example, *The Works of John Knox*, ed. David Laing (6 vols., Edinburgh, 1846–64), I, 298–300; Alec Ryrie, *Being Protestant in Reformation Britain* (Oxford, 2013), 335.

groups which emerged in both settings; Particular Baptists; General Baptists – where can we confidently draw a line?

In particular, as the Servetus case itself reminds us, the repeated surfacing of anti-Trinitarianism in Reformed Protestantism is no coincidence. Even Calvin had found himself in a tangle on this point in 1537, when he rashly tried to defend the doctrine of the Trinity without resorting to the precedents or terminology of the fourth- and fifth-century Councils, and even refused to sign the Athanasian Creed.[23] That was simply brash overconfidence, but the same qualms that led him there took others further. It was among the Reformed and the Reformed-influenced, from the Italian *spirituali* through to Transylvania and Poland, that serious anti-Trinitarianism first began to appear, and to garner such markers of establishment respectability as, in the Polish case, a university and a printing press. Some of the Dutch Remonstrants were drawn by anti-Trinitarianism, and some aligned themselves with the Mennonite offshoot, the Collegiants. William Chillingworth was accused of it. It was a Dutch Reformed theologian, and suspected Remonstrant sympathiser, Gerardus Vossius, who first proved that the Athanasian Creed was not actually written by Athanasius.

Blurring the boundary between radical and magisterial Protestants (and especially between radicalism and Calvinism) does not change the fact that radicalism was numerically small during the sixteenth and seventeenth centuries. It does mean we cannot treat it as marginal to the story, as, especially, anglophone historians are too inclined to do. The contemporary panic about radicalism was not minor, any more than the panics about witches and atheists were minor. And perhaps this panic, at least, was rational. There may not have been many actual radicals, but the ideological boundary between magisterial and radical reformers was porous and to a degree arbitrary. The *potential* for radicalism was everywhere. Only constant vigilance could keep it in check. With hindsight, Servetus's execution looks like an act of wanton brutality. In the early 1550s, when the very stability of the still-fragile Reformed Protestant identity was still unclear and radicals were turning up like, as the witch-hunters would say, worms in a garden, it seemed like a stand had to be taken against a mortal threat.

To allow the confessionalisation thesis to set the terms in which we describe post-Reformation Christianity is to risk assuming that a contingent set of politically determined divisions had some deep religious logic underpinning them. There is a good case to be made that the long alliance between magisterial Protestantism and the state masked, rather than revealed, Protestantism's nature. The best evidence for this

---

[23] Diarmaid MacCulloch, 'Calvin: Fifth Latin Doctor of the Church?', in *Calvin and his Influence, 1509–2009*, ed. Irena Backus and Philip Benedict (Oxford, 2011), 33–45.

is what happened when the alliance began to break down. Spener's *Pia Desideria*, the 1675 tract that launched Lutheran Pietism, now reads as a collection of bland platitudes. This was one of the reasons for its success: no revolutionary manifesto has ever been so reassuring. But it is also because one of the things which made it so shocking was an omission, a shuddering, gonging silence running through the book: in this call for renewal of the church, Spener made no mention of the magistrate at all. Pietism did have powerful princely sponsors, but it did not depend on them for its successes, and indeed it had much the most impact beyond their territories. Its successes in reaching populations who had been left without any access to Protestant ministry after the Thirty Years War was a striking embarrassment to the princely churches of Protestant orthodoxy, which simply had no way of tackling such an enterprise.[24]

It is to some extent a matter of taste how we see the established Protestant churches of the sixteenth and seventeenth centuries: as the result of a real alignment of interests between churches and princes; as a Faustian pact; or as a simple power-grab by emerging states. Examples to fit each case could be rehearsed. My point, however, is that the alliance with temporal power profoundly shaped magisterial Protestantism, but did so in ways that often had nothing to do with its theology. The plainest example of this is how, when Protestant state churches were set up, large amounts of church property were seized by the state and secularised. The consequences of that act of asset-stripping resonated for centuries. Amongst its many long-term consequences was the problem of overseas mission. It is well known that pre-eighteenth-century Protestants did very little missionary work. To be more precise, some individuals and some theologians did, but no institutions did. The problem was not essentially a theological one. Although Calvinist doctrines of predestination have sometimes been blamed for lack of missionary zeal, in fact Calvinists showed more concern for mission than Lutherans. The deeper problem seems to have been institutional. There were no Protestant equivalents to the Catholic religious orders, which could provide the continuity, the training, the logistics and above all the funds necessary to run a missionary enterprise. Serious missionary work is expensive, and the money was gone. Such Protestant missionaries as there were, were moonlighting from jobs with trading companies. A handful of Dutch ministers in Sri Lanka and Taiwan were actually employed to minister to the local populations, but were pitifully under-resourced. Generally, though, state- or commercially controlled Protestant establishments were reluctant to permit missionary work even if someone else was paying. It could stir up local trouble with either local or colonial populations, as would-be missionaries from

[24] W. R. Ward, *The Protestant Evangelical Awakening* (Cambridge, 1992); Philip Jacob Spener, *Pia Desideria*, trans. and ed. Theodore G. Tappert (Philadelphia, 1964).

Sri Lanka to New England discovered. It could also be politically risky: hence, the fierce opposition of the orthodox establishments in the empire to any kind of cross-border missionary work. Protestant missions only took root once they developed the institutions necessary to bypass the state. In the religious free-for-all of 1640s England, there was a wave of donations to support missionary work in New England, providing a very respectable annuity to two missionaries to the Native Americans, and endowing an admittedly shortlived Indian College at Harvard. And it was the Pietist University of Halle which both undertook the initiative of and raised the money for sending missionaries to India in 1706, the first Lutheran overseas mission.[25]

The nature of Protestantism

Instead of mapping Protestantism in the confessional age as a pair of tidy confessional entities and a scattering of radicals out beyond the pale, I am, therefore, suggesting we think of confessionalised Lutheranism rubbing up against a broad, discursive and dangerously soft-edged Calvinism, with the latter especially tending to leak into radicalism – especially when an active state was not on hand to keep piling up the sandbags. In which case, what is the rationale for treating this whole messy ecosystem as a single entity, which can usefully be described as *Protestant?*

There are several possible features that could be seen to unite Protestantism. There is simple genealogy, common descent from the Reformation moment – which is true, but not in itself very useful. Another, more significant argument, a long-standing claim which has been central to influential recent interpretations of Protestantism, is that it is Bible Christianity: the religion of *sola scriptura*, which finds ultimate authority in the unmediated Word of God. For Alister McGrath, that is Protestantism's underpinning genius. For Brad Gregory, that is what condemns Protestantism to irresoluble chaos.[26]

But this is not so. Protestantism is both less and more fluid than this approach suggests. Less so, because in practice it is of course much less theologically open than *sola scriptura* implies. *Sola fide* is logically and chronologically prior to *sola scriptura*. Although the dating of Luther's theological insights is perennially disputed, it is at least clear that he arrived at something very like his mature doctrine of salvation before he accepted, in 1519, that an Ecumenical Council cannot authoritatively

[25] Alec Ryrie, 'Mission and Empire: An Ethical Puzzle in Early Modern Protestantism', in *Sister Reformations II: Reformation and Ethics in Germany and in England*, ed. Dorothea Wendebourg and Alec Ryrie (Tübingen, 2014), 181–206.
[26] Alister McGrath, *Christianity's Dangerous Idea: The Protestant Revolution* (2007); Brad S. Gregory, *The Unintended Reformation: How a Religious Revolution Secularized Society* (Cambridge, MA, 2012).

determine the interpretation of Scripture. Of course, he already had a high doctrine of Scripture, and it was through his encounter with Scripture that he arrived at the doctrine of *sola fide*: but that doctrine then became, for him, not only the key to Scripture but its beating heart. He rejected ecclesiastical authority over the interpretation of the Bible because that authority had contradicted the doctrine he had learned from the Bible, and had therefore – in his eyes – proven itself to be false.

If Protestantism's starting point had genuinely been a blank slate of *sola scriptura*, it could have gone in far more and more varied directions than it in fact has. As various syncretistic movements that emerged in various parts of the world in the twentieth century demonstrate, only a minority of a set of all possible Bible-based religions are recognisable variants on historic Christianity. Protestantism's plurality is both extensive and irreducible, but it is not infinite. As Gregory has argued, it is characterised by proliferating doctrinal chaos, but the chaos is more fractal than random in nature; that is, the same patterns continuously recur, albeit in new configurations. Or, to use a different image: we can talk meaningfully about Protestantism not because of a shared genealogy, but because of shared genes.

Yet Protestantism is also more fluid than the Bible Christianity model suggests. Plainly, the Bible has been crucial to Protestants, but its authority has operated in many ways. Luther's idiosyncratic use of the Bible is well known. As well as notoriously dismissing the Epistle of James as mere straw, he also reportedly told a student that 'I almost feel like throwing Jimmy into the stove.' He could be equally robust with the rest of the canon. He reckoned that Hebrews, Jude and Revelation, like James, were not of apostolic authorship, and sent all four to a relegation zone at the end of his New Testament. He also wanted to expel the book of Esther. He doubted whether Moses wrote the Pentateuch; he reckoned that the books of Chronicles were less reliable than the books of Kings; he thought that Job was largely fiction, that the prophets had made mistakes, that the numbers in some Old Testament accounts were exaggerated. And he was favouritist about other books, notably John's Gospel and the Epistle to the Galatians.[27] No other mainstream reformer was quite so brazen, but Luther's libertine intimacy here demonstrates that this is more than self-serving caprice. Luther treated the Bible this way because it fits with his understanding of what the Bible was. In 1530, he advised Bible-readers

---

[27] Martin Luther, *Luther's Works*, XXXIV: *Career of the Reformer IV*, ed. Lewis W. Spitz (Philadelphia, 1960), 317; Martin Luther, *Luther's Works*, XXXV: *Word and Sacrament I*, ed. E. Theodore Bachmann (Philadelphia, 1960), 361–2, 397; Martin Luther, *Luther's Works*, LIV: *Table Talk*, ed. and trans. Theodore G. Tappert (Philadelphia, 1967), 79–80, 373, 424, 452; Reinhold Seeberg, *Textbook of the History of Doctrines*, trans. Charles E. Hay (2 vols., Grand Rapids, 1958–61), II, 300–1.

to 'search out and deal with the core of our Christian doctrine, wherever it may be found throughout the Bible. And the core is this: that without any merit, as a gift of God's pure grace in Christ, we attain righteousness, life, and salvation.'[28] *That* was the message: the Gospel. The reason he called the Epistle of James straw was that, although it contains sound moral teaching, 'it contains not a syllable about Christ'. Luther applied the doctrine of the Incarnation not only to the Eucharist, but to the Word of God: 'The Holy Scripture', he wrote, 'is God's Word, written, and so to say "in-lettered", just as Christ is the eternal Word of God incarnate in the garment of his humanity'; he even called the Bible 'the swaddling cloths and the manger in which Christ lies'.[29] As such, its incidental content is almost insignificant.

Calvin was more cautious, but he did not fundamentally disagree. He was happy to accept that the creation story in Genesis did not fit the science even of his own day, and to explain that the account was written to fit what its original readers could understand. He was apparently untroubled by the textual glitches he found in Scripture. When in schoolmasterly mode, he could not only chide St Luke for mistaking the name of a high priest or St Paul for writing an almost incomprehensible sentence, but also point out that the New Testament writers were sometimes very sloppy in quoting the Old Testament. Calvin's comment on these regrettable lapses, which he clearly did not regard as very important, tells us a good deal about his own attitude to the Bible: 'with respect both to words and to other things which do not bear upon the matters in discussion, [the Apostles] allow themselves wide freedom'.[30] So for Calvin, too, the authority of Scripture was the authority of its core message, not its incidentals. Hence his strange reluctance to argue that the Bible is authoritative. All he will say is that, through 'the secret testimony of the Spirit . . . Scripture is indeed self-authenticating . . . We feel that the undoubted power of his divine majesty lives and breathes there, . . . a feeling that can be born only of heavenly revelation.'[31] Likewise, as Scott Hendrix has suggested, 'the authority of Scripture for Luther was not like a mathematical theorem which can be proven . . . by the use of self-evident axioms . . . Rather . . . Luther approached Scripture as we would

[28] Martin Luther, *Luther's Works,* XIV: *Selected Psalms III,* ed. Jaroslav Pelikan and Daniel E. Poellot (St Louis, 1958), 36.

[29] Jack B. Rogers and Donald K. McKim, *The Authority and Interpretation of the Bible: An Historical Approach* (San Francisco, 1979), 78; Brian A. Gerrish, 'The Word of God and the Words of Scripture: Luther and Calvin on Biblical Authority', in his *The Old Protestantism and the New: Essays on the Reformation Heritage* (Chicago, 1982), 51–68 at 55.

[30] John T. McNeill, 'The Significance of the Word of God for Calvin', *Church History,* 28 (1959), 131–46, esp. 143–4.

[31] John Calvin, *Institutes of the Christian Religion,* ed. John T. McNeill, trans. Ford Lewis Battles (Philadelphia, 1960), 78–81.

approach a great work of art.'[32] This is an authority which cannot be demonstrated by argument. Either it is perceived, or it is not.

Such views have been seized upon by liberal Protestants keen to look for historical justification for non-literalist views of Biblical authority, which is fair enough, although these are crumbs of liberal comfort gathered from beneath a vast table groaning with evidence that the early Reformers used the Bible as a proof-text with precise literalism. Fortunately, historians can keep out of that fight. For our purposes, some more modest observations will suffice. The view that the Bible's authority derives from its message, and that, as Luther put it, Christ is king over Scripture, is distinguished from the literalist view less by logic than by function. The former view is devotional and inspirational rather than polemical. It is also primary: it is how the Reformers learned their theology, and how Scripture first authenticated itself to them. However, it works much better for one believer's spiritual crisis than for building an institutional church or for fighting a religious war. So, inevitably, as Luther and his colleagues were pressed on their doctrine of authority, the polemical use of Scripture came to the fore. Yet this meaning too was, in origin, not strictly about textual literalism either. It was about exclusion: Luther's declaration that he rejected all authorities *except* Scripture, and Scripture as understood by his own conscience, a double negative echoed by Lutheran and Calvinist formularies throughout the sixteenth century.[33] This doctrine of the sufficiency of Scripture is a claim, not about the authority of the Bible, but about the absence of authority outside the Bible. *Sola scriptura* began as a polemical tool for rejecting all authorities from which any contradiction might arise.

For many Protestants, it swiftly became much more than that. Especially in the Reformed tradition, whose humanism made it more textually conservative, increasingly strong (or rigid) doctrines of Biblical authority emerged, which in the seventeenth century became close to what in modern times is called inerrantist. As Peter Harrison's shrewd history of the Scientific Revolution suggests, the paring away of allegorical and other 'higher' interpretations of Scripture tended to change its value to a set of propositional statements.[34] However, this tendency within Protestantism has rarely been unchallenged: especially if, as we must, we allow that the radicals are genuinely a part of the Protestant family. In the first generation, Anabaptist polemicists were skewering Lutheran and Reformed theologians for defending infant baptism without Biblical warrant (proof, if it were needed, that theology

---

[32] Scott Hendrix, *Tradition and Authority in the Reformation* (Aldershot, 1996), II, 147.

[33] Paul Lehmann, 'The Reformers' Use of the Bible', *Theology Today*, 3 (1946), 328–44 at 329; Gerrish, 'Word of God', 59. Cf. article VI of the Anglican Thirty-Nine Articles.

[34] Peter Harrison, *The Bible, Protestantism and the Rise of Natural Science* (Cambridge, 1998).

trumps prooftexting). Yet they were of course doing the same thing: discerning Scripture's inner meaning and using that inner meaning to interpret and where necessary discard Scripture. In 1524, Jörg Haugk complained that 'many accept the Scriptures as if they were the essence of divine truth; but they are only a witness to divine truth which must be experienced in the inner being'. Hans Hut insisted that the Bible could only be understood through the Holy Spirit; otherwise, he argued, the text bristled with contradictions, of which he provided a substantial list.[35]

The 'magisterial' reformers were scathing about this, and appealed to their learning, which gave them the right to be heard when they interpreted Scripture. As Protestant universities became established, that would become a regular refrain. Equally regular, however, was the response from those who did not have access to a theological education, but who nevertheless would not accept theological disenfranchisement. For the self-taught Nuremberg Anabaptist Hans Hergot, Luther and his allies were 'Scripture wizards' whose hairsplitting subtleties blinded them to the simple truth. Very similar language resurfaced in the English Revolution, when the Ranter prophet Abiezer Coppe dismissed the voice of his own inner textual nitpicker as the 'holy Scripturian whore'. Other Ranters supposedly distinguished between the *history* of Scripture – its dead word – and the *mystery* of Scripture – its living, hidden essence. The early Quakers were scathing about the university-educated clergy whom they called ministers of the Letter, as distinct from the Word: 'not the letter, nor the writing of the Scripture, but the ingrafted Word is able to save your soules', George Fox preached.[36] A couple of centuries later again, at the beginning of the nineteenth century, we find a freed American slave and self-taught preacher named Elizabeth condemning the kind of 'great scripturian' who comes to sermons to take notes and analyse doctrine rather than to meet God.[37] All of these people took their Bibles extremely seriously, but in a spiritualising and sometimes allegorising fashion which made them sources of inspiration rather than of hard theological argument. Those who could not or would not wield the Bible as a polemical weapon tended to fall back on its primary Protestant use as a medium for God's message.

So we might accept Chillingworth's dictum that the Bible is the religion of Protestants: but neither in the polemical sense he meant, that the Bible

[35] *Sources of South German/Austrian Anabaptism*, ed. Walter Klaassen, Frank Friesen and Werner O. Packull (Kitchener, ON, 2001), 19, 24–9.

[36] *Ibid.*, 44–5; *A Collection of Ranter Writings from the Seventeenth Century*, ed. Nigel Smith (1983), 102; A. L. Morton, *The World of the Ranters: Religious Radicalism in the English Revolution* (1970), 82; George Fox, *A Declaration of the Difference of the Ministers of the Word from the Ministers of the World; Who Calls the Writings, the Word* (Wing F1790, 1656), 12.

[37] 'Memoir of Old Elizabeth, a Colored Woman', in *Six Women's Slave Narratives*, ed. William L. Andrews (New York, 1988), 16.

is the banner around which the anti-Catholic cause might gather, nor in the polemical sense his Victorian enthusiasts meant, that anyone who questions Biblical literalism is not a real Protestant. We might, more helpfully, say that Protestantism is and has been a religion of the Bible. Better still, Protestantism is a religion within which the Bible appears to be self-authenticating. That is, it is a religion which hinges on the unmediated encounter with God's grace. Not all Protestants have formulated their understanding of that grace in the same theological terms: Luther's *sola fide* was enduringly influential but has never had the field to itself. Yet that sense of a direct meeting with grace through the individual believer's faith is fundamental, in different ways, to Lutheranism, Calvinism, Methodism, Pentecostalism, Mennonitism, Quakerism, Unitarianism, Adventism and more. There are some religious traditions which are genealogically Reformation-derived but which lack that central emphasis on unmediated grace – for example, Anglo-Catholicism or Mormonism; and these, importantly, are the traditions hardest to describe as Protestant. The remainder, for all their huge diversity, bear an unmistakable family resemblance. The best word we have for that family is 'Protestant'.

Transactions of the RHS 26 (2016), pp. 79–101 © Royal Historical Society 2016
doi:10.1017/S0080440116000062

TALL HISTORIES: HEIGHT AND GEORGIAN MASCULINITIES*

By Matthew McCormack

READ ON 15 JUNE 2015

AT THE UNIVERSITY OF NORTHAMPTON

ABSTRACT. Height is rarely taken seriously by historians. Demographic and archaeological studies tend to explore height as a symptom of health and nutrition, rather than in its own right, and cultural studies of the human body barely study it at all. Its absence from the history of gender is surprising, given that it has historically been discussed within a highly gendered moral language. This paper therefore explores height through the lens of masculinity and focuses on the eighteenth century, when height took on a peculiar cultural significance in Britain. On the one hand, height could be associated with social status, political power and 'polite' refinement. On the other, it could connote ambition, militarism, despotism, foreignness and even castration. The article explores these themes through a case-study of John Montagu, earl of Sandwich, who was famously tall and was frequently caricatured as such. As well as exploring representations of the body, the paper also considers corporeal experiences and biometric realities of male height. It argues that histories of masculinity should study both representations of gender and their physical manifestations.

Let us begin with two sandwiches. These are two versions of a caricature from 1788 depicting John Montagu the earl of Sandwich, literally 'sandwiched' by two young women (Figures 1 and 2). Sandwich was one of the most prominent statesmen of his day, but nowadays tends to be remembered for three things: first, for the snack that he supposedly invented; second, for running the Admiralty during the disastrous American War; and third, for his scandalous lifestyle. He lived openly with his mistresses, one of whom was publicly murdered by an admirer. As we will see, his shortcomings as a public man were commonly related to those in his private morality – and, as such, he was one of the most caricatured people of his day. Caricature plays on appearance in order to exemplify personality, and Sandwich provided promising material for this since his defining physical feature was that he was very tall. The artist here is trying to make a comic point about the ageing libertine consorting

* I would like to thank Michèle Cohen, the journal's referees and audiences in Northampton, Oxford and London for their feedback on this article.

Figure 1 'A Sandwich' (1 Jan. 1788). British Museum Satires 7421. © The Trustees of the British Museum.

Figure 2 (Colour online) 'A Sandwich' (8 Feb. 1788). British Museum Satires 7421.A. © The Trustees of the British Museum.

with two young singers: Sandwich was a patron of music who was known to take singers for mistresses, and the print contains an obvious sexual innuendo. As we can see, in the first version they are of equivalent height, but the artist has redrawn the image in order to exaggerate the height difference. Why did the artist do this and what point were they trying to make? In order to explain this, we have to attend to the wider historical significance of male height, and to think critically about how historians have studied masculinity and the body. We will return to Sandwich at the end of this article, since he provides a telling case-study for why tallness was so rich in meaning in Georgian Britain.

I

Tallness is part of our everyday parlance for talking about men. This often carries implied moral evaluations, suggesting pride (to 'walk tall'), rectitude ('upright') or greatness (someone 'to look up to'). As Fanny Burney remarked of the duke of Wellington before Waterloo: 'He looked remarkably well ... Since his return to military command, he has an Air the most commanding, a high, superior *port*, & a look of animated spirit. I think he is grown taller!'[1] By contrast, Wellington's adversary Napoleon Bonaparte epitomises the negative associations of male shortness, being probably the most famous example of 'short man syndrome'. In reality, Napoleon was about five feet six, which was average for the time and not much shorter than Wellington, but the symbolism was more important than the reality here. British caricaturists consistently mocked 'little Boney', suggesting that he was an ambitious usurper, whose aggressiveness overcompensated for this stature.[2] Lilliputian caricatures of Napoleon served to puncture his Romantic image as an epic warrior, reassuring Britons that this was a threat that could be defeated.

Given these strong associations, it is notable that historians rarely talk about height. It is part of the shorthand of the biographer, as we will see, but is not taken seriously in scholarly studies. In archaeological studies of the body, height is discussed only as a biological fact that relates to evolutionary changes or big shifts in the organisation in human society, such as the shift from hunting to farming.[3] The history of the body posits that the cultural meanings and the lived experience of bodies are contextually specific and loaded with political importance,

---

[1] Quoted in Nick Foulkes, *Dancing into Battle: A Social History of the Battle of Waterloo* (2007), 96.

[2] Andrea Franklin and Mark Philp, *Napoleon and the Invasion of Britain* (Oxford, 2003).

[3] John Robb and Oliver Harris, *The Body in History: Europe from the Palaeolithic to the Future* (Cambridge, 2013), 35.

but height plays little role in key sociological studies of the body.[4] Given its strong gendered associations, its absence from the histories of women and masculinity is striking, and epitomises gender historians' neglect of the actual fabric of body in general.[5] Sabine Geiske's article on the height differential between men and women in heterosexual couples is a fascinating exception here: she argues that it was only in the eighteenth century that a tall woman being with a short man became an object of mockery, hinting at wider shifts in the power relations between the sexes.[6] On the other hand, we will see that height did not just signify dominance, and this is also an example of where masculinity is defined most powerfully in relation to other men, rather than to women.

The one branch of history that takes height seriously is demography. The eighteenth century is very significant for this field, since for the first time the modern state started to collect biometric data from institutionalised populations such as soldiers, convicts and the poor.[7] Demographers do not study height in its own right, but for what it indicates. Roderick Floud and others have made the case for an 'anthropometric history', where height is a key statistical marker of health and nutrition in a large population over a long period. Poor health and nutrition have a depressive effect upon height, and dips in average height occurred during periods of deprivation in Britain, such as the 1790s and the later nineteenth century.[8] In particular, age is an important variable here, as nutrition affects the growing years. People who are healthy and well fed reach their potential height sooner: nowadays it is typically age sixteen in girls and eighteen in boys, but in the eighteenth century, plebeian men continued to grow into their early twenties.[9] The

[4] It is ignored in Bryan Turner's pioneering *The Body and Society* (Oxford, 1984) and mentioned only in passing in Anthony Synott's *The Body Social: Symbolism, Self and Society* (1993). Tellingly, the key work here is in the genre of popular sociology: Ralph Keyes, *The Height of Your Life* (Boston, MA, 1980).

[5] As noted by Lyndal Roper: 'Beyond Discourse Theory', *Women's History Review*, 19 (2010), 307–19 at 316.

[6] Sabine Geiske, 'The Ideal Couple: A Question of Size?', in *Feminism and the Body*, ed. Londa Schiebinger (Oxford, 2000), 375–96.

[7] Stephen Kuntz, 'Making a Long Story Short: A Note on Men's Height and Mortality in England from the First through the Nineteenth Centuries', *Medical History*, 31 (1987), 269–80 at 270.

[8] Roderick Floud, Kenneth Wacher and Annabel Gregory, *Height, Health and History: Nutritional Status in the United Kingdom* (Cambridge, 1990), 29, 151. See also Stephen Nicholas and Richard Steckel, 'Heights and Living Standards of English Workers during the Early Years of Industrialization', *Journal of Economic History*, 51 (1991), 937–57; Stephen Nicholas and Deborah Oxley, 'The Living Standards of Women during the Industrial Revolution', *Economic History Review*, 46 (1993), 723–49; Nikola Koepke and Jeorg Baten, 'The Biological Standard of Living in Europe during the Last Two Millennia', *European Review of Economic History*, 9 (2005), 61–95.

[9] Floud, Wacher and Gregory, *Height, Health and History*, 10.

eighteenth-century military continued to measure men's heights into their early twenties, as they recognised that their young recruits continued to grow. More could be said about the cultural significance of the growing lifecycle: it is striking, for example, that men reach their age of 'majority' when they attain their full height – twenty-one in the eighteenth century, and eighteen today. Maturity equals height: we all 'grow up'.

Archaeological and demographic studies of height therefore have their limitations. On the other hand, they should remind us that we are dealing with a corporeal fact here, rather than just a facet of representation. People's height can relate in very real ways to their access to nutrition, and thence to their social class. Furthermore, height is a lived experience: the world looks different from different vantage points, and bodies of different sizes and shapes are different to inhabit and coordinate. As Floud notes, 'height is a salient characteristic, one of our primary means of identification, one of the features of the body which it is most difficult to disguise'[10] – but men do try to disguise it, by wearing elevator shoes or altering their posture. *The Gentleman's Magazine* of 1798 contained an obituary of a schoolmaster who measured seven feet eight inches: 'His breadth was in proportion to his length; but he was not athletic, nor, upon the whole, healthy. He died under 30 years of age, and a bachelor. Till within these last few years he appeared ashamed of his height, and contrived to stoop, that the disparity might not be seen.'[11] Very tall or short people alike can be subject to ridicule or social disadvantage, and bear the psychological weight of that.[12] Slang dictionaries from the eighteenth century contained numerous insults for tall men, including 'gawkey', 'Jack of Legs', 'Gilly Gaupus' and 'Duke of Limbs', the latter meaning 'a tall awkward ill made fellow'.[13]

Where the history of masculinity is concerned, therefore, the study of height presents an opportunity to reconnect the representation of gender with lived experience and bodily practice.[14] There are, unfortunately, a frustrating lack of sources where men reflect on their own experience of being tall or short: I have not found many for the eighteenth century, and this may be a classic case of an aspect of human life that was not written down, with all of the methodological challenges that this implies.

---

[10] *Ibid.*, 1.

[11] *The Gentleman's Magazine*, July 1798, 626. I am grateful to Gillian Williamson for this reference.

[12] Keyes, *Height of Your Life*, chs. 4 and 5.

[13] Francis Grose, *A Classical Dictionary of the Vulgar Tongue* (London, 1785), GIL, JAC, GIM, DUK.

[14] As recently advocated by John Tosh: 'The History of Masculinity: An Outdated Concept?', in *What is Masculinity? Historical Dynamics from Antiquity to the Contemporary World*, ed. John Arnold and Sean Brady (Basingstoke, 2011), 17–34.

Nevertheless, the use of more public and biometric sources can give us an insight into the significance that height had for eighteenth-century men.

As this brief survey shows, the history of height has largely been ignored. The obvious contrast here is with the history of weight, since there is a wealth of work on this by historians of medicine, gender and social policy. This is a hugely politicised area: fat is a feminist issue,[15] but also one that relates in important ways to class, race and corporate power.[16] In contrast with the history of weight, the history of height is currently written as quantitative rather than qualitative, natural rather than political, and biological rather than moral. As a corrective to this, this study will attempt to demonstrate that tallness is a facet of masculinity that has historically had a peculiar cultural significance.

II

Tall people have been recorded since ancient times. The Bible contains numerous giants of mythical heights, although some modern scholars put Goliath at a realistic six feet nine inches.[17] In the eighteenth century, it was generally believed that men had roughly been of the same height since the Creation, so giants were 'Rarities and Wonders'.[18] There are numerous recorded instances of exceptionally tall people in Britain in the seventeenth and eighteenth centuries, some of whom lived normal lives and others who were exhibited for money.[19] One such was Charles Byrne, the famous 'Irish Giant', who was so concerned that his body would be acquired by surgeons for dissection that he requested a burial at sea. His wishes were not carried out and his skeleton (measuring seven feet seven inches) is still on display at the Royal College of Surgeons.[20]

Up to the early modern period, height could be understood in terms of the humoral body. Whereas the phlegmatic person was 'short and thick' and the sanguine was 'naturally fat', height was identified with the choleric type. As the much-reprinted *Sanitatis Salerni* put it:

---

[15] Susie Orbach, *Fat is a Feminist Issue* (London, 1984).

[16] For example: Sander Gilman, *Obesity: The Biography* (Oxford, 2010); Christopher Forth, 'Fat, Desire and Disgust in the Colonial Imagination', *History Workshop Journal*, 73 (2012), 211–39; *Fat: Culture and Materiality*, ed. Christopher Forth and Alison Leitch (2014).

[17] J. Daniel Hays, 'Reconsidering the Height of Golaith', *Journal of the Evangelical Theological Society*, 48 (2005), 702–15.

[18] *Every Man Entertained: Or, Select Histories: Giving an Account of Persons who have been Most Eminently Distinguish'd by their Virtues or Vices, their Perfections or Defects, either of Body or Mind* (1756), 41.

[19] 'The true effigies of the German Giant, now to be seen at the Swan near Charing-Cross, whose Stature is nine foot and a half in height, and the Span of his Hand a Cubit compleat. He goes from place to place with his Wife, who is but of ordinary Stature, and takes Money for the Show of her Husband' (handbill, 1668).

[20] Robb and Harris, *The Body in History*, 177. Caroline Nielsen has pointed out to me that Byrne is a *cause célèbre* in heritage studies, regarding the ethics of displaying human remains.

Choler is such a humor as aspires,
With most impetuous, insolent desires,
He covets to excel all other men,
His mind outsteps beyond a Kingdom's ken.
Lightly he learns, eats much and grows tall,
Magnanimous, and somewhat prodigall.
Soon mov'd to anger though upon no cause,
His own will is his reasons largest laws.
Subtle and crafty, seldom speaking fair,
A wasting unthrift, overgrown with hair.
Bold spirited, and yet but lean and dry,
His skin most usual of a Saffron dye.[21]

Within the humoral scheme, all bodies contained the four humours in different proportion, which combined physical attributes with personality types. Differences within and between genders were on a sliding scale: women possessed some choler, but it is notable that this 'tall' humour was primarily associated with masculinity.[22] A healthy body maintained a balance between the humours, so excessive height could be a sign of unhealthiness. Indeed, anxieties about the healthiness of the tall male continued throughout the eighteenth century.[23] And with good reason: tall bodies are inefficient, fragile, weaker and more prone to disease than shorter ones.[24]

Aspects of the humoral body continued to coexist with its modern anatomical equivalent. Eighteenth-century physiology located the vital fluid for life in the semen, so excessive loss of semen was physically depletive.[25] The contemporary panic about masturbation therefore concerned bodily health as well as morality.[26] The anti-masturbation tract *Onania* of 1716 relates a letter from a young man who 'learned the vicious Practice of SELF-POLLUTION' at the age of fifteen, and who physically suffered for it: 'I han't grown either in Strength or Stature since I was about 17. I suppose by my cruelty to my self, I crush'd my

---

[21] *Regimen Sanitatis Salerni: Or, The School of Salernes Regiment of Health* (1649).

[22] Thomas Laqueur, *Making Sex: Body and Gender from the Greeks to Freud* (New Haven, 1990).

[23] A treatise of military medicine of 1797 noted that tall soldiers are more prone to leg ulcers and are less able to bear tropical climates: Everard Home, *Practical Observations on the Treatment of Ulcers on the Legs, Considered as a Branch of Military Surgery* (1797).

[24] Keyes, *Height of Your Life*, 37–9.

[25] Roy Porter, *Flesh in the Age of Reason: How the Enlightenment Transformed the Way we See our Bodies and Souls* (2003), 234.

[26] David M. Turner, 'The Body Beautiful', in *A Cultural History of the Human Body in the Enlightenment*, ed. Carol Reeves (2010), 113–32 at 123.

before flourishing Nature.'[27] In a period when men would continue to grow into their twenties, this was stunting indeed.

The emerging body of the Enlightenment was conceived of more mechanistically, and the location of personality was shifting away from the guts – the repository of humoral fluids – and towards the brain and the nerves.[28] Nevertheless, the physical body was still linked to inner character in the eighteenth-century mind. The Sandwich cartoons show how caricature sought to ridicule individuals by exaggerating aspects of their appearance that were suggestive of their personality. As Amelia Rauser has argued, caricature was 'a kind of personality x-ray machine . . . to look deep beneath the surface of a man and avoid the dangers of entrapment by a deceptive, artificial character'.[29] In this context, male height could retain its humoral associations with ambition, covetousness, boldness and craftiness: the language of the humours persisted as a way to describe personality. The satire 'The Levee' of 1783 mocked the Fox–North ministry, but singled out the tall earl of Hertford (Figure 3). His height here alludes to his reputation for avarice: the earl of Bristol noted that Hertford 'has a constant appetite for all preferments for himself and family'.[30] As we will see, the humoral associations of tallness were remarkably enduring. A political handbill of 1820 cast aspersions on the character of the candidate for Newcastle: 'He is a tall, thin, hungry-looking Young Man, apparently well calculated for filling a good sinecure Place.'[31] A lean figure suggested ravenousness, which was highly suspect in a political culture that prided independence and disinterestedness.

Nevertheless, male height was bound up with social class and political power. Economic historians have aggregated archaeological evidence of male height, charting the extent of height differences at any one time

[27] *Onania: Or, the Heinous Sin of Self-Pollution, and all its Frightful Consequences (in Both Sexes) Consider'd*, 6th edn (1730), 145.

[28] Porter, *Flesh in the Age of Reason*, 60.

[29] Amelia Rauser, 'Hair, Authenticity and the Self-Made Macaroni', *Eighteenth-Century Studies*, 38 (2004), 101–17 at 107.

[30] Quoted in John Brooke, *The Chatham Administration, 1766–68* (1956), 71. Contemporary satires to this effect included John Combe's *The Diaboliad: A Poem, Dedicated to the Worst Man in His Majesty's Dominions* (1777), 4–5:

> To lure the Statesman from his deep-lay'd scheme,
> To wake the Courtier from his golden dream,
> And make the [Chamberlain] desire to hold
> Hell's weighty Sceptre, for 'tis made of gold.
> Sure he'd resign for such a tempting fee!
> HELL's Sceptre far outweighs the Golden Key!
> But cautious [Hertford] shrinks, when risks are run,
> And leaves such Honours for his ELDEST SON.

Note the allusion at the end to his stooping frame, also rendered in the caricature.

[31] 'Stolen or Strayed' (handbill: Newcastle, 1820): British Library 8135.e.3(24).

Figure 3 Edward Topham, 'The Levee' (21 Apr. 1783). British Museum Satires 6218. © The Trustees of the British Museum.

as an indicator of health inequality, and therefore social inequality. This accelerates after the early Middle Ages until it is much more pronounced during the early modern period.[32] This also had a geographic dimension: during the industrial revolution, the English urban working-class male was notably shorter than his rural counterpart.[33] Roy Porter notes that 'the upper classes of society were literally taller – superiority of height enshrined and blazoned forth superiority of spirit: the lower classes were meant to look up to their betters'.[34] Their higher station in life was confirmed by their bodies. Being better fed and above manual labour, men of the aristocracy grew taller and did so younger, and their bodies were deliberately cultivated to develop an elegant and elongated frame.[35]

Height was not just a matter of actual stature, since the elite had access to a range of strategies to emphasise a 'tall' body shape. Tailored clothing encourages the wearer to stand up straight, and since the medieval period men's clothes had become increasingly fitted, emphasising the shapeliness

[32] Koepke and Baten, 'Biological Standard of Living', 83–4.
[33] Nicholas and Steckel, 'Heights and Living Standards', 945.
[34] Porter, *Flesh in the Age of Reason*, 246–7.
[35] Chandra Mukerji, *Territorial Ambitions and the Gardens of Versailles* (Cambridge, 1997), 245.

of the leg in particular.[36] In the eighteenth century, the three-piece suit became the uniform of the upper-class Englishman, embodying their moral and political authority in a particular silhouette.[37] Elite men wore heeled shoes, aping Louis XIV whose *talons rouge* symbolised his ability to trample his opponents. Heeled mules and equestrian boots gave men of the upper classes a significant height advantage over their inferiors, so linked masculinity to class in a material way.[38] (High heels – and the body shape, distinctive walk and impracticality that come with wearing them – would not acquire their current association with femininity until the Victorian period.[39]) Finally, height could be enhanced by posture. Conduct literature emphasised the importance of 'mien' and 'a good air' as signs of good breeding. David Turner notes that this 'combined dignity, ease, grace, and a lack of affectation'.[40] Although the intended effect was to appear 'natural', this could paradoxically only be achieved through careful cultivation. As Jane Desmond has argued, 'the postural and gestural maintenance of class distinction was a necessary skill to be learned'.[41]

The fact that it could be learned, however, potentially opened up the status associated with bodily refinement to humbler groups of people. The vogue for 'politeness' sought to refine manners beyond the world of the court, in order to promote social harmony and rational discourse. Bodily comportment was central to this project, since a pleasing exterior would facilitate refined interaction, and would present an individual's real virtues to their best advantage. As Stephen Philpot wrote in 1747, 'Learning is, without doubt, absolutely necessary to qualify a Person designed for any Profession or genteel Employment . . . But, in order to give this valuable Accomplishment its proper Lustre, there must be added to it a polite and graceful Behaviour.' Outer refinement should therefore be synchronised with inner virtue. He argued that parents should engage a dancing master for boys at an early age:

> For if their Children have any Aukwardness in their Gait, or otherwise, when they are grown pretty large, it may be difficult to break them from such contracted ill Habits; or at least they will never be able to perform those graceful Actions of the Body, with that Ease and Unaffectedness as they would otherwise have done, had they begun sooner; but their Motions will always appear stiff and unnatural. Besides, when they are grown

[36] Karen Harvey, 'Men of Parts: Masculine Embodiment and the Male Leg in Eighteenth-Century England', *Journal of British Studies*, 54 (2015), 797–821 at 797.

[37] David Kuchta, *The Three-Piece Suit and Modern Masculinity: England 1550–1850* (Berkeley, 2002).

[38] For example, a pair of men's silk brocade mules from *c.* 1707 have heels measuring 60mm. Northampton Museum P.53.1971.

[39] Elizabeth Semmelhack, *Heights of Fashion: A History of the Elevated Shoe* (Reading, 2008).

[40] Turner, 'The Body Beautiful', 114.

[41] Jane C. Desmond, 'Embodying Difference: Issues in Dance and Cultural Studies', *Cultural Critique* (Winter 1994), 33–63 at 38.

pretty big, they are apt to be ashamed to learn; and perhaps their Aukwardness will be so settled and fixed, that it may not be in the Power of any Master to alter them.

Philpot considered that English boys were characterised by 'excessive Bashfulness' and fail to 'hold up their heads, keep themselves upright, walk so, look at People who speak to them, or pay them a compliment' for fear of being considered '*proud or impudent*': his regime of dance and comportment sought to correct these failings in character and stature.[42]

Philpot was not alone in focusing on the young, since medical treatises 'advocated firmness but tenderness with infants' bodies' so as to promote straightness.[43] Much of this focused on the spine. Nicholas Andry's *Orthopædia: Or, the Art of Correcting and Preventing Deformities in Children* (1743) argued: 'When the Spine is straight, well set, and finely turned, it makes a handsome Body; and when it is crooked and ill turned, the Body is deformed.'[44] Alun Withey argues that, whereas the correction of bodily shape could formerly be condemned as vanity or interfering with God's work, from the second half of the eighteenth century the practice was not only acceptable but desirable. A range of postural devices were commercially available, from stays and trusses, to steel 'monitors' that painfully corrected the slouch. Precisely what bodily ideal they were aiming for is unclear, since this was not explicitly defined,[45] but eighteenth-century aesthetics tended to emphasise classical proportion and symmetry. Andry, for one, suggested that 'The Body, when it is neither too fat nor too thin, is five times as tall as it is broad.'[46] A tall body should therefore be appropriately proportioned: if caricature is a guide to deviance, then tall bodies that were too fat or (more usually) too thin were not ideal.

One of the most notorious proponents of polite behaviour was Lord Chesterfield, who famously instructed his illegitimate son Philip in the minutiae of refinement with a view to easing his progress into society. Chesterfield had himself laboured under the disadvantages of a 'short stature, large head, and unprepossessing figure', which hindered his progress at court as a young man, and he wished better for his son.[47] Chesterfield's 400 letters often dwelt on the bodily aspects of politeness and he took a close interest in his son's height. When his son was sixteen, he wrote: 'The messenger told me, you were much grown, and, to the

[42] Stephen Philpott, *An Essay on the Advantage of a Polite Education Joined with a Learned One* (1747), 73, 28–9.

[43] Alun Withey, *Technology, Self-Fashioning and Politeness in Eighteenth-Century Britain: Refined Bodies* (2016), 27.

[44] Nicholas Andry, *Orthopædia: Or, the Art of Correcting and Preventing Deformities in Children* (1743), 77.

[45] Withey, *Technology*, 28, 22.

[46] Andry, *Orthopædia*, 63.

[47] Samuel Shellabarger, *Lord Chesterfield and his World* (New York, 1971), 109.

best of his guess, within two inches as tall as I am; that you were plump, and looked healthy and strong.'[48] And the following year: 'He tells me that you are taller than I am, which I am very glad of: I desire that you may excel me in everything else too.'[49] This was not just a father's pride in a growing lad, since a tall body was a polite body, suited to refined comportment and to impressing in company.

When these private letters were published in 1774, they caused a storm. Towards the end of the eighteenth century, politeness fell from vogue. Chesterfield's letters – which would have been more acceptable when they were written in the 1740s – now appeared to be cynical and self-serving, and to epitomise the superficiality of politeness in general. The new fashion for 'feeling' emphasised that men should be sincere, straightforward and independent.[50] This was commonly bound up with a critique of the ruling class, whom radicals and 'patriots' alleged were effeminate and culturally foreign. The rash of 'macaroni' caricatures, depicting tall, stooped and spindly bodies, therefore had a political edge. As we will see, this later-Georgian suspicion of exterior polish would have implications for the tall body.

III

Height in the English civilian man also took on connotations from other spheres, and the most important of these was the military. Historians of war have shown how the military and civilian society had shared values and experiences in the eighteenth century, to the extent that they were not yet regarded as being separate spheres.[51] The military carefully recorded the height of its recruits and this data is essential for modern demographic studies of the century. It is worth noting, however, that this data does have certain flaws for deducing the height of the civilian population as a whole.[52] Clearly, this only provides data for males, creating a 'false universal' for anthropometric history. The military had minimum height requirements, so shorter men do not appear in the returns, and furthermore the height standard varied according to the fluctuating demands for manpower. As a circular from the Adjutant General's Office put it when Britain was gearing up for war in December 1792:

[48]Chesterfield to Stanhope, 30 Dec. 1748: *Lord Chesterfield's Letters*, ed. David Roberts (Oxford, 1992), 130.

[49]Chesterfield to Stanhope, 27 Sept. 1749: *Chesterfield's Letters*, ed. Roberts, 165.

[50]Matthew McCormack, *The Independent Man: Citizenship and Gender Politics in Georgian England* (Manchester, 2005), ch. 5.

[51]David Bell, *The First Total War: Napoleon's Europe and the Birth of Modern Warfare* (2007), ch. 1.

[52]As noted by Nicholas and Steckel. They instead use data collected from transported convicts, which they argue is more representative of the wider population, not least because it includes women: 'Heights and Living Standards', 942.

> His M[ajesty] having thought it proper to order an augmentation of 10 private men per company in the Regts of Foot on the British Estabt. to take place immediately, it is His M's further Pleasure, that the Standard for Recruiting on the present occasion, is to be lowered to 5 feet 6 inches for Men not exceeding 30 years of Age; Growing, well made Lads may be taken as low as 5 feet 5 inches.[53]

These changing demands undermine demographers' attempts to use this data to chart long-term changes in the height of the population. Furthermore, the military was highly selective in who it recruited as it was anxious to maximise the height of its recruits. Indeed, the fact that Irishmen and Scotsmen were taller than Englishmen in the eighteenth century may provide a biometric explanation for their disproportionate representation in the British army.[54]

Military historians have long noted the eighteenth-century military's obsession with height.[55] There were good practical reasons for this. Regiments required men of broadly equivalent height in order to deploy volley fire on the battlefield. Tall men were better able to push a bayonet, throw a grenade, 'jump a ditch, climb a breastwork and engage in other exertions' required of eighteenth-century warfare.[56] Furthermore, the complex physical manoeuvres required to load a musket and to march in geometric formations required a body that was elongated and supple as well as disciplined and strong. As well as recruiting tall men, the army improved the stature of the men it already had through exercise, a protein-heavy diet and tailored clothing that forced them to stand up straight: humble redcoats had the famous upright bearing that their social betters would have to engage an expensive dancing master to acquire.[57]

Tall soldiers were therefore prestigious and commanders jealously eyed the height of rival regiments. Taller recruits would serve in grenadier companies, who would flank the regiment at parade in their elaborate, towering hats. In part, tall soldiers were for show, since they showed off the tailored uniform to better effect (in a similar way to tall male servants, who were similarly sought-after as impressive footmen). As a manual from the 1770s noted:

> A Soldier's Coat should be always tight over the breast (without restraint) for the sake of shewing his figure to more advantage ... nothing more effectually exposes an ungraceful figure, than not having the hip buttons considerably lower than the upper part of the

[53] Circular from the Adjutant General's Office, 10 Dec. 1792: The National Archives, Kew, London, WO3/11 fo. 15.

[54] Floud, Wacher and Gregory, *Height, Health and History*, 201.

[55] C. E. Warnery, quoted in Christopher Duffy, *The Military Experience in the Age of Reason* (1987), 94–6.

[56] Quoted in *ibid.*, 94.

[57] Matthew McCormack, 'Dance and Drill: Polite Accomplishments and Military Masculinities in Georgian Britain', *Cultural and Social History*, 8 (2011), 315–30.

hip-bone: a long-waisted coat is in general allowed an addition to the genteelest shape, therefore should always be the military mode.[58]

Military dress did change in line with civilian fashions, however. The end of the eighteenth century witnessed a shift from long to short coats, which in turn changed the proportion of the male body from short- to long-legged.[59] This more classical style served to emphasise the shapeliness of the leg, the prominence of the genitals and the overall height of the wearer. By the Napoleonic Wars, the British redcoat was sporting the short coatee, which sat above the waist. This was both more comely and more practical than long skirts – something the British army learned to their cost in the bushfighting of the American War. The Napoleonic redcoat also wore a tall cylindrical shako rather than the flat tricorne hat, further emphasising his height.

This preoccupation with tallness was taken to a ludicrous extreme by Frederick William of Prussia who, according to the British ambassador to Berlin, had an 'unaccountable passion for great wellmade men'. He collected tall men from all over Europe for his Potsdam Lifeguards, which boasted grenadiers of seven feet tall. Neighbouring states could curry favour with Frederick William by sending him presents of tall men: in 1721, the British government sent him fifteen huge Irishmen which, the ambassador noted, was well received, 'tho' they are not of a size with some of the monsters there'.[60] Reputedly, Frederick William dressed his soldiers in coats, hats and breeches that were deliberately too small, in order to emphasise the visual impression of their height. It was not as if these were particularly effective soldiers, since they were known for being slow and feeble, so he never risked them in battle: indeed, this was one of the most peaceable periods in Prussia's history. In Britain, his obsession with tall soldiers came in for critical comment, since it appeared to epitomise the worst excesses of German absolutism and militarism (and was therefore implicitly critical of Britain's own military-obsessed Hanoverian monarchs). As a correspondent to the *London Magazine* put it:

> His passion for tall men was extravagant, beyond belief; to recruit his great useless regiment of giants, he spared no expence, although covetous to excess, in his own disposition; nor in order to inveigle, or even kidnap a tall man, did his officers stick at fraud, perfidy or the grossest violations of the laws of society and of nations . . . But he exerted the natural roughness, and unfeelingness of his disposition, in breaking his troops to an obedience, and severity of discipline, unheard of before in Europe; which transformed men in to mere machines.[61]

---

[58] Bennett Cuthbertson, *A System for the Compete Interior Management and Oeconomy of a Battalion of Infantry* (1779), 52.

[59] Anne Hollander, *Seeing through Clothes* (Berkeley, 1993), 227.

[60] Quoted in F. L. Carsten, 'British Diplomacy and the Giant Grenadiers of Frederick William I', *History Today* (Nov. 1951), 55–60 at 57.

[61] *London Magazine, Or Gentleman's Monthly Intelligencer*, 28 (1759), 723.

This epitomised the popular image of the German soldier – and, indeed, the German in general given their close association with professional soldiering. Caricatures of German soldiers were invariably of tall, marionette-like automatons, broken to obedience by absolutism, poverty and harsh discipline.[62]

There is a further sense in which tallness could be associated with foreignness and unmanliness in Georgian Britain. Castrati from Italy were popular on London's operatic stage in the mid-century. Boys with promising voices were castrated so as to retain their soprano vocal range, and stars such as Farinelli and Tenducci had famously brilliant voices. Castration also had other physical effects: it disrupted the endochrine system which affected physical development and often resulted in them growing very tall.[63] Lack of testosterone also prevented bone joints hardening, so their ribcage continued to grow and their lungs were abnormally large: this helped them to perform their vocal acrobatics, but contributed to their distinctive physical appearance, which also included long limbs and small heads.[64] This is truly an example of where the body is plastic rather than being a biological constant. Farinelli was famously tall and clumsy with it: for all his vocal talents, he was a poor actor. As one commentator noted: 'What Extasy to the Ear! But, Heavens! What Clumsiness! What Stupidity! What Offence to the Eye!'[65] The physical shape of the castrato was seized upon by caricaturists, who tapped into the 'patriot' charge that Italian opera was a popish foreign import, patronised by an unpatriotic and degenerate ruling class.[66]

The question of whether castrati were unmasculine is more complex. They usually played heroic male roles on the stage, and they exuded a unique erotic appeal (which is dwelt upon in the 1994 feature film *Farinelli*). In the early modern period, the castrato arguably occupied a middle ground between men and women, within the sliding scale of 'one sex' gender difference.[67] As the century wore on, however, the castrato was an anomaly in a world that defined male citizenship in terms of domestic patriarchy and virile heterosexuality. The proceedings to annul Tenducci's marriage in the London courts in 1775 hinged on the question

---

[62]Michael Duffy, *The Englishman and the Foreigner* (Cambridge, 1986), 15.

[63]Berta Joncus, 'One God, so many Farinellis: Mythologizing the Star Castrato', *British Journal for Eighteenth-Century Studies*, 28 (2005), 437–96 at 440.

[64]Nicholas Clapton, 'Carol Broschi Farinelli: Aspects of his Technique and Performance', *British Journal for Eighteenth-Century Studies*, 28 (2005), 323–38 at 325.

[65]Roger Pickering, *Reflections upon Theatrical Expression in Tragedy* (1754), 63.

[66][Attr. William Hogarth,] 'Berenstadt, Cuzzoni and Senesino' (1723): British Museum Satires 1768.

[67]Roger Freitas, 'The Eroticism of Emasculation: Confronting the Baroque Body of the Castrato', *Journal of Musicology*, 20 (2003), 196–249.

of whether a castrato could be a husband and, by extension, a man.[68] The tallness of the castrato became an increasingly jarring visual sign of their foreignness and gender deviance.

Male height in the eighteenth century was therefore a complex business. On the one hand, it had its familiar associations with dominance and power, although this was much more bound up with class difference than it is today.[69] On the other hand, excessive height could also take on much more negative character associations, within a political discourse that was suspicious of foreignness, despotism, militarism, luxury and popery. Nor were these merely representations: there were hundreds of castrati in Europe and thousands of German troops based in Britain, not to mention the tens of thousands of tall men who lived in a culture that was frequently hostile to them.

IV

With all this in mind, let us return to the earl of Sandwich. By taking his height seriously, it is possible to understand why he was such a controversial character at the time, and also why his reputation in the historiography has been so chequered. As his biographer N. A. M. Rodger has noted, Sandwich got a very rough deal from the Whig historians. For the Victorian constitutional historians, Sandwich did everything wrong. He was a government man and a career politician, at a time when public men were supposed to be politically and financially independent. He ran the Admiralty during one of Britain's most humiliating military defeats, a tenure that one Victorian biographer described as 'disastrous':

> He now held this office for eleven years, during which time his conduct was as great a scandal to the public as it had all along been to private morality. Throughout his long administration he rendered the business of the admiralty subservient to the interests of his party, and employed the vast patronage of the office as an engine for bribery and political jobbery.[70]

Moreover, he persecuted John Wilkes, the darling of the Whig historians. Sandwich led Wilkes's prosecution for obscene libel for the publication of his pornographic *Essay on Woman*. This led to charges of treachery and hypocrisy, as Wilkes and Sandwich were acquaintances and members of the libertine club the Monks of Medmenham, and Sandwich's domestic

---

[68] Helen Berry, *The Castrato and his Wife* (Oxford, 2011).

[69] It is worth noting that the height of manual workers today is lower than that of non-manual workers: M. Walker, A. Shaper and G. Wannamethee, 'Height and Social Class in Middle-Aged British Men', *Journal of Epidemiol Public Health*, 43 (1988), 299–303.

[70] J. K. Laughton, 'Montagu, John, Fourth Earl of Sandwich (1718–1792)', in *Dictionary of National Biography*, ed. Sidney Lee (1894): www.oxforddnb.com/view/olddnb/19026, accessed 21 July 2015.

arrangements were hardly conventional.[71] Sandwich was therefore a gift
to the Victorian Whig historians, who required politicians to be virtuous in
both public and private, and who wished to distract from the unpromising
moralities of their heroes Wilkes and Charles James Fox.[72]

This is not the place to reevaluate Sandwich's political record, as
Rodger and others have already done so: in particular, he is now regarded
as a very capable naval administrator. What is striking, however, is
how systematically Sandwich's height has been emphasised by people
trying to describe his character, both at the time and since. Victorian
biographers alluded to his 'uncouth', 'shambling' and 'not prepossessing'
appearance.[73] His contemporary Horace Walpole was characteristically
unkind, and linked his awkwardness (a common metonym for height) to
his public conduct:

> Lord Sandwich was rapacious, but extravagant when it was to promote his own designs.
> His industry to carry any point he had in view was so remarkable, that for a long time
> the world mistook it for abilities; but as his manner was most awkward and unpolished,
> so his talents were but slight, when it was necessary to exert them in any higher light
> than in art and intrigue.[74]

Even affectionate portrayals, such as that by his friend John Cradock,
dwell on his height and clumsiness:

> Lord Sandwich, when dressed, had a dignified appearance, but to see him in the street,
> he had an awkward, careless gait. Two gentlemen observing him when at Leicester, one
> of them remarked, 'I think it is Lord Sandwich coming;' the other replied that he thought
> he was mistaken. 'Nay,' says the gentleman, 'I am sure it is Lord Sandwich; for, if you
> observe, he is walking down both sides of the street at once.'

Sandwich himself was typically good humoured about this. He often
related the anecdote about his dancing master in Paris, who requested
that he should never tell anyone who taught him to dance.[75]

Sandwich may have been ungainly but he was not shy about his
height. He was known for being physically exuberant: 'Stretching out
his strong legs and arms, whilst playing at skittles, Lord Sandwich
would exult amazingly, if by chance he was able to knock down all
nine.'[76] He was a keen sportsman and was particularly enthusiastic
about cricket. Caricatures of Sandwich often identify him with a cricket
bat. One of his political enemies was Sir George Townshend, who was

[71] 'Public opinion rightly condemned the men who for mere party ends thus sacrificed
the ties of friendship.' Laughton, 'Montagu'.

[72] N. A. M. Rodger, *The Insatiable Earl: A Life of John Montagu, 4th Earl of Sandwich* (1993),
xvi; see also John Brewer, *Sentimental Murder: Love and Madness in the Eighteenth Century* (2004),
101.

[73] Laughton, 'Montagu'.

[74] Horace Walpole, *Memoirs and Portraits*, ed. Mathew Hodgart (1963), 27.

[75] J. Cradock, *Literary and Miscellaneous Memoirs* (4 vols., 1828), IV, 165–6.

[76] *Ibid.*, IV, 163.

a talented caricaturist as well as a leading opposition politician. He sketched Sandwich as skinny and hunched, with a cricket bat over his shoulder (Figure 4). Tellingly, Sandwich is dressed in the uniform and pointed hat of a Hanoverian grenadier: his tallness is here equated with German militarism. There was a political point to this, since Townshend was the champion of the New Militia, which sought to create a citizen army as an alternative to the standing army and the unpopular policy of deploying Hanoverian soldiers within England. Townshend's sketch was later incorporated into the satirical print, 'The Recruiting Sergeant: Or Britannia's Happy Prospect' (1757), which was one of the most famous anti-government caricatures of the day.[77] Sandwich is a browbeaten 'recruit' to the government, which is parading past a statue of a belligerent duke of Cumberland. Oddly, Sandwich here is not very tall in relation to the other figures: the print was assembled by the printseller from Townshend's sketches, and scale is rarely realistic in the early, emblematic tradition of caricature. But his physical build, small head, posture and military dress still signal his tallness.

Most caricatures of Sandwich were hostile, as they tended to be towards government figures. Predictably, portraits that Sandwich commissioned of himself were more sympathetic, but even these made no attempt to conceal his height. Portraits of Sandwich in his robes of state are imperious and imposing, but Sandwich's physical build is rendered more realistically in Zoffany's informal portrait. Here, we see his elongated frame and sloping shoulders, but he still appears 'the public man, suave and self-assured'.[78] He is portrayed here at his desk: he was very diligent and this is apparently how he wanted to be remembered. The story of the invention of the sandwich is relevant here. The story used to go that during a marathon gaming session he did not wish to leave the table, so requested a slice of beef between two pieces of toast.[79] An alternative explanation is that he snacked at his desk at the Admiralty, where he worked very long hours.[80] This encapsulates how his masculinity has played out in the historiography: Whig history portrays him as a debauchee, whereas Tory history portrays him as the original workaholic. His very industry, however, made him a problematic figure in Georgian public life. Sandwich inherited some parlous family finances, so the life of an independent statesman was not an option for him: he had to get by on his talents and seek paid administrative posts in government. Critics of Sandwich's status as a public man often highlighted his physical build: contemporaries and

---

[77] Eileen Harris, *The Townshend Album* (1974), figs. 23 and 24a.

[78] Rodger, *Insatiable Earl*, caption to fig. 6.

[79] P. J. Grosley, *A Tour to London*, trans. T. Nugent (2 vols., 1772), I, 149.

[80] Rodger, *Insatiable Earl*, 79.

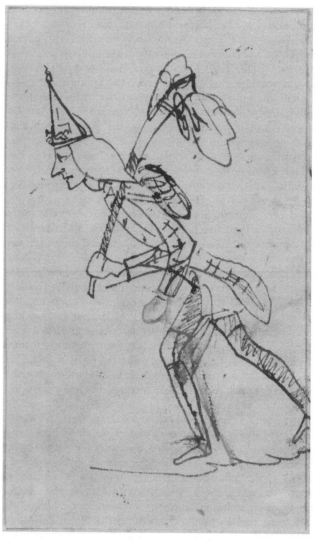

Figure 4 George Townshend, sketch of John Montagu, 4th earl of Sandwich (1750s). National Portrait Gallery 4855(23). © National Portrait Gallery, London.

biographers alike allude to his 'lean and hungry look' in order to insinuate his ambition and dependence, harking back to the humoral associations of the 'choleric' man.[81]

Sandwich's public reputation was further compromised by his reputation as a libertine.[82] John Wilkes, who was hardly one to talk, attacked his private life when he took his revenge in the *North Briton* in 1763:

> His conduct, with respect to women, was not only loose and barefaced, but perfidious, mean, and tricking. He was restrained by no considerations of private character, nor checked by any regard to public decorum. Frauds of the lowest nature, enforced by perjuries and falshoods, were his only arts. With respect to men, he had early lost every sentiment of honour, and was grown exceedingly necessitous from the variety of his vices, as well as rapacious from the lust of gratifying them. Nature denied him wit, but gave him a species of buffoonery of the lowest kind, which was ridiculous in a man of fashion.[83]

Here, we have the 'patriot' critique of Sandwich in a nutshell: avaricious, dependent, oppressive and clownish – all features that symbolically relate to his height. The reality of Sandwich's personal life was rather different. He had been happily married, but his wife suffered from mental illness so they lived apart while she was nursed by her sister. Subsequently, he lived with the singer Martha Ray, in a public and quasi-marital arrangement. Famously, Ray was murdered by a jealous suitor in the crowded foyer of the Royal Opera House. This sensational event served to define Sandwich thereafter,[84] and reinforced his reputation for libertinism at a time when private vice was becoming more problematic in public men. In the 1760s, Wilkes could flaunt his sexual freedom as a libertarian statement, but even he had to reinvent himself as a 'reformed rake' in the more sober 1780s.[85]

Let us finally return to our opening question of how Sandwich was caricatured alongside women. In 'The Contrast – A Park Scene' of *c*. 1780, he towers over his unidentified female companion, who barely comes up to his belly. Sandwich is here the polite man at a time when politeness was becoming problematic. He is elegant but elongated, charming but somewhat sinister, aristocratic but a bit of an anachronism.[86] He is, though, portrayed more flatteringly here than in 'A Sandwich' of 1788. An older Sandwich appears hunched and haggard, his phallic walking cane drooping downwards. The original version (Figure 1) is the more realistic

---

[81] *Ibid.*, 320.
[82] Brewer, *Sentimental Murder*, 112.
[83] *The North Briton from No. I to No. XLVI Inclusive* (1769), 161.
[84] Brewer, *Sentimental Murder*.
[85] McCormack, *The Independent Man*, 110.
[86] Robert Dighton, 'The Contrast – A Park Scene' (1780): British Museum Satires 9665.

of the two, since in the redrawn image (Figure 2) the women's heads and torsos have been shrunk out of proportion, whereas he appears huge.

In the light of what we have discussed here, however, it is comprehensible why the artist should have chosen to do this. It is not just a question of underlining men's 'natural' dominance over women, to follow Geiske's argument: indeed, male height here serves to criticise character and undermine status.[87] Sandwich's height was shorthand for many of his supposed personality traits, in a culture where excessive male height was loaded with political, national and gendered meaning. When Sandwich started his political career in the 1740s, his tall frame may have been an asset in the polite world of Westminster, but by the time of the American War, it fell foul of an opposition political culture that was increasingly hostile to the manners and morals of the traditional ruling class. By then, the 'polite' frame of the tall man suggested a superficial public front: men were increasingly expected to be virtuous in both their public and their private lives, ushering in the Victorian morality that would be so unforgiving to men like Sandwich.

The Victorians expected men to possess moral manliness, rather than polished gentlemanliness, and had quite different ideals of the male body.[88] Whereas the Georgians prided elegance and proportion, Victorians valorised muscular power. Manly bodies were 'robust, stout, hard bodies',[89] emphasising the industrious arm rather than the shapely leg. The ideal military body changed in line with this, at a time when imperial militarism pervaded social values as never before. Whereas eighteenth-century warfare required elongated bodies that could move swiftly and elegantly on open ground, the nineteenth century saw the rise of light infantry tactics, where soldiers used individual initiative and took advantage of the terrain. Seven foot grenadiers were now a liability, whereas compact and tough bodies would be able to take cover and survive in the field. A military manual of 1901 warned recruiters that 'the effectiveness of a force depends on its vigor rather than its size'. 'It is a demonstrated fact that very tall men cannot for long support the fatigues of arduous military service', and worse still, they 'require proportionately more food than do those of smaller stature, besides presenting a larger surface to the bullet of the enemy'. The author

[87] Geiske, 'The Ideal Couple'.

[88] John Tosh, 'Gentlemanly Politeness and Manly Simplicity in Victorian England', *Transactions of the Royal Historical Society*, 12 (2002), 455–72.

[89] Joanne Begiato, 'Manly Bodies in Eighteenth- and Nineteenth-Century England', Royal Historical Society website, 4 Sept. 2015: http://royalhistsoc.org/joanne-bailey-manly-bodies-in-eighteenth-and-nineteenth-century-england/, accessed 31 Mar. 2016. See also Joanne Begiato, 'Between Poise and Power: Embodied Manliness in Eighteenth- and Nineteenth-century British Culture', *Transactions of the Royal Historical Society*, 26 (2016), 125–47.

therefore wondered whether the infantry should follow the cavalry in introducing maximum height requirements, turning the priorities of eighteenth-century recruiters on their head.[90]

The tall male body could therefore be problematic in the nineteenth century as well as in the eighteenth, but for subtly different reasons. We therefore have to study carefully the specific meanings and physical experiences of the body in its particular era. Some historians of masculinity have recently expressed the concern that the field has become too preoccupied with representation, and that it has lost its ability to engage with real 'events and experiences'.[91] Histories of embodiment therefore promise to re-ground the history of masculinity in the material, the physical and the personal. This article has shown how the experience of living in a tall body is qualitatively distinct from that of a shorter one, and that Georgians actively moulded the body through exercise, posture and material appurtenances. On the other hand, the case of male height also suggests that the cultural meanings attributed to bodies could change almost irrespective of the nature of bodies themselves. Frankly, few things could be more 'corporeal' than tallness, so this provides wider lessons for the field. Gender historians need to attend both to the representational and the corporeal, not least because Georgians were prone to tell tall stories about height.

---

[90] Edward L. Munson, *The Theory and Practice of Military Hygiene* (1901), 1, 12–13.
[91] Tosh, 'History of Masculinity', 20.

Transactions of the RHS 26 (2016), pp. 103–123 © Royal Historical Society 2016
doi:10.1017/S0080440116000074

SLAVERY AND THE BIRTH OF WORKING-CLASS RACISM IN ENGLAND, 1814–1833

The Alexander Prize Essay

By Ryan Hanley

ABSTRACT. This paper examines racist discourse in radical print culture from the end of the Napoleonic Wars to the passing of the Abolition of Slavery Act in Britain. Acknowledging the heterogeneity of working-class ideology during the period, it demonstrates that some radical writers actively sought to dehumanise enslaved and free black people as a means of promoting the interests of the white working class in England. It argues that by promoting a particular understanding of English racial superiority, radical intellectuals such as John Cartwright, William Cobbett, and Richard Carlile were able to criticise the diversion of humanitarian resources and attention away from exploited industrial workers and towards enslaved black people in the British West Indies or unconverted free Africans. Moreover, by presenting a supposedly inferior racial antitype, they sought to minimise the social boundaries that were used to disenfranchise English working men and reinforce their own, seemingly precarious, claims to parliamentary reform and meaningful political representation.

In Britain, the early nineteenth century saw the emergence of both a distinctive working-class political identity and new ideas about human difference. The two were not completely discrete phenomena. During this period, the abolition of slavery and the suppression of the transatlantic slave trade entered popular discourse as manifestations of Britain's inherent national moral supremacy.[1] Nevertheless, the textures and referents of this patriotism – specifically who and what it was that made Britain so great – were contested. While the industrial working classes in Britain were intellectually as heterogeneous as any social group, a particular strand of radical discourse became dedicated to spreading ideas of a different type of natural English superiority among the nation's disenfranchised workers. This discourse drew ideas about race and nation together with attacks on well-to-do parliamentary abolitionists, and in some cases led to a thoroughgoing pro-slavery position by the early 1830s. For these radicals, enslaved black people in the West Indies neither deserved the attention of British philanthropists, nor were they

---

[1] See Linda Colley, *Britons: Forging the Nation 1707–1837* (New Haven, 1992), 327–71; Seymour Drescher, *Abolition: A History of Slavery and Antislavery* (Cambridge, 2009), 267–93; Robin Blackburn, *The Overthrow of Colonial Slavery, 1776–1848* (1988), 419–72.

intellectually or morally equipped to appreciate it properly. In their eyes, the money and attention being poured into the abolitionist movement would have been better spent on the equally exploited, but inherently more deserving, white British workers.

Racial prejudice, in the form of the assumed superiority of white Europeans over black Africans, was highly orthodox in early nineteenth-century Britain. For the purposes of this article, therefore, a particular distinction should be drawn between racist discourse – that which actively encouraged or manifested discrimination against, and attempted to subordinate to whites, black people both free and enslaved – and that which, in common with almost all European discourse on race during the period, merely assumed white superiority.[2] Of course, these two types of racial discourse were often interdependent, and both fed off other political preoccupations and discourses. In the context of early nineteenth-century popular politics in Britain, racist discourse emerged primarily in relation to questions of patriotism and nationalism on the one hand, and the ongoing debates over West Indian slavery on the other. During the so-called 'Peterloo years' of the mid- to late 1810s, English radicals criticised abolitionists for ignoring the political rights of Englishmen and focusing attention instead on a distant and less deserving ethnic Other.[3] Over the course of the 1820s, as demands for an extended franchise became more urgent, the black slave was increasingly represented to emergent working-class readerships as being essentially different from, and inferior to, them. These comparisons ultimately comprised a form of racism that was eventually to inform plebeian opposition to abolition in the 1830s and 1840s.

Between 1814 and 1833, theoretical debates over human difference took on a unique aspect in Britain. The climatic theories characteristic of eighteenth-century natural philosophy, which held that differences in climate, diet, culture and degree of 'civilization' were the primary actuators of physical variations like skin colour and hair texture, proved more enduring in Britain than elsewhere on the continent.[4] In general, this 'monogenetic' approach – so called because it insisted that all

---

[2] Comparative historians of racism emphasise the necessity of active discrimination, as against purely theoretical hierarchizing, in defining racist discourse and behaviour. See Francisco Bethencourt, *Racisms: From the Crusades to the Twentieth Century* (Princeton, 2013), 1; George M. Fredrickson, *Racism: A Short History* (Princeton, 2015), 5–6.

[3] For patriotism and English exceptionalism in the radical movements, see Colley, *Britons*, 341–57.

[4] For human difference in eighteenth-century British culture, see, for example, Dror Wahrman, *The Making of the Modern Self: Identity and Culture in Eighteenth-Century England* (New Haven, 2013), 83–156; Anthony Barker, *The African Link: British Attitudes to the Negro in the 17th and 18th Centuries* (1978), 157–93; Bethencourt, *Racisms*, 247–70; Ivan Hannaford, *Race: The History of an Idea in the West* (Baltimore, 1996), 205–15; Felicity Nussbaum, *The Limits of the Human: Fictions of Anomaly, Race, and Gender in the Long Eighteenth Century* (Cambridge, 2003),

human beings shared a single genesis in the Garden of Eden – accommodated preexisting assumptions about the cultural, intellectual and moral superiority of white over non-white peoples. Indeed, by the turn of the nineteenth century, efforts were underway to consolidate these notional hierarchies within the ancient framework of the 'Great Chain of Being'.[5] This theory held that all living creatures were ranked in terms of complexity, forming a chain of imperceptibly small gradations descending from God, through angels, men, 'brute creation' and down to vegetable life. In this model, given a particular racial dimension in Britain by Charles White in his 1799 *Account in the Regular Gradation in Man*, Africans did share a lineage with Europeans that could be traced back to Adam in the Garden of Eden, but had been so degraded by their lack of civilisation that they occupied a lower link in the Great Chain, between white humans and apes. White was particularly concerned to emphasise the superiority of the European specifically over the African, who for him approached 'nearer to the brute creation than any other of the human species'.[6] Individual variations of the specific positions occupied by the various races of mankind abounded, but invariably, white Europeans were placed at the top, nearest the angels.

Perhaps because of an ingrained Protestant conservatism, British theorists were hesitant to embrace new polygenetic explanations for human difference when they emerged in continental Europe during the first three decades of the nineteenth century.[7] Polygenesis, in suggesting that races actually constituted distinct and separately developed types of human being, posed a potentially dangerous challenge to the literal interpretation of the book of Genesis.[8] For similar reasons, during the first two decades of the nineteenth century in particular, British natural historians reacted against 'Great Chain' proponents like White and took great care to emphasise an essential divide between man and animal – though the perceived hierarchies between the various races of mankind remained more or less intact within this model.[9] The default position for British racial theorists during this period held that Africans

135–256; Roxann Wheeler, *The Complexion of Race: Categories of Difference in Eighteenth-Century British Culture* (Philadelphia, 2000), 1–49; George Boulukos, *The Grateful Slave: The Emergence of Race in Eighteenth-Century British and American Culture* (Cambridge, 2008).

[5] Nancy Stepan, *The Idea of Race in Science: Great Britain, 1800–1960* (1982), 1–19.

[6] Charles White, *An Account in the Regular Gradation in Man* (1799), 41–138, quotation at 42.

[7] Early polygenesis is often associated with Georges Cuvier, a translation of whose *Lectures in Comparative Anatomy* appeared in Britain in 1802, though he was in fact a monogenist. His mentee and, later, bitter rival Louis-Antoine Desmoulins was, however, a leading polygenist. See George Cuvier, *Lectures in Comparative Anatomy*, trans. W. Ross (1802); Louis-Antoine Desmoulins, *Histoire naturelle des races humaines du nord-est de l'Europe* (Paris, 1826).

[8] For anxieties over the scriptural ramifications of polygenism, see Colin Kidd, *The Forging of Races: Race and Scripture in the Protestant Atlantic World, 1600–2000* (Cambridge, 2006), 121–67.

[9] George W. Stocking, *Victorian Anthropology* (New York, 1987), 43–4.

were undoubtedly morally and intellectually inferior, and some thought their degeneration was irrevocable. But what separated white from non-white peoples was largely thought to be due to long-term circumstances rather than as a consequence of separately developed biological makeup. Africans were undoubtedly human beings, if unequal to Europeans. To enslave them was therefore morally indefensible and beneath the ethical dignity of the European race.[10]

However, as the first half of the nineteenth century wound on, an orthodox ethnic chauvinism crystallised in popular culture which was to influence the next generation of racial theorists. While full-blown polygenism made only slow progress in Britain during the 1820s, preconceived intellectual characteristics that had traditionally been attributed to different ethnic groups started, gradually, to be seen as organic, hereditable and unchangeable. This was related to an increasing nationalistic tendency in much British popular culture, including in some of the radical press. As Nancy Stepan has demonstrated, '[i]n most respects science followed rather than led public opinion on race. The cosmopolitanism of the eighteenth century . . . was being replaced in the early nineteenth century by a more parochial and nationalistic outlook which increased the temptation to think in exclusive terms and to despise non-white peoples.'[11]

Victory in the Napoleonic Wars had secured Britain's global imperial ascendancy, but like the Union of 1800–1 this had served to diversify rather than homogenise what 'British' actually meant at the personal level. This prevented the notion of an essentialist or biological 'national character' from spreading too quickly. Among conservatives, as Peter Mandler has suggested, a sense of Britain's preeminence in political and moral development emerged as a unifying patriotic identifier instead.[12] This emphasis on 'civilisation' was attractive to conservative interests because it enabled the expansion of British cultural hegemony without necessarily requiring greater access to political participation, either through the extension of the franchise at home or by granting greater autonomy to colonial assemblies. Meanwhile, after 1823, the abolitionist movement

---

[10] For example, the very first sentence of White's *Gradation in Man* was a reassurance that the author 'hopes that nothing advanced will be construed so as to give the smallest countenance to the pernicious practice of enslaving mankind, which he wishes to see abolished throughout the world'. Even William Lawrence, among the most strident advocates of African racial inferiority, advanced his theories 'without the fear that you will find in them either apology or excuse for Negro slavery'. White, *Gradation in Man*, iii; William Lawrence, *Lectures on Physiology, Zoology, and the Natural History of Man* (1819), 364.

[11] Stepan, *Race in Science*, 4–5.

[12] Peter Mandler, *The English National Character: The History of an Idea from Edmund Burke to Tony Blair* (2006), 29–38; see also Krishnan Kumar, *The Making of English National Identity* (Cambridge, 2003), 187–96; Gerald Newman, *The Rise of English Nationalism: A Cultural History, 1740–1830* (New York, 1997), 123–56.

began making steady progress in the amelioration of conditions for the enslaved, including measures for the abolition of Sunday working and preventing excessive corporal punishment.[13] What offended some metropolitan radicals about these developments was that they effectively equated British plebeian political rights and (so the reasoning went) working conditions to those of the slaves in the West Indies. The question facing radicals in the 1820s then, was this: why did they deserve political advocacy more than slaves? Over the course of the decade, some radicals, anticipating mid-century nationalist rhetoric, chose to adapt conservative civilisational language and an exclusive definition of British patriotism to promote a new type of political nation: one drawn along the lines of ancestral heritage and racial unity.[14]

To what extent did these important perspectival shifts affect specifically working-class attitudes towards slavery and race? From the outset, it should be emphasised that no consistent, universal position on abolition emerged across the entire British industrial workforce during the early nineteenth century. Indeed, scholars have tried in vain to settle the question of what radicals thought should be done about slavery. James Walvin, Iain McCalman and Michael Turner, for example, have all suggested that the early affinity shared by abolitionism and reform in the 1780s and 1790s inspired 'a new generation of radical leaders with ultra- and antislavery sympathies' well into the new century.[15] In contrast, Patricia Hollis and Marcus Wood have highlighted instances of consistent hostility towards the enslaved populations of the Caribbean in English radical discourse, from the 1780s to the Chartist period.[16] More

---

[13] For a full discussion of amelioration developments, see Caroline Quarrier Spence, 'Ameliorating Empire: Slavery and Protection in the British Colonies, 1783–1865' (Ph.D. thesis, Harvard University, 2014), 193–243. For the broader abolition context, see Blackburn, *Overthrow*, 419–72.

[14] For working-class nationalism in this period, see Linda Colley, 'Whose Nation? Class and National Consciousness in Britain, 1750–1830', *Past and Present*, 113 (1986), 97–117. For xenophobia in nineteenth-century British popular culture, see *Fear, Loathing and Victorian Xenophobia*, ed. Marlene Tromp, Maria Bachman and Heidi Kaufman (Columbus, OH, 2013), 1–27.

[15] Quotation from Iain McCalman, *Radical Underworld: Prophets, Revolutionaries and Pornographers in London, 1795–1840* (Cambridge, 1988), 196–7; Michael J. Turner, '"Setting the Captive Free": Thomas Perronet Thompson, British Radicalism and the West Indies, 1820s–1860s', *Slavery and Abolition*, 26 (2005), 115–32; James Walvin, 'The Impact of Slavery on British Radical Politics: 1787–1838', *Annals of the New York Academy of Sciences*, 292 (1977), 343–55.

[16] Patricia Hollis, 'Anti-Slavery and British Working-Class Radicalism in the Years of Reform', in *Anti-Slavery, Religion, and Reform: Essays in Memory of Roger Anstey*, ed. Christine Bolt and Seymour Drescher (Folkestone, 1980), 294–315; Marcus Wood, 'William Cobbett, John Thelwall, Radicalism, Racism and Slavery: A Study in Burkean Parodics', *Romanticism on the Net*, 15 (1999), 1–26. Available from: www.erudit.org/revue/ron/1999/v/n15/005873ar.html, accessed 18 Jan. 2016.

recently, social historians of abolitionism have come down somewhere in the middle, acknowledging the fractured, fractious and discontinuous progress of both the anti-slavery and domestic reform movements.[17] In a broad sense, support for abolitionism among reformers, and indeed social connections between the two movements, seems to have been more easily identifiable before the turn of the century than after – though, as McCalman and others have demonstrated, there were a few exceptions.[18] By the 1840s, certainly, the default radical position appears to have shifted from one where abolitionists were natural allies in the struggle for a more egalitarian domestic politics, to one where they represented the very 'old corruption' that radicalism existed to challenge.

The question of race in the early nineteenth-century English reform movement has received far less scholarly attention, but such that exists is similarly polarised. Satnam Virdee, for example, situates 'the emergence of a growing antagonism between the English and minority worker' very carefully in the 1830s and 1840s, and argues that during the preceding 'heroic age of the proletariat', radicals remained 'relatively free of contamination by the ideology of white supremacy'.[19] Wood, on the other hand, maintains that 'the slave population were cut off from a claim to the political rights of radicalism, and the mechanism by which this severance was achieved is a crude racism, by which Blacks are not seen as part of the class struggle, because they are not seen as human'.[20] A particular difficulty in this debate is presented by the piecemeal and sometimes idealising nature of studies into the popular reform movements. The charismatic ultra-radical and former slave Robert Wedderburn, for example, was a central figure in mobilising plebeian abolitionist and anti-racist sentiment during the late 1810s and early 1820s, but he has only assumed his fair share of visibility in scholarly literature relatively recently.[21] On the other hand, classic studies of working-class history, including the foundational work of E. P. Thompson, have always been criticised for their lack of attention to the 'flag-saluting, foreigner-hating, peer-respecting side of the plebeian mind'.[22] More recent work by Peter

---

[17] See, for example, Drescher, *Abolition*, 245–67.

[18] Robert Wedderburn is often used as an example of radical sympathy with anti-slavery activism. See Peter Linebaugh and Marcus Rediker, *The Many-Headed Hydra: The Hidden History of the Revolutionary Atlantic* (2000), 287–327; Iain McCalman, 'Anti-slavery and Ultra-radicalism in Early Nineteenth-Century England: The Case of Robert Wedderburn', *Slavery and Abolition*, 7 (1986), 99–117.

[19] Satnam Virdee, *Racism, Class and the Racialized Outsider* (Basingstoke, 2014), 25–6.

[20] Wood, 'Burkean Parodics', 12.

[21] Wedderburn is virtually absent from the history of English radicalism prior to McCalman's pioneering work in the late 1980s.

[22] The quotation is from Geoffrey Best, 'Review: *The Making of the English Working Class*', *Historical Journal*, 8 (1965), 278, cited in E. P. Thompson, *The Making of the English Working Class* (1968).

Linebaugh and Marcus Rediker has similarly been accused of taking too ideological an approach in its insistence on the importance of an antiracist 'transatlantic proletariat'.[23] Radical biography, in particular, can be just as susceptible to hagiography as 'establishment' histories. This perhaps helps to explain why, for example, William Cobbett's virulent and entrenched anti-black racism is only occasionally acknowledged and rarely subjected to detailed scrutiny.[24] Ultimately, attempts to fix upon a single overarching narrative of the relationship between radicalism and race before 1830 remain, for good reason, contested and problematic.

What follows, then, should not be taken as an attempt to represent the opinions of the whole of the exploited industrial workforce of early nineteenth-century Britain. The 'working-class racism' at stake in this article is not necessarily reflective of a monolithic plebeian or artisan world-view, but rather of some of the attempts to formulate one. This paper explores how certain metropolitan radical elites adopted, adapted and promoted new forms of racially hierarchical ideology to a readership whose collective identity and common objectives were still assuming their mature form. Through this type of investigation, it becomes possible to chart the emergence and consolidation of a specifically *working-class* racism in radical print culture – even if those producing it may not have been themselves socially or educationally representative of their own readership. In other words, this study is not of the racism *of* the emergent English working class, but rather of the racist discourse produced *for* the emergent English working class. This discourse opposed the interests of black people, both free and enslaved, to those of the white English industrial labourer. Through the deployment of specifically racial signifiers of national belonging, it attempted to stabilise an emerging working-class socioeconomic identity and legitimise its claims to meaningful political representation. In order to justify the working-class stake in the national interest, radicals needed to identify a negative against which their proposed, expanded political nation could be defined. For many, the despotism of the deposed Bonaparte regime provided an answer.[25] For some radicals, racial hierarchy provided another.

---

[23] For criticism of Rediker and Linebaugh, and their response, see David Brion Davis, Marcus Rediker and Peter Linebaugh, '"The Many-Headed Hydra": An Exchange', *New York Review of Books*, 20 Sept. 2001.

[24] As well as Wood, 'Burkean Parodics', see Arthur Scherr, '"Sambos" and "Black Cut-Throats": Peter Porcupine on Slavery and Race in the 1790s', *American Periodicals*, 13 (2003), 3–30. For Cobbett's equally entrenched anti-Semitism, see Karl W. Schweizer and John W. Osborne, *Cobbett in his Times* (Leicester, 1990), 70–7.

[25] See, for example, Colley, *Britons*, 306–25.

1814–1819

The artisan, liberal radicalism of the early 1790s resurged stronger and with a new plebeian dimension in the years after the end of the Napoleonic Wars. In E. P. Thompson's words, 'it is as if the English nation entered a crucible in the 1790s and emerged after the Wars in a new form... Almost every radical phenomenon of the 1790s can be found reproduced tenfold after 1815.'[26] Post-war economic depression, outsized national debt, widespread underemployment and wage cuts occasioned by the sudden mass demobilisation of military personnel generated widespread unrest among urban working-class populations. This environment provided an opportunity for members of the 'old guard' of 1790s radicalism to reach a new popular audience. Thomas Spence, for example, had stayed true to the cause throughout the Wars, and before his death in September 1814 he had drawn a new generation of radical leaders, including black men like Robert Wedderburn and William Davidson, into his organisation.[27] Indeed, the black presence in the 'Spencean Philanthropists' during the late 1810s and early 1820s has, for some scholars, suggested that the egalitarian principles of the reform movement as a whole extended to anti-racism.[28] This is certainly true of Wedderburn and Davidson themselves, whose speeches and writings from this period powerfully combine contemporaneous British radical discourse with praise for the revolution in St Domingue and personal testimony of the horrors of West Indian slavery.[29] For these black radical-intellectual pioneers, the old rhetorical device of equating the lack of political representation with slavery took on an unanswerably powerful personal dimension. Wedderburn's attacks on slavery, in particular, were bound up with his identification of the racist underpinnings of the institution. Indeed, for these radicals, abolition and domestic political reform were inextricably linked ends to be achieved by the same means.

Anti-slavery sentiment was indeed widespread throughout most of the British radical movement during this period, just as it was among the plebeian and artisan demographics from whom it drew the core of its support. This, too, was related to the end of the war with France. A treaty signed at the Congress of Vienna in September 1814 had included a clause which would allow the French to continue trading in slaves freely

[26] Thompson, *Making of the English Working Class*, 209.

[27] McCalman, *Radical Underworld*, 7–180; Malcolm Chase, *'The People's Farm': English Radical Agrarianism 1775–1840* (Oxford, 1988), 45–120.

[28] McCalman, 'Anti-slavery and Ultra-radicalism', 99–117.

[29] See, for example, Robert Wedderburn, *The Horrors of Slavery and Other Writings*, ed. Iain McCalman (Princeton, 1992); Anon., *An Authentic History of the Cato-Street Conspiracy with the Trials at Large of the Conspirators* ([c. 1820]), 318–25.

for another five years without interference from the Royal Navy.[30] Even though the operation was in its relative infancy, the Navy's suppression of the transatlantic slave trade had by this time already infiltrated the popular consciousness as a much-lauded example of Britons' shared love of liberty.[31] Sensing the national mood, Samuel Romilly, the former solicitor general and a parliamentary advocate for moderate reform, made a speech attacking Lord Castlereagh, the British negotiator at Vienna, for allowing the French to continue in the trade.[32] Meanwhile, the popular press was vociferous in condemning the provision, especially as it was widely perceived at the time to hand an economic advantage to the old enemy across the Channel. While all couched their opposition to the provision in moral terms, many also explicitly cited the 'effects which the introduction of large numbers of slaves into the French colonies, while they are excluded from our own, may have on the prosperity of the latter'.[33] Popular support for the abolition of the slave trade thus came to be matched, in some measure, with British patriotism, Francophobia and a hard-headed concern for the protection of colonial economic interests.

Some 'old guard' radicals drew on this popular dissatisfaction in an attempt to garner support for parliamentary reform. At a public meeting of reformers held in London in June 1816, Major John Cartwright criticised Castlereagh and the prime minister, Lord Liverpool, 'for giving a renewed sanction to the selling of *African* slaves', claiming that the opposition voiced in parliament by Romilly and others two years previously was only possible through the support of 'the people'.[34] However, Cartwright's support for the abolition and suppression of the slave trade was only sincere for as long as it helped make his point about the exploitation of English workers. In reality, his true wish was that abolitionists would stop playing 'the part of *African patriots*', and 'aid us [reformers] with their powerful eloquence, in our efforts for putting an end to the selling of the people of England!'.[35] There was no doubt that the distinction he hoped to draw in order to declare the Englishman's superior right to parliamentary advocacy was racial. He

[30] Paul Michael Kielstra, *The Politics of Slave Trade Suppression in Britain and France, 1814–48* (2000), 22–55.

[31] For the early history of Royal Navy slave trade suppression, see *ibid.*, 25–33; Mary Wills, 'The Royal Navy and the Suppression of the Atlantic Slave Trade, c. 1807–1867: Anti-slavery, Empire and Identity' (Ph.D. thesis, University of Hull, 2012).

[32] See, for example, Samuel Romilly [pseud. Liber], *Observations on the Late Treaty of Peace with France; as far as it Relates to the Slave Trade* (1814).

[33] Anon., *Remarks on that Article in the Late Treaty of Peace, which Permits a French Slave Trade for Five Years* (1814), 8.

[34] *Cobbett's Political Register*, 15 June 1816, 754.

[35] *Ibid.*

imagined using abolitionist campaigning tools for the benefit of the more deserving English labourer:

> The whole solution of their sympathy you have in Mr. Wedgewood's medallion of an imploring *Negro* in chains, inscribed 'Am I not a man and a brother?' – But to parliamentary Patriots of *England*, is not an *Englishman* somewhat more than an *African Negro?* – Let such patriots then imagine the medallion of an indignant Englishman, not in the crouching attitude of a kneeling supplicant, but erect, and thus apostrophising: 'Are we not joint heirs of the same inheritance, and is not that inheritance in the hands of robbers?'[36]

Cartwright's comparison between the crouched, 'imploring Negro' and the upright, 'indignant Englishman' reveals much about how the limits of popular empathy had shifted since Wedgwood's famous cameo had first been mass produced in 1787. Quite aside from the bald assertion of English superiority, Cartwright's adjustment of the sympathetic subject's posture – from the kneeling supplication of the 'Negro' to the upright indignation of the 'Englishman' – articulated the comparative statuses of their respective claims to humanitarian attention. The African's claim to common humanity, 'Am I not a man and a brother?', was overwritten by Englishmen's demand to be recognised as 'joint heirs' of an essentialised political 'inheritance'. This English inheritance was exclusive of any number of national, religious and ethnic groups (not to mention all women), but the specific one against which Cartwright had chosen to define it was the black slaves in the West Indies.

As Marcus Wood has pointed out, Cartwright was not the only radical who 'defined the Caribbean slave as the personification of the opposite of British Liberty'.[37] Perhaps the best-known advocate for British working peoples' rights during the early nineteenth century, William Cobbett was also one of the most outspoken and committed racists of the period. Cobbett had begun his journalistic career as a staunch anti-Jacobin writer, attacking the French revolutionaries and vociferously supporting the transatlantic war against France. The virulent and racially inflected nature of his 1804 attack on the slave-led Haitian Revolution might most generously be read in this context.[38] Arthur Scherr has certainly read both Cobbett's attack on the Haitian revolutionaries and his pro-slavery stance in the 1790s as evidence of his broader 'ultraconservatism'.[39] By 1817, Cobbett had largely moved away from his initial anti-radical position and began supporting the cause of moderate reform.[40] His entrenched

---

[36] *Ibid.*

[37] Wood, 'Burkean Parodics', 1.

[38] Wood, at least, is certainly not so minded: his characterisation of Cobbett as the 'the most ingeniously post-Burkean negrophobe' of the period is unequivocal. *Ibid.*, 4.

[39] Scherr, 'Peter Porcupine on Slavery', 3–30.

[40] See, for example, James Grande, 'William Cobbett: Dimensions of Patriotism', in *William Cobbett, Romanticism and the Enlightenment*, ed. James Grande and John Stevenson

anti-black racism, however (much like his well-documented anti-Semitism and hatred of the Scottish) had not softened.[41]

In the aftermath of 'Bussa's Rebellion', a relatively large-scale slave uprising in Barbados in April 1816, Cobbett published an open letter addressed to the abolitionist William Wilberforce, which accused him of fomenting the insurrection. 'It was notorious', he claimed,

> that the Negroes were in a state of profound ignorance; it was notorious that they had no such thing as moral sentiment; it was notorious that, though susceptible of the vindictive feelings with which you and your tribe endeavoured to fill their breasts, they were incapable of justly valuing the benefits which they derived from the care and protection of their masters.[42]

Cobbett was promoting a particular belief about what the Barbadian slaves were and were not intellectually capable of. His description suggested that enslaved people could *feel* vindictive towards planters in an instinctive or primal way. Reflecting their emotional, acerebral nature, these feelings of anger and resentment proceeded from the 'breast', rather than the mind. The more sophisticated evaluative task of 'justly valuing the benefits' of slavery, and the cultivation of a mature form of morality, were seen as simply beyond the enslaved. Ironically, Cobbett's prioritisation of the slaves' 'profound ignorance' implied a belief that these limitations were, at least partially, the result of the degrading effects of slavery itself. His diatribe against Wilberforce epitomised the racialised circular logic at the heart of anti-abolitionist reasoning: because the 'negroes' were enslaved, they were unfit for freedom; because they were unfit for freedom, they must remain enslaved.

However, an important differentiating factor between this and other forms of pro-slavery and racial thought was the explicit depiction of degraded black humanity as a comparator against which white, specifically working-class, intellectual or moral superiority could be claimed. Like Cartwright, Cobbett encouraged British workers, politically disenfranchised by an unreformed parliament, economically exploited by expanding industrialisation, and socially atomised by ongoing urbanisation, to shore up their precarious claim to national belonging by defining themselves negatively against racial outsiders. His racism was profoundly inflected by an antipathy towards the parliamentary anti-slavery movement, and the arch-conservative evangelical Wilberforce in particular. Arguments over the proper distribution of humanitarian attention thus quickly became framed in reference to the supposedly

(2015), 45–61; *The Opinions of William Cobbett*, ed. James Grande, John Stevenson and Richard Thomas (Farnham, 2014), 55–77.

[41] John Stevenson, 'William Cobbett: Patriot or Briton?', *Transactions of the Royal Historical Society*, 6 (1996), 123–36.

[42] *Cobbett's Political Register*, 11 Sept. 1817, 546.

limited intellectual and moral capacity of black slaves. While this did not necessarily preclude a grudging form of *sympathy* for the enslaved, it did prefigure a more uncompromising form of racial chauvinism that was to become more common in the 1820s. Cobbett described the enslaved as animalistic, and suggested that their suffering was therefore less acute than that experienced by the more intellectually and morally sensitive white English working class. Again, he articulated this type of discourse most clearly in his public letters to Wilberforce:

> [T]his argument was used, it was the *mind*, you said; it was the *consciousness of his being a slave*; this was the dreadful evil. Now, Sir, I wish by no means to underrate this suffering even in the mind of the grossly ignorant negro, who rises even in mental capacity, generally speaking, not many degrees above that of numerous inferior animals. Even in this sort of being I am not disposed to underrate the suffering arising from the consciousness of being a slave. But while your feelings are so acute upon this subject, you appear to be as dead as a stone to the feelings of the intelligent and ingenious people of England, which are all alive, in every relationship of life: whose friendship is so ardent, whose gratitude is so lasting, whose resentment is so open and so quick; and who, which is more than all the rest, have been accustomed from their very infancy to hear boasts of English freedom and security.[43]

Again, Cobbett was interacting with a host of established and emerging conceptions about the differences between black and white people. He did not make the claim – as would later nineteenth-century racial theorists – that the key sites of difference between the two were biological. Rather, he maintained that they were moral and intellectual. The distinction became one of national character. Specifically, he implied that the 'intelligent and ingenious people of England' were capable of reasoned, socialised responses (friendship, lasting gratitude and open and quick resentment) to Wilberforce's actions, accentuated by – indeed, proceeding from – their acculturation to the celebrated 'national' virtues of 'freedom and security'. In typical Cobbettian fashion, English patriotism here denoted moral capacity. The grudging concession that the 'grossly ignorant negro' had the intellect and moral sophistication to feel anguish as a result of their enslavement was undercut by the implication that slaves' supposed animalistic lack of 'mental capacity' protected them in some measure from fully appreciating the horror of their own exploitation.

Cobbett may not have been explicitly engaging with racial theory in this passage, but his broad assumptions about black people's lacking 'moral sentiment' and being less sensitive to mental anguish than whites chimed with the most overtly 'racist' of contemporaneous British comparative autonomy. In a series of lectures delivered between 1817 and 1819, anthropologist William Lawrence cited travel accounts as evidence of an

---

43 *Ibid.*, 547.

African predisposition towards irrationality.[44] He claimed that Africans 'exhibit generally a great acuteness of the external senses', but also 'display gross selfishness, indifference to the pains and pleasures of others... and an almost entire want of what we comprehend altogether under the expression of elevated sentiments, manly virtues, and moral feeling'. Europeans, on the other hand, were distinguished by their 'pre-eminence' in 'moral feelings and mental endowments'.[45] These observations were, in part, extrapolated from the type of specific, encoded examples Cartwright and Cobbett had sought to provide. The kneeling, supplicant African and the upright, apostrophising Englishman; the ingratitude and vindictiveness of the rebellious Barbadian slave and the intellectual resentment of the exploited British worker: none of these referred to any particular individual. Rather, they were expressly intended as symbolic of the putatively more legitimate claims for empathy for white English workers over black slaves – a relation that was still commonly understood to have emerged as a result of differential levels of 'civilization' and consequent disparities in 'moral sense' or 'mental capacity'. Their political function was to ensure that popular agitation was directed towards domestic political reform, explicitly to the cost of humanitarian intervention on behalf of black people, including slaves. In that sense, these passages can be understood as early and influential contributions to the development of racial prejudice in British popular politics.

1819–1830

After the infamous Peterloo massacre of 16 August 1819, in which over a dozen pro-reform protesters were killed and over 400 injured by the Manchester yeomanry, the home secretary Lord Sidmouth introduced a new raft of repressive anti-democratic measures known as the Six Acts.[46] These measures included restrictions on meetings of over fifty people, compulsory registration for publishers, increased taxation on all periodicals and more capacious definitions of seditious and blasphemous utterances and publications. Reformers, especially ultra-radicals, initially railed against the new laws. They were all to pay the price for doing so. In 1820, Davidson, the young black Spencean, was involved in a plot to assassinate the prime minister Lord Liverpool and his cabinet:

[44] It should be noted that Lawrence was an outlier in British anthropological science at this point, though this was less to do with his assumptions of African intellectual inferiority than his 'insistence that life could not be discussed independently of animal body nor mind independently of brain'. Stocking, *Victorian Anthropology*, 43.

[45] Lawrence, *Lectures on Physiology*, 476.

[46] The exact events and consequences of 16 Aug. 1819 are still the subject of scholarly and popular debate. For some recent research, see *Return to Peterloo*, ed. Robert Poole (Lancaster, 2014).

the so-called 'Cato Street Conspiracy'. Davidson was hanged and then beheaded on 1 May for his part in the plot, along with four others.[47] His associate Wedderburn spent two years in Newgate after being prosecuted under the new seditious blasphemy laws. Richard Carlile, a leading radical publisher who had stood beside Hunt at the hustings at Peterloo, spent most of the period 1819–25 in prison on various charges of sedition and blasphemy.[48]

Wilberforce, among the most conservative (religiously and politically) of the elder Tories, took a special interest in the prosecution of seditious blasphemers. He visited Wedderburn in gaol to try to convince him, with some limited success, to concentrate his considerable oratorical and literary talents on the anti-slavery campaign instead of domestic radicalism.[49] The aging evangelical also visited Carlile in his cell at around the same time, though he was rebuffed, one imagines, in no uncertain terms. Wilberforce may have felt offended; he soon saw to it personally that Carlile's wife, Jane, who had taken over publishing her husband's periodicals while he was in gaol, was also arrested and imprisoned for two years for printing seditious libel.[50] Through his involvement in the Society for the Suppression of Vice, Wilberforce also took a leading role in enforcing the heightened level of tax on periodical publications – a measure designed to hobble the radical press.[51] Wilberforce was at this time still a leading parliamentary abolitionist, and in any case his name had been synonymous with the British campaign against slavery since the success of slave trade abolition in 1807. His personal intercessions against the radical movement during the 1820s, as much as his high church evangelicalism and his patronising position on improving the morality of the 'lower orders', could hardly have endeared him or his cause to men like Carlile. Indeed, British radicals were never to forgive him; after Peterloo, they increasingly saw their aims and ambitions as incompatible with the parliamentary abolitionist movement.

Sidmouth's repressive measures, effectively and at times vindictively enforced by Wilberforce and others in the Liverpool cabinet, necessitated a change of approach for the reform movement. Once dismissed as a quiescent period for proletarian activism, sandwiched between the more turbulent Peterloo years and the reform acts of the 1830s, the 1820s is now

[47] Anon., *Authentic History of the Cato-Street Conspiracy*, 368–92.

[48] See McCalman, *Radical Underworld*, 181–91.

[49] McCalman, 'Introduction', in Wedderburn, *Horrors*, 1.

[50] See Wilberforce House, Hull, Wilberforce Letters, 16/15 'William Wilberforce to Olivia Sparrow, 20 July 1820'.

[51] Gregory Claeys, 'Early Socialism as Intellectual History', *History of European Ideas*, 40 (2014), 893–904. For a general discussion of the Society for the Suppression of Vice, its activities and its detractors, see M. J. D. Roberts, 'Making Victorian Morals? The Society for the Suppression of Vice and its Critics, 1802–1886', *Historical Studies*, 21 (1984), 157–73.

recognised as the decade in which a coherent working-class intellectual milieu crystallised in Britain. This so-called 'march of the mind' was characterised by a shift away from the rough-and-ready, tavern-based plebeian debating culture of the Peterloo years and towards the pursuit of 'respectability', sober intellectual self-improvement, religious scepticism and the early adoption of new modes of scientific and philosophical thought such as phrenology and freethinking religious scepticism.[52] This environment lent itself to a kind of humanitarian liberalism that generated a parallel, self-consciously extra-parliamentary anti-slavery movement among some radicals, most notably Wedderburn.[53] For similar reasons, many English radicals in the 1820s (including Cartwright) were also relatively sympathetic to the idea of Catholic emancipation.[54] Thus, Irish Catholic reformers such as Daniel O'Connell were, in the spirit of solidarity, seen by many as allies in the broader campaign for political reform – though in O'Connell's case, his close association with parliamentary abolitionists generated some friction.[55] While anti-Irish sentiment was certainly present in English plebeian culture during the 1820s, the influx of immigration precipitated by the Great Famine was still over a decade away, and as such the explicitly racial 'Othering' of the Irish in England had not yet reached the essentialising nadir of the mid-Victorian period.[56] Anti-black racist rhetoric, however, was already represented in a small but tenacious sector of radical print culture. The 'march of the mind' thus saw some radicals adopt more overt approaches to racial hierarchy, including attempts to popularise the relatively novel notion of permanent racial categories and hereditable African inferiority.

Once again, Cobbett was at the forefront of British popular racism. Evading prosecution in Britain for seditious libel, he had travelled in America between 1817 and 1819, and considered the free black population

[52] David Magee, 'Popular Periodicals, Common Readers and the "Grand March of Intellect" in London, 1819–34' (D.Phil. thesis, University of Oxford, 2008); McCalman, *Radical Underworld*, 181–203.

[53] See Wedderburn, *Horrors*, 1–61, 153–4.

[54] Robert Hole, *Pulpits, Politics and Public Order in England, 1760–1832* (Cambridge, 1989), 230–2. Cobbett also supported Catholic emancipation, but 'he promptly reversed his attitude in 1825 when the Catholic leaders accepted a policy which was opposed to the strict principles of parliamentary reform'. G. I. T. Machin, *The Catholic Question in English Politics, 1820–1830* (Oxford, 1964), 8.

[55] See, for example, Wedderburn's attacks on O'Connell in *An Address to Lord Brougham and Vaux*, cited in Ryan Hanley, 'A Radical Change of Heart: Robert Wedderburn's Last Word on Slavery', *Slavery and Abolition*, 37 (2016), 438. For O'Connell and English parliamentary abolitionists during this period, see Christine Kinealy, *Daniel O'Connell and the Anti-Slavery Movement: 'The Saddest People the Sun Sees'* (2011), 13–27.

[56] For anti-Irish racial stereotyping in the 1840s, see, for example, Charlotte Boyce, 'Food, Famine, and the Abjection of Irish Identity in Early Victorian Representation', in *Fear, Loathing and Victorian Xenophobia*, ed. Tromp, Bachman and Kaufman, 153–80.

there 'a disorderly, improvident set of beings'.[57] He and his son, John Morgan Cobbett, were dismayed when they arrived at their estate on Long Island in June 1818. 'There is one thing here that I cannot bear at all', the younger Cobbett wrote to his mother a few days after their arrival, 'that is that all the servants, male and female are Black, Oh, the Sacre Blacks.'[58] William Cobbett was equally mistrustful of the servants – he suspected them of stealing linen and employed a white maidservant to secure the valuables under lock and key.[59] By the time he returned to Britain late in 1819, his view of black Americans was intractable. '[T]hey are the *thieves of the country*', he foamed, 'they form nine-tenths of the paupers and criminals... not a word that they say can be believed;... with regard to them, *falseness* is the rule and *truth* the exception.'[60]

Cobbett was not satisfied with attacking the character of free black Americans: he wanted to prove that they were fundamentally different beings to white men. In an extended harangue addressed to the Liverpool Quaker abolitionist James Cropper, and published in his *Weekly Political Register* in August 1821, he set out his position explicitly:

> That the Negroes are a race of beings *inferior* to white men I do not take upon me to assert; for black is as good a *colour* as white; and the Baboon may, for any thing I know or care, be *higher* in the scale of nature than man. Certainly the Negroes are of a *different sort* from the Whites. An almost complete absence of the reasoning faculties, a sort of dog-like grin, and a *ya-ya-ya* laugh, when spoken to, may be, for any thing that I know, marks of *superiority*... I am, therefore, not presumptuous enough to take upon me to assert, that the Blacks are not the *superior* beings; but I deny all *equality*. They are a *different* race; and for Whites to mix with them is not a bit less odious than the mixing with those creatures which, unjustly apparently, we call beasts.[61]

In terms of the prevalent understandings of racial difference, this was a synthetic stance. The confusion, for example, over whether 'Negroes' more closely resembled apes or dogs was reminiscent of Charles White's outdated *Account in the Regular Gradation in Man*, which contained a comparative chart of the skulls of different races of men and animals (see Figure 1). In White's taxonomy, derived from the earlier work of Petrus Camper, intellectual faculties were expressed in the angle of the face – the more acute the angle, the less intellectually developed the specimen.[62] For humans, the anatomical model of perfection, the 'Grecian Antique',

[57] William Cobbett, *A Year's Residence in the United States of America* (3 vols., 1819), II, 378.

[58] Nuffield College Library, Oxford, Cobbett papers, box 32/XXX/44, 'John Morgan Cobbett to Nancy Cobbett, 6 June 1818', 1.

[59] *Ibid.*, box 32/XXX/48, 'William Cobbett to Nancy Cobbett, 19 June 1818', 2.

[60] *Cobbett's Weekly Political Register*, 4 Aug. 1821, 148.

[61] *Ibid.*, 147

[62] Camper's ideas were published in England in 1794 as *The Works of the Late Professor Camper, on the Connexion between the Science of Anatomy and the Arts of Drawing, Painting, Statuary &c.* (1794).

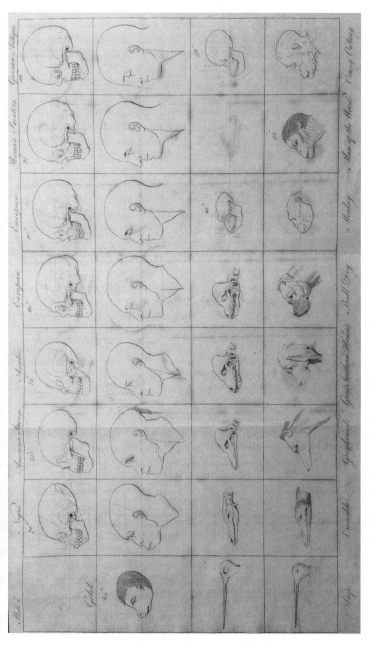

Figure 1 From Charles White, *An Account in the Regular Gradation in Man* (1799).

had a facial angle of 100 degrees, while at the bottom end of the scale, the 'Negro' had a facial angle of only 70 degrees. The only other mammals given for comparison in this illustration were apes and dogs, whose facial angles ranged from 58 degrees ('Orang Outang') to the pointed snout of the greyhound.

Cobbett's pretended rejection of the increasingly popular notion of a fixed racial hierarchy was transparently disingenuous. His suggestion that an 'almost complete absence of the reasoning faculties' corresponded to 'a sort of dog-like grin' suggests at least a passing familiarity with Camper's or White's illustration – perhaps through the more recent writings of James Cowles Pritchard, who found the model 'to agree with facts'.[63] Elsewhere in the same article, he hinted towards a (rather bigoted and unsophisticated) interest in comparative anatomy, suggesting that East Indians were less fit for slavery than Africans because they had 'hair upon their heads instead of wool; had human faces, and the smell of other men'.[64] What he added to preexisting ideas of human difference was a personal dislike of black people, and the desire to organise social relations, at least as far as humanitarianism and sexual pairings, in a racialised order.

If Cobbett's engagement with racial theories in the early 1820s was at times allusive, other leading radicals were to draw upon them more explicitly as the decade wound on. Richard Carlile, whose family had suffered so much from Wilberforce's personal interventions on behalf of the Tory administration, is a case in point. Carlile had little time for Cobbett himself, but much of his own racism was similarly bound up in a dislike of abolitionists and a prioritisation of the plight of the English working classes. This stemmed as much from his staunch support for religious freethinking, deism and, eventually, atheism, as it did from his personal antipathy towards Wilberforce and his fellow 'Saints'.[65] Both polygenetic racial theory and 'Great Chain' arguments had long been considered blasphemous in Britain, and Carlile's views on human difference seem to have been inflected by his personal dislike of evangelical Christianity. Indeed, it was in reportage about Christian missionaries going to Africa that Carlile's racial discrimination took on its most violently bigoted articulacy. 'Is not the saving of a white soul at home, as good as that of a black soul abroad?' he asked, 'And why not send missionaries to the monkeys of South America? Who is to say to

[63] James Cowles Pritchard, *Researches into the Physical History of Man* (1813), 48; for Pritchard's racial theory, see Hannah Franziska Augstein, *James Cowles Prichard's Anthropology: Remaking the Science of Man in Early Nineteenth-Century Britain* (Amsterdam, 1999), 129–56.

[64] *Ibid.*, 160.

[65] See, for example, Carlile's attack on the 'religion and black humanity of Mr. Wilberforce' as being 'entirely of a foreign nature' in his introduction to the 'Memoir' of Robert Blincoe, a child worker in a Lancashire cotton mill. *The Lion*, 1:5 (1 Feb. 1828), 145.

what grade of animals the soul extends? Or where the human species ends, and that of the monkey begins? Some beings, called human, are lower in character than a portion of the beings, called monkeys.'[66]

Like Cobbett and Cartwright before him, the heart of Carlile's racial discourse was a series of ironic comparisons intended to dehumanise the African object of humanitarian intervention and thus elevate the exploited English worker by means of comparison. His ironic, quasi-scientific overtones were intended to achieve two specific purposes. First, by explicitly dehumanising those whom, elsewhere in the same article, he called the 'red, brown and black savage animals abroad', he ridiculed the very notion of missionary work.[67] Who, after all, could take Christian humanitarianism seriously when the intended beneficiaries were not even really human? Secondly, he demanded the redirection of resources towards the 'dirty white-brown' workers of Britain.[68] Indeed, he signed off this report with what would become the mantra of selfish working-class conservatism: 'if this distribution and teaching of the Bible be a charity, like other charities, it should begin at home'.[69] For Carlile, the situation of the English working class was too desperate for resources to be wasted on those he considered sub-human, and unable to enjoy them. In this respect, part of his reforming ideology was predicated on the notion of an explicitly racial hierarchy.

In common with British comparative anatomists – and indeed the vast majority of British people – most radicals nevertheless remained opposed to slavery in the abstract until at least the end of the decade. For Cobbett, the anti-radical and industrialising tendencies of the parliamentary West Indies interest made them as natural enemies as the abolitionists. Consequently, even his most racist diatribes were tempered with assurances that

> I detest the slave traffic; not so much, however (for I will be no hypocrite) on account of the slaves themselves, if they be *well fed and well treated*, as on *our own account*; knowing well as I do, that whatever the vile miscreants wring from the carcasses of slaves abroad, they use for the purpose of making us slaves at home.[70]

Carlile was rather more half-hearted, but did include some backhanded approval of the abolitionist Thomas Clarkson in his published work. In an aside to an 1829 story about Robert Southey, the Poet Laureate, ranking radical reformer Robert Owen alongside Clarkson as 'one of the moral regenerators of the age', he bemoaned that 'greater men, as moral regenerators, might have been associated with him', who were 'as

---

[66] *Ibid.*, 1:19 (9 May 1828), 577.
[67] *Ibid.*, 578.
[68] *Ibid.*
[69] *Ibid.*
[70] *Cobbett's Weekly Political Register*, 4 Aug. 1821, 170.

ardent as Clarkson was in the other case, in seeking the emancipation of all the slaves to feudal despotism and vicious habits at home'.[71] As with their attacks on parliamentary abolitionists, these grudging anti-slavery concessions were framed, with almost monomaniacal obsessiveness, in reference to the working-class experience 'at home'. In contrast to the dynamic, egalitarian, anti-slavery ultra-radicalism of the late 1810s, the self-improving and self-consciously respectable radicals of the late 1820s could only barely bring themselves to voice any opposition to slavery. When they did, they were careful to do so without troubling the racial boundaries of empathy they had worked so hard to delineate.

Conclusion

British radical sympathy for the emancipation movement was put under considerable strain after 1830. When the slave emancipation act was finally passed in 1833, the British government agreed to compensate the slave-owners, to the amount of around £20,000,000, for the loss of their human 'property'. This money was to come out of tax revenue.[72] While moral support for slave emancipation remained widespread, this provision could hardly have been better calculated to set working-class reformers against the parliamentary abolitionists. Writing in *The Poor Man's Guardian* in June 1833, the influential Chartist Bronterre O'Brien summed up some of the objections: 'We have said enough to show that we are no enemies to colonial emancipation; all we require is that when negroes are emancipated, it *shall not be* at the expense of those who are greater slaves than themselves.'[73] For his part, Carlile quickly took to printing pro-slavery tracts written by former slave-owners.[74] Cobbett was met with applause when, during a public lecture in 1830, he expressed his 'indignation' at hearing MPs 'whine over the sorrows of the fat and greasy negro in Jamaica ... while our own countrymen are found in such a condition under their very eyes'.[75] Even Wedderburn, the ultra-radicals' most outspoken opponent of slavery during the 1810s and 1820s, turned about-face and wrote an anti-abolitionist pamphlet, *An Address to Lord*

---

[71] *The Lion*, 4:26 (25 Dec. 1829), 807.

[72] Full records of the compensation payments and claimants are available online at *Legacies of British Slave-Ownership* (online), available from: www.ucl.ac.uk/lbs/, accessed 22 Mar. 2016. See also Catherine Hall, Nicholas Draper, Keith McClalland, Katie Donington and Rachel Lang, *Legacies of British Slave-Ownership: Colonial Slavery and the Formation of Victorian Britain* (Cambridge, 2014); Nicholas Draper, *The Price of Emancipation: Slave-Ownership, Compensation and British Society at the End of Slavery* (Cambridge, 2013).

[73] *The Poor Man's Guardian*, 15 June 1833.

[74] For example, he published Henry Simmons, *Third Letter to the Right Hon. Earl Grey, First Lord of the Treasury &c. on the Question of Negro Emancipation* (1834).

[75] William Cobbett, *A Third Lecture on the French Revolution* (1830), 11.

Brougham, in 1831.[76] Neither did the jubilation of the slaves when they were finally emancipated in 1838 soften British working-class attitudes. By the early 1840s, as Patricia Hollis puts it, 'breaking up an anti-slavery meeting had become a statement of class consciousness by working-class radicals'.[77]

The collapse of support for anti-slavery activism among much of Britain's working-class population at the very moment of emancipation may, in some measure, be accounted for by the racism of leading radicals in the 1810s and 1820s. Cartwright, Cobbett, Carlile – these were not marginal figures in early nineteenth-century British radicalism. They and their ideas were deeply significant in the formation of British working-class identity. Expounding an ever-narrower nationalism, they questioned the very humanity of enslaved and free Africans in the same pages that their plans for a politically and socially reformed Britain took shape. The idea of an apparently fundamentally different and inferior racial antitype made the mere social distinctions used to disenfranchise and exploit English workers seem far less significant by comparison. In this way, the English working class came to understand itself as the white working class, almost from its very inception. As Virdee suggests, white supremacist ideology may not have been universal, or even widespread, among England's working people until the 1840s.[78] But some radicals made a specific effort to make it so. The Chartists' antipathy towards abolitionism had roots in the radical movements of the 1810s and 1820s. Racism in Britain was never wholly confined to the wealthy and powerful.

---

[76] Hanley, 'A Radical Change of Heart', 423–45.
[77] Hollis, 'Anti-Slavery and British Working-Class Radicalism', 295.
[78] Virdee, *Racism*, 38.

Transactions of the RHS 26 (2016), pp. 125–147 © Royal Historical Society 2016
doi:10.1017/S0080440116000086

BETWEEN POISE AND POWER: EMBODIED MANLINESS IN EIGHTEENTH- AND NINETEENTH-CENTURY BRITISH CULTURE*

By Joanne Begiato

READ ON 18 JUNE 2015

AT THE UNIVERSITY OF NORTHAMPTON

ABSTRACT. This paper explores representations of the manly body and the ways in which its relationship with masculine identity and embodied selfhood changed over time and class. It spans a period in which different types of masculinities were dominant, from the later eighteenth-century man of feeling to the later nineteenth-century muscular Christian, and proposes that an embodied approach offers a more nuanced consideration of the ways in which ideals of masculinity were culturally viewed and utilised. First, it provides a chronology of the manner in which the ideal manly body changed over the two centuries, demonstrating that abstract masculine values were always rooted in male bodies. Secondly, it proposes that although most idealised masculine identities were elite, attention to the more corporeal aspects of gender offers evidence that there were features of the manly body, for example hardness, that appealed across social ranks.[1] Elite men valorised idealised working-class men's bodies and saw in them something to emulate. Moreover, working-class men used classically inspired figures to represent themselves when formulating class and gender identities.

Samuel Johnson defined exercise in his 1755 *Dictionary of the English Language* as 'Habitual action by which the body is formed to gracefulness, air, and agility.'[2] A century and a half later, Eugen Sandow explained his exercise regime to readers of *Strength and How to Obtain It* (1897) in rather dissimilar terms:

---

* I would like to thank a number of people for their contributions to this paper. First, my thanks to Tim Reinke-Williams for inviting me to give the lecture upon which it is based, and to the participants at the RHS Symposium: Masculinity and the Body in Britain, 1500–1900, for their questions and observations. I am also grateful to Matthew Craske, Christiana Payne and Andrew Spicer for their support and judicious comments. Finally, sincere thanks to Michael Brown for discussing and reading the paper in its several versions.

[1] Stuart Hogarth, 'Reluctant Patients: Health, Sickness and the Embodiment of Plebeian Masculinity in Nineteenth-Century Britain. Evidence from Working Men's Autobiographies' (unpublished Ph.D., London Metropolitan University, 2010), ch. 1.

[2] Cited in Julia Allen, *Swimming with Dr Johnson and Mrs Thrale: Sport, Health and Exercise in Eighteenth-Century England* (Cambridge, 2012), 5.

Exercise, indeed, without using the mind in conjunction with it, is of no use. It is the brain which develops the muscles. Physical exercise must be commenced by degrees first bringing into play one muscle, then two, then three, and so on, being careful all the time to put the mind into every movement. Let me strongly advise every student to study well the anatomical chart which is published with this book. By its aid you will be able not only to receive a useful lesson in anatomy, but you will be able to see at a glance the exercise which each muscle may be developed.[3]

Exercise in these cases produced two strikingly different bodies: one created a body that was graceful, poised and agile, the other a body that was muscled, powerful and strong. Although Sandow noted the importance of brain and will power in developing a body, it was increased size that was the desired result. Indeed, Sandow included his own spectacular bodily measurements in the book, and offered prizes to readers for the greatest strength or the best development attained from using his physical culture regime, determined by before and after measurements of their biceps, triceps, thighs and chest.[4] This paper traces these ideal bodily styles for men, to argue that poise and power were two, not always oppositional, aspirational models of manly bodies across the two centuries, which could be used by men from different social classes to construct individual and collective identities.

To date, scholars have scrutinised male bodies in a number of ways. Those who investigate the culture of war show that the state and nation literally and figuratively shaped men's bodies. Military demands and techniques of war required certain types of manly form, shaped by uniform, training and drill.[5] Moreover, the idealised male body came to represent abstract notions such as the strength of nation and progress, and symbolised ideologies underpinning empire and various political movements.[6] In most cases, these were idealised, whole bodies. The damaged male body, however, has also been scrutinised. Historians of emotions, war, labour, health and safety and disability reveal the many ways in which fighting and working men were psychologically and physically damaged by their activities. All reveal the significance of bodies

---

[3] Eugen Sandow, *Strength and How to Obtain It* (1897), 'Introduction'.

[4] *Ibid.*, 27.

[5] Padhraig Higgins, '"Let Us Play the Men": Masculinity and the Citizen-Soldier in Late Eighteenth-Century Ireland', in *Soldiering in Britain and Ireland, 1750–1850*, ed. Catriona Kennedy and Matthew McCormack (Basingstoke, 2013), 179–99; Catriona Kennedy, *Narratives of the Revolutionary and Napoleonic Wars: Military and Civilian Experience in Britain and Ireland* (Basingstoke, 2013), ch. 2; Matthew McCormack, *Embodying the Militia in Georgian England* (Oxford, 2015), particularly ch. 4; George L. Mosse, *Fallen Soldiers: Reshaping the Memory of the World Wars* (Oxford, 1990).

[6] Michael Brown and Chris Lawrence, 'Quintessentially Modern Heroes: Surgeons, Explorers, and Empire, c. 1840–1914', *Journal of Social History*, published online 2016; Mosse, *Fallen Soldiers, passim*; R. A. Nye, 'Review Essay: Western Masculinities in War and Peace', *American Historical Review*, 112 (2007), 417–38.

to masculine identity, since maimed or incapacitated men were unmanned in their own and society's eyes.[7] Histories of sex and reproduction also provide insights into changing medical understandings of bodies and the ways in which gender attitudes shaped them.[8] Scholars of the print culture of erotica and pornography, and work on same-sex desire, address the eroticised male body to reveal its cultural force.[9]

Histories of consumption and material culture indicate that men's bodies were the site of debates about luxury and anxieties over effeminacy.[10] Similarly, historians of fashion and clothing explore the ways men dressed and fashioned their bodies and hair as external markers of sex, virility, maturity, civility and masculinity.[11] In the history of art and literature, men's bodies are discussed as part of varying aesthetics, genres and gender. Though these studies are predominantly representational, more recent scholarship on personal, class and racial identities exposes the ways working men used their bodies as a canvas. For example, by the early nineteenth century, nearly all seamen were tattooed to illustrate identity, travelling experiences, sense of belonging and also manliness, since it demonstrated their capacity to withstand pain.[12] Historians of sport expose the changing shape of men's bodies and expectations

[7] Joanna Bourke, *Dismembering the Male: Men's Bodies, Britain and the Great War* (1996); A. Callen, 'Man or Machine: Ideals of the Labouring Male Body and the Aesthetics of Industrial Production in Early Twentieth-Century Europe', in *Art, Sex and Eugenics*, ed. F. Brauer and A. Callen (2008); S. Koven, 'Remembering and Dismemberment: Crippled Children, Wounded Soldiers, and the Great War in Britain', *American Historical Review*, 99 (1994), 1167–202; Arthur McIvor and R. Johnston, 'Dangerous Work, Hard Men and Broken Bodies: Masculinity in the Clydeside Heavy Industries', *Labour History Review*, 69 (2004), 135–52; Michael Roper, *The Secret Battle: Emotional Survival in the Great War* (2008); David M. Turner, *Disability in Eighteenth-Century England: Imagining Physical Impairment* (New York, 2012).

[8] Mary E. Fissell, *Vernacular Bodies: The Politics of Reproduction in Early Modern England* (Oxford, 2004); Thomas Laqueur, *Making Sex: Body and Gender from the Greeks to Freud* (Cambridge, MA, 1990).

[9] Karen Harvey, *Reading Sex in the Eighteenth Century: Bodies and Gender in English Erotic Culture* (Cambridge, 2004); Matt Houlbrook, *Queer London: Perils and Pleasures in the Sexual Metropolis, 1918–1957* (Chicago, 2005).

[10] Matt Houlbrook, 'Queer Things: Men and Make-up between the Wars', in *Gender and Material Culture in Britain since 1600*, ed. Hannah Grieg, Jane Hamlett and Leonie Hannan (Basingstoke, 2016), 120–37.

[11] K. Honeyman, 'Following Suit: Men, Masculinity and Gendered Practices in the Clothing Trade in Leeds, England, 1890–1940', *Gender and History*, 14 (2002), 426–46; D. Kuchta, *The Three-Piece Suit and Modern Masculinity. England, 1550–1850* (Berkeley, 2002); Christopher Oldstone-Moore, *Of Beards and Men: The Revealing History of Facial Hair* (Chicago, 2016).

[12] Claire Anderson, 'Empire, Boundaries, and Bodies: Colonial Tattooing Practices', in *A Cultural History of the Human Body*, V: *In the Age of Empire*, ed. Michael Sappol and Stephen P. Rice (2014), 171–90; Matt Lodder, '"Things of the Sea": Iconographic Continuities between Tattooing and Handicrafts in Georgian-era Maritime Culture', *Sculpture Journal*, 24 (2015), 195–210.

associated with them, as they chart the diets, training, 'civilising' and professionalisation of sports like boxing, rugby and cricket.[13]

Given this apparent plenitude of scholarship on men's bodies, why do we still need to engage critically with male bodies and masculinity? It is necessary because there is a tendency to see some attributes of masculine identity as largely associated with abstract qualities rather than bodies, and with specific classes. Acknowledging that manliness could be defined as merging the ethical and the physical, Tosh argues that nineteenth-century writers nonetheless located it in the mind rather than the body. Thus, he observes that 'the Victorian code of manliness made scant acknowledgement of the body', for its predominantly elite cultural form gave it a 'cerebral and bloodless quality'.[14] He suggests that it was not until the later nineteenth century that the manliness of muscular Christianity incorporated the hearty, sturdy, male body.[15] This was a style of masculinity that associated virtue and morality with a healthy body cultivated through sport and piety, which prevailed throughout the second half of the nineteenth century. Admittedly, manliness was an ideal and an aspiration, conveying prized values including virtue, piety, courage, endurance, honesty and directness. John Tosh has identified manliness as a 'cultural representation of masculinity rather than a description of actual life'.[16] Yet, as the survey of studies of male bodies above shows, bodies symbolised abstract values and thus it is important to question how far manliness was primarily cultural rather than embodied.[17]

Furthermore, this scholarship is scattered across diverse fields of history, making it difficult for the historian of masculinity to construct an overarching chronology of embodied manly identities. Moreover, discussions of the gendered body in this corpus of work are only one element of a wider investigation. Historians of art, for example, focus on the male form in several types of art, but are predominantly interested in genre conventions, the origins of the iconography utilised and the ways in which the visual product was interpreted, rather than its role in

---

[13] Roberta J. Park, 'Muscles, Symmetry and Action: "Do You Measure Up?" Defining Masculinity in Britain and America from the 1860s to the Early 1900s', *International Journal of the History of Sport*, 22 (2005), 365–95; Roberta J. Park, 'Biological Thought, Athletics and the Formation of a "Man of Character": 1830–1900', *International Journal of the History of Sport*, 24 (2007), 1543–69.

[14] John Tosh, 'What Should Historians do with Masculinity? Reflections on Nineteenth-century Britain', in John Tosh, *Manliness and Masculinities in Nineteenth-Century Britain. Essays on Gender, Family, and Empire* (Harlow, 2005), 32–3.

[15] *Ibid.*, 33.

[16] *Ibid.*, 32.

[17] For an overview of the value of embodied history to understanding masculinity, see Christopher Forth, 'Manhood Incorporated: Diet and the Embodiment of "Civilized" Masculinity', *Men and Masculinities*, 11 (2009), 578–601, at 582.

shaping masculinities.[18] Other scholars treat men's bodies as idealised, aesthetic forms or positive stereotypes and symbols of normative meaning and values. Where this scholarship engages with or contributes to the embodied turn in history, it is driven by other agendas.[19] Michael Budd's ground-breaking work on physical culture *c.* 1850–1918 is an early example of this field, but is predominantly concerned with a Foucauldian body politics, and the ways in which nations control, shape and oppress human bodies.[20] This is crucial, but there is more to be said about the formulation of gender identities.

Alternatively, scholars see some men as bearers of stigmatised inadequate bodies that mark them as ethnic, racial, sexual or class outsiders. For example, working-class men's bodies are treated collectively, for the most part, as passive objects of surveillance by authorities and discipline in work and institutions from schools, to prisons, to insane asylums.[21] They identify the utility of manhood, which led to attempts to control men through manipulating their health, physical shape and fitness.[22] As Matthew McCormack observes, for example, eighteenth-century militia authorities deliberately attempted to improve the militia's 'physical stock', categorising recruits on their physical appearance, health and wholeness of bodies.[23] By the twentieth century, as Joanna Bourke argues, men's bodies were the objects of state and employers' surveillance to keep them useful and functional.[24] This raises questions about the scrutinised men and how they saw their own body 'type' and the extent to which they were simply passive victims of corporeal politics.[25]

Moreover, partly because of the fragmented nature of the work described, the vexed relationship between representation and experience

[18] For example, Tim Barringer, *Men at Work: Art and Labour in Victorian Britain* (New Haven, 2005).

[19] For an overview of the history of the body, see Michael Sappol, 'Introduction: Empires in Bodies; Bodies in Empires', in *Cultural History of the Human Body*, ed. Sappol and Rice, 1–35.

[20] Though it should be noted that he is also interested in the way individual men viewed and deployed their own bodies, such as Eugen Sandow. Michael Budd, *The Sculpture Machine: Physical Culture and Body Politics in the Age of Empire* (Basingstoke, 1997).

[21] Ava Baron, 'Masculinity, the Embodied Male Worker, and the Historian's Gaze', *International Labor and Working-Class History*, 69 (2006), 143–60; Craig Heron, 'Boys Will Be Boys: Working-Class Masculinities in the Age of Mass Production', *International Labor and Working-Class History*, 69 (2006), 6–34.

[22] For the focus on improving the health of men's and women's bodies, see Pamela K. Gilbert, 'Popular Beliefs and the Body: "A Nation of Good Animals"', in *Cultural History of the Human Body*, ed. Sappol and Rice, 125–48.

[23] McCormack, *Embodying the Militia*, 86–7.

[24] Bourke, *Dismembering the Male*, passim.

[25] Also see Mark Jenner and Bertrand Taithe, 'The Historiographical Body', in *Companion to Medicine in the Twentieth Century*, ed. Roger Cooter and John Pickstone (New York, 2003), passim.

remains unresolved. It is only recently that men's somatic experience is being examined. An embodied approach potentially offers a better understanding of individual men's personal experience of their bodies and health, since, as Karen Harvey argues, the body is 'an instrument that performs socially or culturally constructed sexed or gendered identities'.[26] Gender is not only performed, it is inhabited through one's body. As such, scholars are increasingly endeavouring to achieve a more corporeal understanding of experience. Thus, Harvey aims to 'study the lived, embodied experience of gender'.[27] Elsewhere, she advocates drawing on one's 'own material experiences', combined with documentary evidence, to investigate the physical experience of labour skills in the past.[28] These are noble aspirations, but problematic. How can the historian divest herself of her own somatic sense, her own social and cultural context, to imagine herself into an actor's very different body and mentality? This paper therefore focuses instead on representations of gendered male bodies, gathered from analysis of the term 'manly' and 'manliness' across a range of publications and visual genres. It aims to assess their impact upon individual and collective masculine identities, in order to offers insights into change over time for historians of masculinities.

This paper deliberately spans conventionally discrete periods in its survey of ideals of manly bodies. Most work, for example, considers either the age of the man of feeling and Christian sensibility from the 1750s to the 1830s or the age of muscular Christianity from the 1840s to the end of the century. This broad chronology also bridges other ways of categorising bodily eras, such as Michael Budd's divisions between the 'epoch of the glorified body' (early modern period to the end of the eighteenth century), and the epoch of 'the age of the sculpture machine' (1820s to 1930s).[29] Instead, this survey of bodily ideals suggests that a range of male body styles have coexisted, which varied between poise and power, often influenced by classical statuary, either of which could be acceptable, depending upon context and prevailing fashions. Secondly, it considers the issue of social classes, since research, whether addressing art, or labour, rarely studies both elite and working-class male bodies, to show that the two shared some features and were constitutive of each other.

---

[26] Karen Harvey, 'Men of Parts: Masculine Embodiment and the Male Leg in Eighteenth-Century England', *Journal of British Studies*, 54 (2015), 801.

[27] *Ibid.*, 800–1.

[28] Karen Harvey, 'Craftsmen in Common: Objects, Skills and Masculinity in the Eighteenth and Nineteenth Centuries', in *Gender and Material Culture*, ed. Grieg, Hamlett and Hannan, 83.

[29] Budd, *Sculpture Machine*, xii–xiii.

A chronology of eighteenth- and nineteenth-century manly bodies

One could infer from scholarship on muscular Christianity that the focus on the male body in the post-Crimean War period was new, the result of militarising and imperialising forces and 'new athleticism'.[30] In fact, men's bodies were just as central to formulations of masculinity in the previous century, although the idealised male form and related masculine values were mutable. Changing practices in war, empire and labour, understandings of science, sports and aesthetic fashions all influenced the relationship between physiques, minds and gender identities.[31]

Despite considerable diversity, the classical body influenced by Greek antique sculptures was at the core of all formulations of male physical beauty and health.[32] Two classical male body-types were especially potent models: the young, slim athleticism of the Ephebes, and the mature, hefty, heroic Herculean form.[33] These images of poise and power were influential throughout the eighteenth and nineteenth centuries and were widely held aesthetic concepts across Europe, since as Michael Hau observes, classicism promoted transnational aesthetic considerations among artists and cultural elites.[34] Martin Myrone's study of masculinities in British art, for example, suggests that Georgian ideals of manly beauty focused upon the less brawny Greek model. Citing a series of history paintings of Virgil's hero Aeneas by Nathaniel Dance, 1766, he comments that unlike the 'brute' Achilles, who killed Hector, and is depicted as a physically massive Herculean, Aeneas bore a form that 'could be recommended for his genteel accomplishments, sheer physical beauty and his dutiful patriotism, which fitted with a moderate image of masculinity in civil society'.[35] The poised bodily form was associated with manners. David Hume, for instance, observed that readers were on the side of Trojans 'now', rather than Greeks, and were much more interested in the 'humane and soft manners of Priam, Hector, Andromache, Sarpedon, Aeneas, Glaucus, nay, even of Paris and Helen, than for the severe and cruel bravery of Achilles, Agamemnon, and the other Grecian

---

[30] James Mangan and James Walvin, 'Introduction', in *Manliness and Morality: Middle-Class Masculinity in Britain and America 1800–1940*, ed. J. A. Mangan and J. Walvin (Manchester, 1987), 3; Joseph A. Kestner, *Masculinities in Victorian Painting* (Aldershot, 1995).

[31] For the diversity of bodily ideals 1800–1920, see Michael Hau, 'The Normal, the Ideal, and the Beautiful: Perfect Bodies during the Age of Empire', in *Cultural History of the Human Body*, ed. Sappol and Rice, 149–50.

[32] This was common across Europe. *Ibid.*, 150, 152.

[33] Kestner, *Masculinities in Victorian Painting*, 54.

[34] Hau, 'The Normal, the Ideal', 152, 164.

[35] Martin Myrone, *Body-building: Reforming Masculinities in British Art, 1750–1810* (New Haven, 2006), 70.

heroes'.[36] By the second half of the nineteenth century, power prevailed as the Herculean body-type came to symbolise muscular Christianity.[37] Nonetheless, by the early twentieth century, the two ideal Greek male body-types were increasingly linked with specialised forms of physical fitness and sports.[38]

In the eighteenth century, manners, feelings and utility dictated men's ideal physiques and associated styles of bodily deportment and ideals. These were influenced by polite sociability, the cult of sensibility and eighteenth-century military techniques. All required a male body that was graceful, slim and able to move in dance-like forms. This dexterous idealised man fitted a commercial, colonial society whose interests were protected by an army trained in linear tactics.[39] Thus, the Georgian manly body was graceful and strong, but not burly. In 1804, *The Lady's Magazine* explained that sixteen-year-old Selina was wooed by Edward whose 'form wore every manly grace; his manners were soft, persuasive, elegant'.[40] This manly body was well proportioned and composed of 'manly' 'parts', which like musical notes, formed a satisfactory whole.[41]

Poise and grace were not coded as feminine, although men needed to be cautious that softness of manner did not become softness of body. In 1783, a newspaper defined effeminacy in men as 'the absence or debilitation of masculine strength and vigour, or the happy metamorphosis of the gentleman turned lady; that is, female softness in the male discovered by outward signs and tokens, in feminine expressions, accent, voice, gesture, dress, and deportment'.[42] Grace and refinement had to be combined with strength and dexterity. Indeed, David Hume described a man as having 'beauty and vigour' because he possessed 'dexterity in every manly exercise . . . farther adorned with a blooming and ruddy countenance, with a lively air, with the appearance of spirit, and activity in all his demeanour'.[43]

Physical exercise produced this nimble manly body through exertion or recreation. This included walking, riding and dancing, rather

[36] Hume, 'Letter to the Authors of the Critical Review concerning the Epigoniad of Wilkie', cited in Myrone, *Body-building*, 71.

[37] For the continuing popularity of the classical forms, see Kestner, *Masculinities in Victorian Painting*, 48. An example is Leighton's 1871 *Hercules Wrestling with Death for the Body of Alcestis*.

[38] Hau, 'The Normal, the Ideal', 165.

[39] McCormack, *Embodying the Militia*, 99–102.

[40] *The Lady's Magazine*, 35 (1804), 146.

[41] John Armstrong, *Miscellanies* (2 vols., 1770), II.

[42] 'Further Gleanings from the Late English Newspapers', in *Independent Journal or the General Advertiser*, Wednesday 28 Jan. 1784, 2. I am grateful to Dane Morrison for directing me to this.

[43] David Hume, *The History of England. From the Invasion of Julius Cæsar to the Revolution in 1688* (12 vols., [1789]), V, 2.

than a specific organised game.[44] In 1750, the *Youth's General Instructor* recommended

> *Dancing*...which gives a graceful motion, and above all things, Manliness, and a becoming confidence to young children, I think it cannot be learned too early, after they are once of an age and strength capable of it. But you must be sure to have a good master, that knows and can teach, what is graceful and becoming, and what gives a Freedom and Easiness to all the motions of the body.[45]

Physical exertions were important to masculinity for two reasons. First, they trained men to be skilful and light on their feet. Secondly, outdoor activities hardened the body which would lead to manliness since physical hardiness was equated with male virtue. In his *Code of Health and Longevity*, published in 1807, John Sinclair observed that air was essential to athletic exercises since the more men 'are in the air, the firmer their flesh becomes'.[46] This was also classically inspired, for example, Samuel Johnson's definition of manly included Juvenal's *mens sana in corpore sano* (via Dryden), meaning a 'sound mind in a sound body'.[47]

The idealised manly body was in transition from the 1790s into the first half of the nineteenth century becoming solid, broader, rugged and perhaps less elegant. There were numerous causes of this shift. The resurgence of classical ideals in neoclassicism influenced clothing fashions, which evoked nude sculpture, and ideal bodily types.[48] This was a more outdoors, less 'feeling' version of the idealised manly body. A 'young man's' letter to the *Lady's Monthly Museum*, 1801, criticising men of fashion, hints at this:

> I have not scrupled to wear brown paint, like other gentlemen, to increase the manliness of my appearance; nor to gape and stare at the women; nor to walk past them without deigning to look at them; nor to assume pride and reserve, or apathy, or rudeness, as suited the caprice of fashion: yes, Sir, all this I have done, but in vain. I never can be a man of fashion, because unfortunately, I am not devoid of feeling.[49]

The brown paint was make-up aimed at making men look more tanned and physically active.

A combination of expanding print culture, industrialisation and consumption, along with the perception of national crisis during the Revolutionary and Napoleonic Wars, also influenced these ideas about the male body. Indeed, the slender, sensible manly form was

---

[44] Allen, *Swimming with Dr Johnson*.

[45] William Richards, *Youth's General Instructor: Or, a Short and Easy Introduction to the Arts and Sciences* (1750?).

[46] Cited in Allen, *Swimming with Dr Johnson*, 35.

[47] My thanks to Stephen Gregg, Matt McDowell, Elaine Chalus and Freya Gowrley for a discussion on this quotation.

[48] Harvey, 'Men of Parts', 812.

[49] To the Editor of the Lady's Monthly Museum, *The Lady's Monthly Museum* (London, England), [Wednesday], [1 Apr. 1801], 285.

viewed as less suitable to sustain and defend a nation. For example, thinness was increasingly associated with poverty and the French enemy. Problematically, while the portly English body of John Bull – the 'common man' – was emblematic of loyalist visions of manliness, he was hardly a fighter.[50] Perhaps unsurprisingly celebrated military and naval men were often depicted as large and/or robust and therefore appealing. Corporal John Shaw, a boxer and life-guardsman was feted for his bravery and sacrificing his life at Waterloo, stood over six feet tall, was admired for his size and was nicknamed by his neighbours as the 'Cossall giant'.[51] Size became a corporeal vehicle through which masculine values were demonstrated.[52] In 1791, it was recorded: 'Before I had learned from the note the name and business of my Visitor, I was struck with the manliness of his person, the breadth of his chest, the openness of his countenance, and the inquietude of his eye.'[53] Similarly, an 'upright' posture conveyed both the sense of an ideal body and high moral behaviours. For instance, the periodical *John Bull*, 1822, paid a tribute to a London lord mayor and member of parliament, praising his 'manly and UPRIGHT conduct'.[54]

From the mid-nineteenth century, the ideal male body was increasingly large, robust and overtly muscular with bulk, sturdiness and stolidity offering bodily signs of fortitude. Physical power was the key to manliness. In 1847, *Bell's Life* commented approvingly on a cricketer of the newly formed I Zingari cricket club: 'he fought to win every inch of ground with mighty manliness'.[55] In 1896, a Macbeth actor was described as possessing 'rugged manliness'.[56] These mighty manly bodies were less likely to be smooth like their predecessors; indeed, they were regularly described as rough, and faces were bearded. Those extremely corporeal adjectives – plucky and hearty – emerged to personify the manly body. Moreover, since the body was also understood to be related to the mind,

---

[50] K. Downing, 'The Gentleman Boxer: Boxing, Manners, and Masculinity in Eighteenth-Century England', *Men and Masculinities*, 12 (2010), 328–52.

[51] Michael Kirkby, 'The Redcoats of Nottinghamshire', https://nottinghamhidden historyteam.wordpress.com/2013/09/03/the-redcoats-of-nottinghamshire/, accessed 17 June 2016; Henry Charles Moore, 'Shaw, John (1789–1815)', in *The Dictionary of National Biography: Supplement, 1901–1911*, ed. Sidney Lee (1920); Edwin Trueman and R. Westland, *History of Ilkeston: Cossall* (1899).

[52] McCormack, *Embodying the Militia*, 88–9.

[53] *Proceedings of the Association for Promoting the Discovery of the Interior Parts of Africa* (1791).

[54] TO JOHN BULL. *John Bull* (London, England), Monday, 29 July 1822, Issue 85, 677.

[55] 'Cricketer's Register', *Bell's Life in London and Sporting Chronicle* (London, England), Sunday, 12 Sept. 1847, 6. This club was founded 1845 by men educated at public school; today it still bears the club rule: Keep your Promise – Keep your Temper – Keep your Wicket up. www.i-zingari.com/history, accessed 12 July 2013.

[56] John Johnson Collection, Theatre programme, 'The seventh performance given by Mr. E. Glossop Such, in aid of the "Home of Rest for Horses", venue: St George's Hall, [London], Langham Place, date of event: 6 May 1896.

it was assumed that strengthening the male body would strengthen the will and character.[57]

Motion and posture were again critical, but significantly different from grace and nimbleness. The manly movement was powerful and brisk. In 1889, *The Fishing Gazette* declared that Norman Fraser of Kildonan, a 'household word throughout the whole of Sutherlandshire' was a 'brisk and manly Highlander'.[58] Such an upright, straight posture was partly influenced by a military carriage and 'New Athleticism'. An advert in 1888 in *The Sporting Times* announced 'the Grandest Show of Manly Sports ever presented to the public' at Her Majesty's Theatre, Haymarket.[59] In the 'cult of sporting manliness', organised sports and games were judged especially likely to produce manliness.[60] They displayed masculinity through physical prowess and skill, manly values through team spirit, and drew links between physical strength, health and moral wellbeing.[61] The classically inspired physique also dominated the physical culture movement. Eugen Sandow, for instance, emulated classical statues in building his own musculature, and posed as a 'living' classical figure for artists and on stage.[62]

Again, nation and empire were critical to these developments.[63] Plucky, hearty male bodies supported an industrialised, imperialised and, increasingly, militarised Britain where new weaponry led to skirmish and light infantry battle techniques.[64] The muscular classical body in an age of empire was deployed to construct hierarchies of race and tied to concerns of imperial power.[65] It was also related to changing economic conditions when new technology and mechanisation, and the rise of sedentary jobs such as salaried office workers, clerks and deskilled manual labour appeared to challenge men's 'physical significance'. All were potentially emasculating and thus physical, rough, tough muscularity outside the workplace was reemphasised.[66]

---

[57] Roberta Park, 'Biological Thought, Athletics and the Formation of a "Man of Character": 1830–1900', in *Manliness and Morality*, ed. Mangan and Walvin, 7–34.

[58] 'Famous Fishermen', *The Fishing Gazette: Devoted to Angling, River, Lake and Sea Fishing and Fish Culture* (London, England), Saturday, 31 Aug. 1889, Issue 645, 129.

[59] *The Sporting Times* (London, England), Saturday, 8 Dec. 1888, Issue 1316, 4.

[60] James Walvin, 'Symbols of Moral Superiority: Slavery, Sport and the Changing World Order, 1800–1950', in *Manliness and Morality*, ed. Mangan and Walvin, 246.

[61] Gilbert, 'Popular Beliefs and the Body', 142–4.

[62] Kestner, *Masculinities in Victorian Painting*, 54.

[63] The ideals were also harnessed to notions of racial purity when they were framed within a Darwinian evolutionary framework by the later nineteenth century, see Hau, 'The Normal, the Ideal'.

[64] Michael Brown, 'Cold Steel, Weak Flesh: Mechanism, Masculinity and the Anxieties of Late Victorian Empire', *Cultural and Social History*, forthcoming.

[65] Hau, 'The Normal, the Ideal', 161.

[66] Baron, 'Masculinity, the Embodied Male Worker', 146–7.

The class dimensions of manly bodies and masculinity

The idealised bodies outlined above were elite: primarily aimed at and understood by educated genteel society. Indeed, the pervasive ideal of muscular Christianity is often envisaged as a middle-class creation, that middle-class and gentry boys engaged with through their public school education, and which was imposed upon lower-ranking men as a way to reform them and society. Thus, the corporeality of Victorian working-class men appears most frequently in scholarship that considers endeavours to 'remake' lower-class men by improving their bodies. The combination of social Darwinism and urban industrialisation led to fears that working-class men were physically deficient, which reached crisis point in England during the South African wars. In his 1905 'Introductory Address on Efficiency' to Charing Cross Hospital, the celebrated Scottish alienist Sir James Crichton-Browne's included a section on 'The National Physique' in which he bemoaned that 'We have on our hands hordes of under-grown, under-fed, blemished, diseased, debilitated men, women, and children . . . who are industrially and socially in-efficient.'[67] Such concern was widespread and prompted institutionalised attempts to salvage the 'degenerate' body of the British working man through the Interdepartmental Committee on Physical Deterioration and in the form of boys' and men's fraternal organisations and school physical education.[68]

The same imperative contributed to new leisure and recreation initiatives aimed directly at the working class.[69] In 1868, the 'respectable' magazine aimed at working-class boys, *Boys of England: A Young Gentleman's Journal of Sport, Travel, Fun and Instruction,* warned:

> Boys of England, in these days of cheap education, cheap standard literature, or cadet volunteer corps, cricket-clubs, and gymnasia; in these days when, even with unaided self-help and perseverance, you may achieve such wonders, it is your own fault if you do not grow up wise and strong men. Scorn aping manliness of mind and body; learn to think, speak, and write, learn to swim, jump, and run, despise skulking laziness, and face hard study and hard hand-labour.[70]

[67] Sir James Crichton-Browne, 'An Introductory Address on Efficiency', *The Lancet,* 7 Oct. 1905, 1014.

[68] A. W. Fitz Roy, *Report of the Inter-departmental Committee on Physical Deterioration* (1904); Budd, *Sculpture Machine,* 18. For similar fears of degeneration in France, Germany and the US, see Hau, 'The Normal, the Ideal', 15–19.

[69] For example, the Young Men's Christian Association, founded 1844, and the National Physical Recreation Society, founded in 1886, which promoted fitness for working-class men, Budd, *Sculpture Machine,* 25.

[70] Crackers for the Ingenious, *Boys of England: A Young Gentleman's Journal of Sport, Travel, Fun and Instruction* (London, England), [Friday], [17 July 1868] Issue 87, 142. For the magazine, see E. J. B. Rebecca Knuth, *Children's Literature and British Identity: Imagining a People and a Nation* (Lanham, Toronto, 2012), 64.

In these accounts, the only agency the working-class man had over his body was to follow instructions. Undoubtedly, the needs of the state and nation were prominent in dictating the idealised male body, and in the deployment of the real male body. Nevertheless, there is evidence that the appeal of the muscular labouring male body could both inspire elite men and offer agency to working men.

The male labouring body was, after all, celebrated in visual, textual and material form, particularly in the imagined forms of the soldier, the sailor, the boxer and the entrepreneurial strongman.[71] These working men's bodies had a broad dissemination, commercialised in decorative, domestic objects intended to be collected and displayed in the home, such as ceramic vessels and plates, and pottery portrait figures, featuring boxers, as well as soldiers and sailors.[72] By the later nineteenth century, such working men were also deployed in advertising to sell products.[73] In examples from the early eighteenth century, the fine body of the labourer was based on classical statuary. This was intended to allude to the natural health and beauty of working men and thereby criticise the more effete, enervated effeminate bodies of those wealthy enough to participate in luxury and consume this art.[74] Joseph Wright of Derby's nocturnal paintings of blacksmiths, for example, include *The Blacksmith's Shop* 1771, in which three fine-figured men labour at the anvil.[75] Perhaps even more overtly indicative of the hearty beauty of male physical labour is the iron founder in Wright's *An Iron Forge*, 1772.[76] Overseeing the power-driven tilt hammer, he stands with his powerful arms crossed over his chest. Not only is he literally a glowing example of male strength, he is also surrounded by his family, indicating his virility and domesticity. As Matthew Craske observes, in these paintings Wright produced the opposite of the grand style of history painting, where the blacksmith stood as the lusty everyman essential to the village, and presumably natural society.[77]

[71] For the labourer more generally, see K. McClelland, 'Some Thoughts on Masculinity and the "Representative Artisan" in Britain, 1850–1880', *Gender and History*, 1 (1989), 164–77.

[72] Kasia Boddy, *Boxing: A Cultural History* (2008), 44–5; Thomas Balston, *Staffordshire Portrait Figures of the Victorian Age* (1958), plate 47 (The Grapplers); P. D. Gordon Pugh, *Staffordshire Portrait Figures and Allied Subjects of the Victorian Era* (1970), 286–97 (soldiers and sailors).

[73] Karen Walker, 'Manly Men and Angelic Women: Gender and Nostalgia in George Elgar Hicks's Watercolour The Sinews of Old England (1857) and in an advertisement for Cadbury's Cocoa (1886)', http://open.conted.ox.ac.uk/resources/documents/manly-men-and-angelic-women-gender-and-nostalgia-george-elgar-hicks%E2%80%99s, accessed 18 June 2015.

[74] Matthew Craske, *Joseph Wright of Derby: Entrepreneur of Gloom*, unpublished book manuscript. My sincere thanks to Matthew for sharing his book manuscript with me.

[75] http://collections.britishart.yale.edu/vufind/Record/1669279.

[76] http://www.tate.org.uk/art/artworks/wright-an-iron-forge-t06670/text-summary.

[77] In this way, his paintings are similar to Chardin's images of dignified working people. Craske, *Joseph Wright of Derby*, ch. 1. For the argument that the forge-man is portrayed as heroic, see Ravenhill-Johnson, *Art and Ideology*, 35.

By the 1840s, the male labouring body was formulated as heroic. Thomas Carlyle, for instance, elevated work to a religion in his chapter in 'Labour', in *Past and Present* (1843). In his view, work made the man, and in so doing saved the individual and national body and soul. He observed:

> Consider how, even in the meanest sorts of Labour, the whole soul of a man is composed into a kind of real harmony, the instant he sets himself to work! Doubt, Desire, Sorrow, Remorse, Indignation, Despair itself, all these like hell-dogs lie beleaguering the soul of the poor dayworker, as of every man: but he bends himself with free valour against his task, and all these are stilled, all these shrink murmuring far off into their caves. The man is now a man. The blessed glow of Labour in him, is it not as purifying fire wherein all poison is burnt up, and of sour smoke itself there is made bright blessed flame![78]

The elevation of the working man to heroic status was widespread in British art and literature in the second half of the nineteenth century. Tim Barringer's 'critical iconography of the working man' suggests that representations of the male labouring body acted as 'the nexus of ethical and aesthetic value'.[79] The two best-known visual examples of the heroic working man are found in George Hicks's *The Sinews of Old England*, 1857, and Ford Madox Brown's *Work*. Hicks's *Sinews of Old England* is a particularly appealing example of the genre of the labouring man at his cottage door. The title refers to the phrase 'the sinews and power of old England', which was used to describe the navy.[80] No doubt this drew connections in viewers' minds with the heroic 'everyman', Jack Tar, whose robust, stout, hard body offered another appealing model of working manhood.[81] The other archetypal depiction of heroic manual labour is Ford Madox Brown's richly iconographic painting *Work*, influenced by Ruskin and Carlyle and so closely linked to Carlyle's views on work that it portrays him as an observer.[82] Work is glorified in the navvies' bodies. In a sonnet that he wrote to accompany the painting, Brown eulogised (Feb. 1865) work as beading the brow and tanning 'the flesh of lusty manhood', thereby 'casting out its devils!'[83] Brown, a radical and socialist, used the central heroic navvy's body whose pose he based on the Apollo Belvedere, to convey the worth of the lower classes over poorer-quality men who did not labour so nobly.[84] Brown described the Apollo-like navvy as being in

---

[78] Thomas Carlyle, 'Labour', *Past and Present* (1843), http://www.online-literature.com/thomas-carlyle/past-and-present/34/, accessed 16 June 2015.

[79] Barringer, *Men at Work*, 1–2.

[80] For the use of the title, see *Men and Times of the Revolution; Or, Memoirs of Elkanah Watson, including Journals of Travels in Europe and America, from 1777 to 1842* (New York, 1856). https://archive.org/details/menandtimesoowatsrich, accessed 16 June 2015 .

[81] Joanne Begiato (Bailey), 'Tears and the Manly Sailor in England, *c.* 1760–1860', *Journal for Maritime Research*, 17 (2015), 117–33.

[82] Barringer, *Men at Work*, 28.

[83] Cited in Gerard Curtis, 'Ford Madox Brown's "Work": An Iconographic Analysis', *Art Bulletin*, 74 (Dec. 1992), 633.

[84] *Ibid.*, 629; Barringer, *Men at Work*, 37.

the 'pride of manly health and beauty', and of course in this combination his figure merged both poise and power.[85]

Such images can be read in several ways in the light of what has been discussed so far. Manly labouring bodies served as moral exemplars for society. In 1770, Arthur Young complained:

> It is not the deficiency of labouring hands, but the progress of sloth and indolence which ought to alarm our fears: it is this which induces the idle part of our people to prefer the less toilsome, but more precarious works of the manufacture to the rough, but more manly exercises of the husbandman.

Here, the labouring rural manly body was the antithesis of an unmanly idleness, that bugbear of social and moral commentators because it damaged productivity.[86] Those like Hicks's domesticated labourer can be seen as moralistic in intention, reinforcing the gendered spheres of home with the man active in the public sphere and his adoring wife waiting in the domestic sphere.[87] Like other similar images, it sentimentalised men's hard labour, in the process making industrious working-class men less threatening to higher-ranking people by valorising their work ethic for their families.[88] Moreover, as with the Jack Tar, this image of the labouring man at the heart of his family embodied the strength of the nation through the motif of familial affection that saturates the painting. Working men's bodies in genre pictures were also didactic in that they were intended to promote manly ideals to their social superiors. For instance, Millais's *The Rescue* painted in 1855 offers a working-class muscular hero: a fearless fireman rescuing two children from a burning house. *The Athenaeum* reviewer of the painting declared the fireman to be 'thoroughly English, cool, determined, and self-reliant . . . resolute, manly, strong as iron, like one accustomed to pass through fire'.[89]

Scholars of labour and art argue that such heroic depictions of male labouring bodies subordinated and objectified men.[90] This firm-jawed fireman not only reinforced patriarchal hierarchies of men and women, he reinforced those between men, by offering an archetype of tough male body which sedentary men were unlikely to reach. Furthermore, Ava Baron characterises working-class men in these images as passive, because, like women, they became the subject of the gaze; their muscular

---

[85] Curtis, 'Ford Madox Brown's "Work"', 631; Barringer, *Men at Work*, 37.

[86] *Ibid.*, 16.

[87] *Ibid.*, 30–1.

[88] For an overview of this in relation to trade union emblem history, see Ravenhill-Johnson, *Art and Ideology*, 36–40.

[89] Cited in Herbert Sussman, *Victorian Masculinities: Manhood and Masculine Poetics in Early Victorian Literature and Art* (Cambridge, 1995), 144, 146.

[90] For the thesis that the labourer in art became increasingly depersonalised and anonymous, see John Barrell, *The Dark Side of the Landscape: The Rural Poor in English Painting 1730–1840* (Cambridge, 1980).

bodies eroticised and therefore pacified.[91] Though handsome, heroic and idealised, Ravenhill-Johnson claims, they 'are still "the other", not of the same class as the purchaser of fine art; their depiction acts as reassurance that workers are sober, industrious and, above all, nonthreatening'.[92]

Yet working bodies need not be read only in terms of condescension, passivity and subordination. These representations were multi-purpose and working-class men's bodies had dynamic cultural power which spanned social classes. Elite men, for example, were inspired by the idealised hardened working male body. Hardening was a feature derived from plebeian working men. Stuart Hogarth explains that plebeian men needed wiry, tough, enduring bodies in order to carry out their manual labour. As such, their paid physical labour not only shaped and made demands upon their bodies, it was intrinsic to the formation of their gender and class identities.[93] Men originally of lower social status, writing in the early nineteenth century, referred in their memoirs to a similar notion of body 'hardening'. Thomas Bewick described compensating for his sedentary life as an engraver during his apprenticeship, and the resulting ill-health it caused, by following medical advice to restrict his diet and train his body through walking to harden it into a manlier form.[94] Francis Place used cold-water therapy to harden his body against illness.[95] Studies of twentieth-century mining, steel working and ship building demonstrate that male workers continued to define their masculine identity through a cult of toughness at work, as well as the ability to take and ignore risks.[96]

Elite men emulated the hardened bodies of plebeian men from the early nineteenth century. Admittedly, this was probably derived from representations of labouring men's bodies rather than reality, since, as Pamela Gilbert observes, this was compromised by the fact that labourers' bodies were formed by hard labour and rarely produced a body conforming to classical ideals.[97] Still, as Barringer argues, visual images formed styles of masculinity as well as articulating them.[98] Examples include elite men who emulated the idealised form of boxers. From the later eighteenth century, competitive boxing defined new sought-after models of male stance, use of the body, appearance and body shape. Karen Downing notes the appeal of the 'gentleman' boxer's body, which was

---

[91] Baron, 'Masculinity, the Embodied Male Worker', 148–9.

[92] Ravenhill-Johnson, *Art and Ideology*, 38.

[93] Hogarth, 'Reluctant Patients', *passim*.

[94] Thomas Bewick, *Memoir*, 1822 (unpaginated manuscript, Adam Matthew Publications Microfilm Series).

[95] *The Autobiography of Francis Place, 1771–1854*, ed. M. Thrale (Cambridge, 1972).

[96] McIvor and Johnston, 'Dangerous Work, Hard Men and Broken Bodies', 142.

[97] Gilbert, 'Popular Beliefs and the Body', 144–5.

[98] Barringer, *Men at Work*, 16.

'able to simultaneously convey strength, refinement, and self-control'.[99] Popular portraits of boxers displayed both male poise and power; as Harvey points out, fighters were posed naked from the waist upwards, but wore trim breeches: a melding of politeness and strength.[100] The boxer's appeal was commercialised in various ways. Boxers marketed their diet and training regimes to elite men, intended to produce this muscular, but elegant physique. Most famously, George Gordon Byron used a boxing regime to lose weight and improve his body. He even materialised his love of boxing in a dressing screen upon which he collaged coloured pictures of prize-fighters and reports of boxing matches.[101]

Wealthy men also adopted plebeian styles of dress from the later eighteenth century, wearing modest and plain clothing which eventually came to be seen as a distinctively English style. The shift from breeches to trousers in men's legwear in the nineteenth century was particularly influenced by working men's trousers.[102] As John Styles observes, men who chose to dress down 'were sharing in a powerful trend towards the rural, the sporting and the plebeian'. In an era of national crisis, this trend personified patriotism through the association with pugnacious plebeian masculinity and English liberty.[103] From the mid-nineteenth century, a generation of more sedentary middle-class men romanticised, and yearned to possess themselves, the bodily markers of the heroic working body. Of course, there were considerable differences between the social classes' adoption of sportsmen's training regimes, body hardening and simpler dress. Stuart Hogarth explains that hardening was a necessity for the labouring classes, but the middle-class men who adopted it when formulating gendered identities did so as 'a reaction against rich living', both in terms of self-indulgence and mental strain.[104] Thus, by the later nineteenth century, as Gilbert proposes, the muscular Christian's 'body was based less on class than on other attributes seen as quintessentially British, and it insisted on a body toughened either by physical labour or physical sport'.[105]

Working men's muscular arms

Tim Barringer describes Brown's *Work* as composed around the three navvies, 'who catch the full force of the July sun that reflects harshly

---

[99] Downing, 'The Gentleman Boxer', 343.

[100] Harvey, 'Men of Parts', 812.

[101] Boddy, *Boxing: A Cultural History*, 49–54

[102] Harvey, 'Men of Parts', 811.

[103] John Styles, *The Dress of the People: Everyday Fashion in Eighteenth-Century England* (New Haven, 2007), 192–3.

[104] Hogarth, 'Reluctant Patients', 73.

[105] Gilbert, 'Popular Beliefs and the Body', 144.

from their bared forearms'.[106] Indeed, perhaps the most potent symbol of working men's labour was the muscular forearm. It was central to the depictions of industrial workers from Joseph Wright's iron-forge workers, to Hicks's agricultural worker, to Brown's Apollo-like navvy. Karen Harvey has focused upon the eighteenth-century elite male clothed leg as a marker of masculinity, conveying meanings of male power, strength, beauty and virility.[107] This article concludes by arguing that the labourer's forearm was equally powerful in cultural meaning, and was extensively deployed by a range of social classes. The raised muscular male arm, with rolled-up sleeve, holding a working tool was originally the sign of the blacksmith; a single raised muscular arm bearing a hammer was used in trade guilds' heraldry.[108] By the early nineteenth century, it became a common icon of skilled labour, adopted for use on friendly societies' and trades unions' ephemera and banners to symbolise pride in labour.[109] Arguably, it only became a more threatening image of class militancy by the twentieth century.[110]

Initially, strong and muscular arms signified generic masculinity, not class- or occupational-specific manhood. An early seventeenth-century poem *A Maid's Revenge* by James Shirley, for instance, reprinted in 1793, has the count de Monte Nigro (who was described as a braggard) ask: 'Wherefore has | Nature given me these brawny arms, this manly bulk, | And these collossian supporters nothing but to sling | The sledge, or pitch the bar, and play.'[111] It was never merely a marker of muscular male strength. The muscular male arm connoted both the capacity to smite and protect. This is demonstrated by a sermon preached following the 1755 Lisbon earthquake, which pronounced that 'He hath a Mighty Arm; strong is his Hand; and high is his right Hand.'[112] It was this mighty arm to which one supplicated, as when Roxana in 'The Rival Queens' pleaded to heaven following her broken heart and rising passions: 'What saving hand, or what a mighty arm | Can raise me sinking?'[113] The notion of the

[106] Barringer, *Men at Work*, 48.

[107] Harvey, 'Men of Parts', *passim*.

[108] Kim Munson, 'The Evolution of an Emblem: The Art & Hammer, 2010', unpublished paper. www.academia.edu/231841/Evolution_of_an_Emblem_The_Arm_and_Hammer, accessed 12 June 2015.

[109] John Gorman, *Banner Bright: An Illustrated History of Trade Union Banners* (Buckhirst Hill, 1986), 78.

[110] G. A. Williams, 'Introduction', in Gorman, *Banner Bright*, 20. For an example, see the Herculean form of a worker wrestling with the serpent of capitalism on the Dockers Union Export Branch banner, painted in the early 1890s, Gorman, *Banner Bright*, 127.

[111] James Shirley, *The Maid's Revenge. A Tragedy* (1793).

[112] Samuel Clarke, *A Sermon Preached at Daventry, December 7, 1755, On Occasion of the Late Earthquake at Lisbon* (1755).

[113] Nathaniel Lee, 'The Rival Queens; Or the Death of Alexandra the Great', in *The British Drama: Comprehending the Best Plays in the English Language, Tragedies* (1804), 173.

protective male arm was also deeply reassuring. Elizabeth Lichtenstein Johnson, for example, recorded her thirteen-year-old daughter's verses that she had written when fearful during a tumultuous sea passage in 1801:

> Oh why am I so much afraid,
> Why does each wave alarm,
> Does not the Lord protect me still
> And guard me by his arm?[114]

From political to popular culture, the nation offered its symbolic muscular arm to defend its subjects. Thomas Quayle, for example, declared that Jersey enjoyed a 'beneficent government; protecting them with a mighty arm, from the ravage, and the insult of the surrounding foe' in his review of agriculture in 1815.[115] Thus, archetypal men might stand in for and defend the nation through their mighty arms. For example, in the popular poem 'The Sailor's Tear', the sailor raises his arm in all three stanzas – in the first two to wipe away a tear as he leaves his loving family, but in the final verse his arm is raised to slay the enemy:

> Ere long o'er ocean's blue expanse,
> His sturdy bark had sped;
> The gallant Sailor from her prow,
> Descried a Sail a-head;
> And then he rais'd his mighty arm,
> For Britain's foes were near,
> Ay then he raised his arm, but not
> To wipe away a tear.[116]

Of course, the viewer was also meant to admire the sinewy muscular forearms of Hicks's and Brown's working men, because they were symbolic of the manly sinews of patriotism and national strength, as well as the steely, hardened fortitude of skilled labour. Indeed, the workers' powerful forearm became a marker of Britain's industrial power. Historians of art, and scholars of friendly societies and trades unions' iconography, for example, suggest that the heroic style of representing the working man from the 1850s was part of a 'new recognition of the

---

[114] *Recollections of a Georgia Loyalist by Elizabeth Lichtenstein Johnston, Written in 1836*, ed. Rev. Arthur Wentworth Eaton (New York, 1901), 101. For similar references to strong paternal arms, see Joanne Bailey (Begiato), *Parenting in England: Emotions, Identities and Generation* (Oxford, 2012), 118–21.

[115] Thomas Quayle, *General View of the Agriculture and Present State of the Islands on the Coast of Normandy Subject to the Crown of Great Britain* (1815), 213.

[116] *Sailor's Tear*, Bodley Ballads, Bodleian Library, Frame 19918. Also see sheet music, Victoria & Albert Collection, S.356–2012, *c.* nineteenth century, https://jscholarship.library. jhu.edu/handle/1774.2/20159, accessed 15 June 2015.

times that the wealth of the nation rested on its industrial output, and the skills of its working men'.[117] The muscular arm, if first associated with particular trades according to which tools it held, became a political symbol of an entire working class late in the nineteenth century.[118]

There were numerous tensions at the centre of this image of working men's strength and identity. Barringer points out that 'Industrial work is portrayed as a celebration of the male body, well-nourished and in good health, rather than as a process that disfigures and ultimately destroys it.'[119] Yet, in some ways, this was recognised, and the concept of the heroic worker was used to ameliorate it. Jamie Bronstein shows how newspapers celebrated working-class men for performing acts of heroism following industrial disasters, casting their actions in terms of self-sacrifice and wartime heroism.[120] During the 1862 Harley Colliery disaster, the *Newcastle Chronicle* described resting rescuers: 'While the ruddy glare of the fire was cast over their broad, manly features and well-moulded forms, they seemed to be the living embodiment of all those attributes of courage and strength which . . . [distinguish] the inhabitants of the British Isles.'[121] If this smacks of glossing over the exploited male labouring body, it is worth remembering that working-class men deployed the narrative themselves for their own ends.[122]

As this hints, this imagined male body had collective social agency for working-class men too. There is evidence from the turn of the eighteenth century that members of the working classes deployed and politicised images such as the handsome, working man resting at his cottage door to demonstrate that labouring men had the independence and respectability to possess a political voice. As much as in his masculine status, this was measured through his manly, temperate body, and physical strength.[123] It was central to the attempts to improve working-class men's bodies through the means of self-help. As the literary scholar Michael Budd comments, the second half of the nineteenth century saw 'the development of a new notion of the embodied self – one emphasizing the possibility of improving the body and character'. He points out that Samuel Smiles promoted this in his 'self-help' regime, which saw mutual connections between

[117] Ravenhill-Johnson, *Art and Ideology*, 28, 38.

[118] Munson, 'Evolution of an Emblem', 9.

[119] Barringer, *Men at Work*, 166–7.

[120] Jamie L. Bronstein, *Caught in the Machinery: Workplace Accidents and Inured Workers in Nineteenth-Century Britain* (Stanford, 2007), 73–7. For the language of military heroism, see Michael Brown, '"Like a Devoted Army": Medicine, Heroic Masculinity, and the Military Paradigm in Victorian Britain', *Journal of British Studies*, 49 (2010), 592–622.

[121] Cited in Bronstein, *Caught in the Machinery*, 75.

[122] *Ibid.*, 74.

[123] Matthew McCormack, 'Married Men and the Fathers of Families: Fatherhood and Franchise Reform in Britain', in *Gender and Fatherhood in the Nineteenth Century*, ed. Trev-Lynn Broughton and Helen Rogers (New York, 2007).

physical steadfastness, bodily health and self-reliance.[124] Whether this was a means of social control is open to debate, but working men certainly used these notions of bodily fitness as a way to improve social status. The physical culture regimens commercialised by 'fitness entrepreneurs' like Eugen Sandow to working-class men with disposable income also thus 'offered lower-class men a body-centred form of self-discipline and respectability'.[125]

Accordingly, there is substantial evidence that working men took up the visual iconography of muscular arms as part of their formulations of self- and class-identity. Harvey observes that industrialisation focused more attention on men as workers and upon their occupations, leading to an identification of working men as both producers and workers. She argues therefore that the iconography of men's tools on ceramic objects and in visual culture helped articulate a collective identity of craftsmen in the first part of the nineteenth century.[126] Muscular arms exposed by rolled-up sleeves ready for labour and grasping tools were the most potent symbol of approved 'heroic' men's labour. Alongside others such as the handshake, symbol of unity and concord, they became central to the iconography of working-class friendly societies, trades unions and political movements like Chartism.[127] Heroic, working men stood at the heart of their bannerettes, banners and certificates; large, noble and elevated, rolled up shirt sleeves showing muscular forearms to present physical strength and health, and occupational identity through the tools they hold.[128] The illustrations of emblems collected in Ravenhill-Johnson's study offers numerous pieces of evidence spanning the century from the 1820s to 1920s.[129] James Sharples's emblem of the Amalgamated Society of Engineers (1851) is an excellent example, featuring two dignified working men, a blacksmith and an engineer, posed in the heroic model of history painting; both have sleeves rolled up.[130]

Crucially, these visual representations of working-class identity and objectives were designed and created by working-class people. The artists were working-class and shared similar artistic conventions of male physiques to their elite counterparts. Often trained in art schools, they too had begun training by copying from antique sculpture, and Old Masters; even lesser artists trained at night school would copy from art primers, pattern books and engravings.[131] The industrial blacksmith

[124] Budd, *Sculpture Machine*, 20–1.
[125] Hau, 'The Normal, the Ideal', 159; Kestner, *Masculinities in Victorian Painting*, 54.
[126] Harvey, 'Craftsmen in Common', 69, 75–8.
[127] Ravenhill-Johnson, *Art and Ideology*, 31.
[128] *Ibid.*, 107.
[129] *Ibid.*, plates 1–90.
[130] Barringer, *Men at Work*, 173–5; Ravenhill-Johnson , *Art and Ideology*, 28.
[131] Ravenhill-Johnson, *Art and Ideology*, 35, 38, 40.

James Sharples, for instance, 'appropriated the vocabulary of high art in order to fashion a corpus of visual self-representation'.[132] He also constructed his public persona in such terms. Samuel Smiles added him to the celebrated lives in the second edition of *Self-Help*, published in 1860. In addition, Smiles requested his photograph to add to his collection of notable self-made men. In the resulting studio portrait, Sharples posed as blacksmith not artist, sleeves rolled up to bare his working man's forearms, holding his hammer.[133] As Ravenhill-Johnson's study of the art and ideology of the trade union emblem demonstrates, their working-class commissioners and creators appropriated Greek and Roman culture to represent their union members.[134] Perhaps a particularly telling example is on the Certificate of the Friendly Society of Iron Founders of England, Ireland and Wales, 1857, by John James Chant. It shows a typical architectural cutaway with working scenes at the bottom, and two ennobled working men at the top, rolled-up sleeves, holding their tools of trade. However, at the centre is a miner hewing an enormous coal face. He is positively Herculean, bare-chested and heavily muscular.[135] Here were both the poised and powerful male bodies.

What is also striking about such emblems is that they were not restricted to banners which were publicly paraded, but were also part of the domestic environment Certificates and emblems were meant to be displayed at home. Others had particularly domestic uses and connotations. A touching example is the emblem of the Friendly Association of Cotton Spinners, a Glasgow society, formed in 1806, and printed on a japanned tin tray in *c.* 1825.[136] The image was a copy of the Association's bannerette. In front of the power spinning machine stands a male worker extending his hand to a female child worker; his sleeves are rolled up above his elbows, he is neatly attired in a waistcoat otherwise. This demonstrated his paternal benevolence and his respectable status as much as his trade, which is represented by the spinning machinery rather than a handheld tool. The Carlisle branch of the Glasgow Association used the same image in its banner, probably around a similar date. The domestic nature of the banner, however, is particularly vivid, since the banner takes the form of a patchwork quilt, with the emblem reproduced in embroidery on an apron at its centre, surrounded by pieced cotton patches. The apron was apparently worn by a local cotton spinner when celebrating the passing of the 1832 Reform Act in a procession

---

[132] Barringer, *Men at Work*, 139.

[133] *Ibid.*, 149–50.

[134] Ravenhill-Johnson, *Art and Ideology*, 2.

[135] *Ibid.*, plate 21. For colour version of engraving, see www.unionhistory.info/Display. php?irn=7000001&QueryPage=AdvSearch.php.

[136] Glasgow Museum, accession no. A.1938.11.du, http://collections.glasgowmuseums. com/starobject.html?oid=139177. Also discussed in Gorman, *Banner Bright*, 70.

through Carlisle.[137] This is a reminder of the ways in which working-class masculinities were formulated in the home as much as the workplace or leisure venue.

There is also evidence of the links between the earlier sturdy heroic labouring man and his later counterparts. J. Havelock Wilson, who founded the Sailors' and Firemen's Union in 1887, recorded in his autobiography that union banners often portrayed national figures of importance to the working-class movement. He recalled frequently seeing his own portrait on the various banners of the seamen's union in all kinds of 'picturesque positions'. One that he specially noted was his portrayal as the '"heroic sailor" Jack Crawford, the hero of the naval battle of Camperdown'. This Sunderland-born sailor became a northern hero thanks to his actions in 1797 in nailing the fleet's colours back onto the mast, and was portrayed on ceramics, and prints through the century.[138] This hints at a long lineage of working-class heroism, rooted in male bodily strength and evolving from a primarily gender to class identity.

Conclusion

Manliness was not cerebral and bloodless, but was carried within and conveyed through men's bodies whose parts, poise and power were encoded with gendered values and qualities. An embodied approach therefore opens up male corporeality to be read as a site for cultural meaning and social practice. This paper demonstrates that manly bodies were reified as symbols, progenitors and defenders of gender, society and nation. These bodies therefore needed to be manipulated and made-over to improve men and their masculine qualities at an individual and collective level and across social classes. Influenced in form by classical aesthetics, depictions of men's bodily styles spanned a spectrum of poise and power, deployed in either or both forms to embody cultural, social, political, economic and military success. Initially, this was a set of codes originating within and circulated among elite groups. However, men who did not use their bodies to earn a living came to emulate the appearance and exercise regimes of muscular men's bodies trained through sport or work. Moreover, the allure of poised and powerful male bodies extended beyond the upper ranks. From the later eighteenth century, working-class men also adapted bodily symbols of muscularity, strength and skill to construct their own masculine, occupational and class identities.

---

[137] Tullie House Museum & Art Gallery, Carlisle http://www.tulliehouse.co.uk/thecollection/cotton-spinners-banner-victorian

[138] Gorman, *Banner Bright*, 113.

Transactions of the RHS 26 (2016), pp. 149–173 © Royal Historical Society 2016
doi:10.1017/S0080440116000098

LAST RESORT OR KEY RESOURCE? WOMEN WORKERS FROM THE NAZI-OCCUPIED SOVIET TERRITORIES, THE REICH LABOUR ADMINISTRATION AND THE GERMAN WAR EFFORT

By Elizabeth Harvey

READ 25 SEPTEMBER 2015

ABSTRACT. Foreign labour was an essential resource for the Nazi war economy: by September 1944, around six million civilian labourers from across Europe were working in the Reich. Any initial readiness on the part of the peoples of Nazi-occupied Europe to volunteer for work in the Reich had quickly dissipated as the harsh and often vicious treatment of foreign workers became known. The abuse and exploitation of foreign forced labourers by the Nazi regime is well documented. Less well understood is why women formed such a substantial proportion of the labour recruited or forcibly deported from occupied eastern Europe: in September 1944, a third of Polish forced labourers and just over over half of Soviet civilian forced labourers were women. This article explores the factors influencing the demand for and the supply of female labour from the Nazi-occupied territories of the Soviet Union, particularly after the appointment of Fritz Sauckel as Plenipotentiary for Labour in March 1942. It explores the attitudes of labour officials towards these women workers and shows how Nazi gender politics and the Nazi hierarchy of race intersected in the way they were treated.

On 16 March 1943, an official in the labour administration in Nazi-occupied eastern Ukraine sent out orders to the local labour recruitment teams. In order to meet the targets of the latest crash programme to deport Soviet civilians as labourers to the Reich, each local district under military administration was with immediate effect to 'recruit' and dispatch to the Reich 500 workers per week, 'primarily women' ('in erster Linie Frauen').[1] Why, one might wonder, would the recruitment teams have been told to recruit 'primarily women'?

The coercive and violent recruitment of labour in occupied Ukraine was one strand in the vast history of forced labour under Nazi rule,

---

[1] Wirtschaftsinspektion Mitte, Chefgruppe Arbeit (an Verteiler), betr. Anwerbung von Ostarbeitern für das Reich, 16 Mar. 1943, Bundesarchiv (BA) Berlin, R3901, 20273.

involving not just mass deportations of prisoners of war and civilians to work in Germany and other countries under Nazi rule, but also forms of forced labour within the occupied countries themselves.[2] To talk of forced labour entails definition, as Mark Spoerer and others have discussed: there were gradations of forced labour, and in wartime Nazi Germany, with its highly regulated labour regime applying also to German men and women, it would be inaccurate to talk of German workers being free of coercion.[3] But for the purposes of the following discussion of foreign forced labour working in the Reich, it is helpful to refer to the criteria outlined by Spoerer that a forced labourer is *unable to terminate their employment of their own accord* and has *little or no control over their conditions of living and working.*[4]

On the basis of that definition, forced labour in Nazi Germany was predominantly foreign: labour was a fruit of conquest. Spoerer estimates the accumulated total of foreign workers (civilians and POWs) deployed in the Reich over the course of the Second World War at around 12 million, of whom 80–90 per cent could be regarded – according to his definition – as forced labourers.[5] Statistics for September 1944 showed 5.97 million foreign civilians working in the Greater German Reich, who at that point constituted 26 per cent of the Reich's (civilian) labour force.[6] Forced labour comprised not only foreign civilian deportees plus prisoners of war (the latter totalling 2.19 million at the start of 1945), but also concentration camp prisoners (including foreign Jews brought to the Reich) and German Jews deployed as forced labourers: including them brings the cumulative total of forced labourers in the Reich during the war to an estimated 13.5 million. A further calculation would bring in additional estimates of forced labour undertaken within the occupied countries under Nazi rule.[7] In the Reich, the atrocious treatment of workers from eastern Europe

---

[2] Pioneering studies include Edward Homze, *Foreign Labor in Nazi Germany* (Princeton, 1967); Ulrich Herbert, *Fremdarbeiter: Politik und Praxis des 'Ausländer-Einsatzes' in der Kriegswirtschaft des Dritten Reiches* (Berlin and Bonn, 1985); *Europa und der 'Reichseinsatz': Ausländische Zivilarbeiter, Kriegsgefangene und KZ-Häftlinge in Deutschland 1938–1945*, ed. Ulrich Herbert (Essen, 1991).

[3] Mark Spoerer, *Zwangsarbeit unter dem Hakenkreuz: Ausländische Zivilarbeiter, Kriegsgefangene und Häftlinge im Deutschen Reich und im besetzten Europa 1939–1945* (Stuttgart and Munich, 2001), 10–19; Mark Spoerer and Jochen Fleischhacker, 'Forced Laborers in Nazi Germany: Categories, Numbers, and Survivors', *Journal of Interdisciplinary History*, 33 (2002), 169–204, here 173–6; Marc Buggeln, 'Unfreie Arbeit im Nationalsozialismus: Begrifflichkeiten und Vergleichsaspekte zu den Arbeitsbedingungen im Deutschen Reich und in den besetzten Gebieten', in *Arbeit im Nationalsozialismus*, ed. Marc Buggeln and Michael Wildt (Munich, 2014), 231–52.

[4] Spoerer, *Zwangsarbeit*, 15.

[5] *Ibid.*, 221.

[6] *Ibid.*, 9, 222.

[7] Buggeln, 'Unfreie Arbeit', 243–51.

was notorious: among civilian forced labourers from the occupied Soviet territories, Spoerer suggests that around 170,000 died.[8]

If historical research on forced labour was relatively sparse in the 1960s and 1970s, since Ulrich Herbert's landmark study in 1985 a huge literature has developed, some studies exploring the role of regime agencies and individual companies employing forced labourers, others tracing how forced labourers were part of local economies.[9] Crucially, this work has increasingly drawn on the testimonies of former forced labourers, many of whom – as Johannes-Dieter Steinert has shown – were dragged to Germany as children and adolescents.[10] Most recently, studies have extended their focus to the labour administration in the occupied territories, asking both about deportations to the Reich and the ways in which people were made to 'work for Germany' in their own countries.[11]

The majority of foreign labourers working in the Reich were male. Women, however, constituted a rising proportion of the total foreign labour force in the course of the war, and these growing contingents were recruited above all from eastern Europe. While foreign women came from across occupied Europe, it was already clear in 1941, before the arrival of civilian workers from the occupied Soviet territories, that the bulk of women workers coming into Germany were from Poland and that the proportion of women among the total of Polish workers in the Reich was higher than among the contingents from other countries.[12] The arrival of civilian labour recruits/deportees from the occupied Soviet territories brought a further upswing in the proportion of foreign workers who were female: already by early summer 1942, it was evident that women were constituting around half of the transports. In September 1944, of the 5.97 million civilian foreign workers deployed in the Reich, one third were

[8] Spoerer, *Zwangsarbeit*, 228.

[9] Recent collections include *Arbeitskräfte als Kriegsbeute: Der Fall Ost- und Südosteuropa 1939–1945*, ed. Karsten Linne and Florian Dierl (Berlin, 2011); *Rüstung, Kriegswirtschaft und Zwangsarbeit im 'Dritten Reich'*, ed. Andreas Heusler, Helmuth Trischler and Mark Spoerer (Munich, 2010); *Zwangsarbeit in Hitlers Europa: Besatzung, Arbeit, Folgen*, ed. Dieter Pohl and Tanja Sebta (Berlin, 2013), and (with a wider comparative dimension) *Zwangsarbeit als Kriegsressource in Europa und Asien*, ed. Kerstin von Lingen and Klaus Gestwa (Paderborn, 2014).

[10] *Hitler's Slaves: Life Stories of Forced Labourers in Nazi-Occupied Europe*, ed. Alexander von Plato, Almut Leh and Christoph Thonfeld (New York and Oxford, 2010); Johannes-Dieter Steinert, *Deportation und Zwangsarbeit. Polnische und sowjetische Kinder im nationalsozialistischen Deutschland und im besetzten Osteuropa 1939–1945* (Essen, 2013).

[11] Karsten Linne, Florian Dierl and Zoran Janjetović, *Pflicht, Zwang und Gewalt: Arbeitsverwaltungen und Arbeitskräftepolitik im deutsch besetzten Polen und Serbien 1939–1944* (Essen, 2013); Tanja Penter, *Kohle für Stalin und Hitler: Arbeiten und Leben im Donbass 1939 bis 1953* (Essen, 2010).

[12] *Der Arbeitseinsatz im Deutschen Reich*, 21 (1941), 5 Nov. 1941, 19.

women.[13] Just over half of all civilian forced labourers from the occupied Soviet territories and a third of the forced labourers from occupied Poland were female, and Polish and Soviet women conversely formed the biggest contingents among foreign female workers. Of the 1,990,367 foreign women working in the Reich in September 1944, 586,091 were from Poland and 1,112,137 were 'Ostarbeiterinnen', the term used by the National Socialist regime for the women brought as labourers to the Reich from the occupied territories of the Soviet Union.[14] Such figures contrast with the lower absolute numbers and the lower proportion of women workers among the labour recruited from occupied western Europe: for instance in September 1944, 29,379 Belgian women and 42,654 French women were working in the Reich, constituting 14.6 per cent of Belgian workers and 6.6 per cent of French workers respectively.[15]

Gender has rarely been in the forefront of the concerns of historians writing about forced labour.[16] Many studies have masked or downplayed the issue. However, references are to be found in the literature to the gender composition of the labour deportees, and one obvious starting point for thinking about patterns in the recruitment and exploitation of female forced foreign labourers is the correlation pointed out by Ulrich Herbert thirty years ago between the proportion of foreign labourers of a particular nationality that were women and the position of that nationality in the Nazi racial hierarchy. The lower the status in that hierarchy, the higher the proportion of women among those recruited.[17] The significance of this correlation, though, demands to be explored further: how self-evident was it that the Nazi labour administration would recruit more women of a 'lower' racial category (Poles, Ukrainians, Belorussians) for work in the Reich than women from the occupied countries of western Europe?

One set of insights into the recruitment of female forced labourers from the Soviet Union derives from studies of labour mobilization policies within the Reich. These policies were shaped by assumptions about priorities in the war economy, about how far prisoners of war and foreign civilians should be brought in to fill gaps, and – at a time when the regime was eliminating the Jews from wartime German society – how incoming 'alien' workers were to be strictly segregated

---

[13] *Der Arbeitseinsatz im Großdeutschen Reich*, 11/12 (1944), 30 Dec. 1944, 11.

[14] Herbert, *Fremdarbeiter*, 272.

[15] *Ibid.*; *Der Arbeitseinsatz im Großdeutschen Reich*, 11/12 (1944), 30 Dec. 1944, 11.

[16] Important exceptions include Gabriella Hauch, 'Zwangsarbeiterinnen und ihre Kinder: Zum Geschlecht der Zwangsarbeit', in *NS-Zwangsarbeit: Der Standort Linz der 'Reichswerke Hermann Göring AG Berlin', 1938–1945*, ed. Oliver Rathkolb, I (Linz, 2001), 355–448; Tamara Frankenberger, *Wir waren wie Vieh: Lebensgeschichtliche Erinnerungen ehemaliger sowjetischer Zwangsarbeiterinnen* (Münster, 1997).

[17] Herbert, *Fremdarbeiter*, 271.

from Germans. Along with the overall dynamic of evolving policy on foreign labour there were changing perceptions of what foreign women, and particularly eastern European women, were good for. Initially, these focused largely if not exclusively on the deployment of Polish women into agricultural and domestic work, but from mid-1942 onwards the incoming 'Ostarbeiterinnen' became seen increasingly in terms of their potential to fill jobs in industry, particularly in armaments-related production. Here, historians have traced how the drive to deploy foreigners, and specifically foreign women, was linked to the difficulty of getting more German women to work in industry above and beyond those already bound, increasingly long term, into industrial work.[18] As these studies have shown, the mass influx of foreign women into semi-skilled and unskilled production-line jobs and their deployment in heavier and more hazardous work relieved some of the pressure on the labour administration to squeeze more under wartime conditions out of German women already working in industry, and to propel additional German women into industrial jobs.[19] However, there is still scope for further probing of the question whether 'Ostarbeiterinnen' were seen by employers and the labour administration as a preferred resource (compared to male 'Ostarbeiter' and/or German women) or simply as a last resort.[20] It is also not clear from studies hitherto whether labour officials thought there were *any* limits on what even women workers deemed to be 'racially inferior' could be expected to do.

Regional studies of German occupation policy shed further light on the reason for the large numbers of women recruited for work in the Reich from the occupied Soviet territories by teasing out the 'push' factors in different regions of Ukraine and Belorussia. The conditions within which deportations took place were shaped by Soviet military conscription and evacuation measures, unemployment, food shortages, economic dislocation and population displacement following German occupation, and subsequently the spread of partisan resistance.[21] German

---

[18] Homze, *Foreign Labor*, 10; Rüdiger Hachtmann, 'Industriearbeiterinnen in der deutschen Kriegswirtschaft 1936 bis 1944/45', *Geschichte und Gesellschaft*, 19 (1993), 332–66.

[19] Hachtmann, 'Industriearbeiterinnen', 348, 350.

[20] See Herbert, *Fremdarbeiter*, 207, on contemporary perceptions of the work performance of 'Ostarbeiterinnen' compared to German women.

[21] Christian Gerlach, *Kalkulierte Morde: Die deutsche Wirtschafts- und Vernichtungspolitik in Weißrußland 1941 bis 1944* (Hamburg, 1999), esp. 449–93; Babette Quinkert, *Propaganda und Terror in Weißrussland 1941–1944: Die deutsche 'geistige' Kriegführung gegen Zivilbevölkerung und Partisanen* (Paderborn, 2009), 257–73; Penter, *Kohle für Stalin und Hitler*, 179–291; Herwig Baum, 'Für die Stadt Kiew wird eine "Fangaktion" vorbereitet . . .: Akteure und Praxis der Zwangsarbeiterrekrutierungen in der Ukraine während des Zweiten Weltkrieges', in *Arbeitskräfte als Kriegsbeute*, ed. Linne and Dierl, 270–302; Dieter Pohl, *Die Herrschaft der Wehrmacht: Deutsche Militärbesatzung und einheimische Bevölkerung in der Sowjetunion 1941–1944* (Munich, 2008), 305–19.

responses to these conditions and the occupiers' assumptions about the existence and scope of 'surplus' or 'unwanted' population in the occupied territories helped determine the scale and composition of the transports to Germany from early 1942 onwards. Women, particularly young women, were a prominent element in the pool of potential labour and subjected along with their fellow-countrymen to inducements, propaganda and direct coercion from the recruiting commissions combing the occupied Soviet territories from the end of 1941. Yet it is still worth asking how far the proportion of women who ended up in labour transports to the Reich was a matter of accident or design.

The 'pull' and 'push' factors at work in the recruitment of 'Ostarbeiterinnen' highlight what may appear as a straightforward logic of substitution that governed Nazi wartime efforts to keep the economy in the Reich and in the occupied territories supplied with labour. At the same time, the insights of gender historians alert us to the singular paradoxes at work in the racist Nazi 'rationality' that constructed Soviet women workers as endlessly flexible and interchangeable 'hands'. These paradoxes may help illuminate further the correlation between the imagined hierarchy of race and the recruitment of female labour. In the 1980s, Gisela Bock showed how theories based on both 'racial hygiene' and racial anthropology attenuated the polarity of the sexes in their construction of 'inferior' human types or racial groupings.[22] She argued that this assumption – that 'inferior races' lacked the polarity of the sexes characteristic of the 'superior' peoples – was at work in the regime's treatment of foreign women workers. Along with Polish women, Soviet women were constructed as the 'other' of German womanhood within the wartime workforce, with Jewish women and Sinti and Roma women being regarded as lower still in the Nazi hierarchy of race. However, such constructions were bizarrely inconsistent: stereotypes of Soviet women could conjure up both the 'asexual phantasm' of an endlessly exploitable 'work hand' and fixate with racist obsessiveness on their supposed hyperfecundity.[23]

The attention paid by historians of gender to the question of women's bodies and their reproductive as well as productive capacity has also

---

[22] Gisela Bock, *Zwangssterilisation im Nationalsozialismus: Studien zur Rassenpolitik und Frauenpolitik* (Opladen, 1986), 135–7. On this idea of a racist 'attenuation' of sexual polarity, see also Gabriella Hauch, 'Die Institutionalisierung der NS-Bevölkerungs- und Sexualpolitik gegen Ostarbeiterinnen und Polinnen: "Modell Oberdonau"?', in *Frauen im Reichsgau Oberdonau: Geschlechtsspezifische Bruchlinien im Nationalsozialismus*, ed. Gabriella Hauch (Linz, 2006), 215–26, here 216–17, and Frankenberger, *Wir waren wie Vieh*, 44–5.

[23] Hauch uses the term 'asexuelle Phantasmen': 'Institutionalisierung', 217. For examples of German stereotypes of Slavic women's alleged hyperfecundity, see Bock, *Zwangssterilisation*, 440–1.

informed research on Nazi policies on race, sexuality and population: this in turn opens further perspectives on the deportation of Soviet (and Polish) women to work in the Reich. In one view, forced labour and mass labour deportations also served to attack the 'biopower' of eastern European peoples.[24] This was a vision expressed at its racist and misogynist extreme by the racial expert Erhard Wetzel in his notorious commentary on 'General Plan East' (*Generalplan Ost*) with its fantasies of mass anti-natalist campaigns in a future occupied Russia.[25] From another angle, the importation of 'Slavic' women alongside men has been interpreted as the effort to create a sexual 'buffer': their presence was, it has been suggested, part of a deliberate strategy to curb sexual contact between German women and the foreign men who were constructed as a threat to the German national body.[26]

Soviet women may thus have appeared to recruiters as an accessible and interchangeable mass of 'pure labour' destined for whatever menial tasks they were set and subject, like their menfolk, to uninhibited force; they may also have been sought as *female* labour for specific sorts of 'women's work'. Women may have figured as an 'unproductive' surplus in the occupied territories, or as a 'biological threat', to be displaced as part of population and spatial restructuring and on that basis destined for potential dispatch to the Reich; they may even have been regarded as a 'sexual buffer' protecting German women from the attentions of eastern European men. This article takes these hypotheses as a starting point for asking how far those in charge of labour deployment and other labour officials explicitly reflected on or expressed their perceptions and motives for recruiting Soviet women for labour in the Reich. It is beyond the scope of this paper to sum up the thinking on these questions on the part of all the agencies involved in the German civilian and military apparatus of occupation and the authorities concerned with the labour question within the Reich. Instead, the following discussion considers examples from official decrees, publications and internal correspondence in order to offer some pointers to the thinking of labour officials about the recruitment and deployment of women from the occupied Soviet territories in the Reich as 'Ostarbeiterinnen'.

---

[24] On labour and labour deportations in the context of anti-natalist measures against eastern European populations: Bock, *Zwangssterilisation*, 445; Homze, *Foreign Labor*, 29–30; Frankenberger, *Wir waren wie Vieh*, 20–1.

[25] Erhard Wetzel, Stellungnahme und Gedanken zum Generalplan Ost des Reichsführers SS, 27 Apr. 1942, in *Vom Generalplan Ost zum Generalsiedlungsplan*, ed. Czesław Madajczyk (Munich, 1994), 50–81, here 73–5; see also Bock, *Zwangssterilisation*, 440–2.

[26] For the suggestion that this was a factor in the recruitment of eastern European women for work in the Reich, see Gisela Schwarze, *Kinder, die nicht zählten: Ostarbeiterinnen und ihre Kinder im Zweiten Weltkrieg* (Essen, 1997), 98; Frankenberger, *Wir waren wie Vieh*, 24.

Questions of supply and demand

In January 1941, Friedrich Syrup, a senior civil servant in the Reich Ministry of Labour, articulated his vision of a multi-national labour pool marshalled and mobilised across the expanding economic space under Nazi domination in such a way that 'reserves' would be tapped and 'surpluses' shifted to areas of demand: the imagery was of flows and streams resulting in supranational cooperation to the benefit of all.[27] Syrup's expansive rhetoric masked both the measures increasingly used to stop western European workers in the Reich terminating their contracts in order to go home,[28] and the by now established practices developed by the German labour offices in Poland of coercion and violence in the recruitment of labour for the Reich. It also passed over the ways in which racial/ethnic restructuring in Poland was implicated in the creation of 'surpluses' of potential labour, and the involvement of the labour administration in these displacements and selections.[29] The recruitment policy in Poland had by the autumn of 1941 brought more than a million Poles to the Reich, just over a quarter of them women, and subjected them to draconian and stigmatising special decrees.[30] The precedent for forcing civilian women alongside men onto labour transports to the Reich was thus in place when German troops invaded the Soviet Union. However, the mass deportation to the Reich of female alongside male civilian labour from the occupied territories of the Soviet Union was not an immediate imperative at the outset of occupation and emerged piecemeal in the winter of 1941/2. The rounding-up of women was part of the wider picture of the quest for any and all 'hands' and reflected perceptions of where a 'surplus' of labour existed, but it also came to include the specific targeting of women as women.

Expecting a quick victory, the regime leadership assumed in the summer of 1941 – despite predictions to the contrary from labour experts in the field as well as in the Reich – that transporting forced labourers from

---

[27] Friedrich Syrup, 'Probleme des Arbeitseinsatzes im europäischen Großraum', *Der Vierjahresplan*, 5, 1–3 (Jan. 1941), 20–1.

[28] Spoerer, *Zwangsarbeit*, 97.

[29] On the involvement of the labour administration in the expulsion and displacement of Poles in the annexed territories and in the General Government, see Karsten Linne, 'Volkstumspolitik und Arbeiterrekrutierung im Reichsgau Wartheland', in *Arbeitskräfte als Kriegsbeute*, ed. Linne and Dierl, 107–38, idem, 'Die deutsche Arbeitsverwaltung zwischen "Volkstumspolitik" und Arbeiterrekrutierung – das Beispiel Warthegau', and idem, '"Sklavenjagden" im Arbeiterreservoir – das Beispiel Generalgouvernement', in Linne, Dierl and Janetović, *Pflicht, Zwang und Gewalt*.

[30] Linne, 'Die deutsche Arbeitsverwaltung'; idem, '"Sklavenjagden" im Arbeiterreservoir'; *Der Arbeitseinsatz im Deutschen Reich*, 21 (1941), 5 Nov. 1941, 19; Diemut Majer, *'Fremdvölkische' im Dritten Reich* (Boppard, 1981), 304–14.

the newly occupied Soviet territories to the Reich would be superfluous.[31] The focus instead was on seizing agricultural produce, in the process depriving the local population to the point of famine and flight from the cities, and forcing the population to work in situ for the Germans.[32] To secure and control this local labour, a network of labour offices was quickly set up both in the areas under civilian administration (Reich Commissariat Ostland and Reich Commissariat Ukraine), and in the areas nearer the front line that remained under military administration.[33] In a succession of decrees from August 1941 onwards, a labour obligation was imposed on both sexes: this initially covered Jews aged 14–60 and non-Jews aged 18–45: the age range for non-Jews was subsequently extended.[34] With the mass murder of Soviet Jews already under way, the Nazi occupiers saw forced labour for Jews as a short-term interlude before these workers, too, would be murdered and replaced as workers by non-Jews.[35] In the first phase of occupation, Jews and non-Jews, the latter including women with children and the elderly, were drafted into 'work columns' deployed on roadbuilding, infrastructure repair or snow clearance.[36]

As the Nazi assault on the Soviet Union stalled from the autumn of 1941 onwards, more and more German men had to be called up to replace the men lost on the Eastern Front, leaving ever more gaps in the war economy.[37] Soviet prisoners of war were the first to be considered as a labour supply, but by the beginning of November 1941 so many POWs were already dead or dying of starvation and murderous neglect that the decision was taken, under Goering's lead as the head of the Four Year Plan apparatus, to recruit civilians.[38] In December 1941, to speed up recruitment of Soviet civilian labour the Reich Labour Ministry dispatched recruitment teams (*Werbekommissionen*) to the occupied Soviet territories, including the former Baltic states, staffed by seconded officials from regional labour offices in the Reich. A new target of more than 600,000 recruits from the occupied Soviet territories was set on 24 February 1942: this would subsequently be raised to between 1.4 and 1.5 million after the appointment of Fritz Sauckel as Plenipotentiary for Labour (Generalbevollmächtigter für den Arbeitseinsatz or GBA)

---

[31] Gerlach, *Kalkulierte Morde*, 456–8. One exception to this was the dispatch of more than 15,000 agricultural workers from Lithuania and Belorussia to East Prussia in July and August 1941.

[32] Penter, *Kohle für Stalin und Hitler*, 186–7.

[33] Baum, "'Fangaktion'", 273–5; Penter, *Kohle für Stalin und Hitler*, 197, 207.

[34] Gerlach, *Kalkulierte Morde*, 452; Pohl, *Herrschaft der Wehrmacht*, 306.

[35] Gerlach, *Kalkulierte Morde*, 454.

[36] Pohl, *Herrschaft der Wehrmacht*, 307.

[37] Herbert, *Fremdarbeiter*, 137–43.

[38] *Ibid.*, 140–3, 148–9.

on 21 March 1942.[39] As targets grew ever more dizzying, patterns of interaction between recruiters and local populations that had been seen in Poland played out once again. Initial efforts at recruitment elicited some compliance among those who believed recruiters' promises and who sought an escape from poverty, hunger and destruction in their immediate surroundings.[40] However, reports quickly filtered back about the horrors of the journey to the Reich, about being treated like prisoners, stigmatised with the OST badge (like the Poles with their P badge), fed starvation rations with mouldy and rotten food, put up in filthy and primitive barracks, abused in the workplace and paid virtually nothing. The readiness to use force had been inherent in the process of recruitment from the start: as this news spread in the occupied territories, recruiters soon came to depend on threats and coercion.[41]

For all the parallels with the deportations of Polish labour, the significant proportion or even preponderance of women among the labour deportees from the occupied Soviet territories was a new departure. Observations by labour administrators based in the occupied eastern territories and those in Berlin, together with comments from the recruitment officials in the field, shed some light on the reasons for this. The recruiting commissions were already finding in early 1942 in their areas of recruitment in the occupied eastern territories a shortage of men: women were for several reasons a significant or predominant element among the civilian population of working age from teenagers upwards. First, the Soviet authorities had in face of the German invasion evacuated plant and skilled manpower eastwards, depleting the adult male workforce.[42] Second, men who had been called up to the Red Army had been killed or captured: among these were the estimated 2.53 million Soviet prisoners who died in captivity, many within the occupied territories.[43] Third, the Wehrmacht, Organisation Todt and the railways administration required labour on the spot in the occupied territories and were quick to snap up any skilled male workers available.[44] From late 1942, the absence of men intensified as the

[39] Ibid., 158; Quinkert, Propaganda und Terror, 259; Pohl, Herrschaft der Wehrmacht, 312.

[40] Penter, Kohle für Stalin und Hitler, 198; Gerlach, Kalkulierte Morde, 467.

[41] Quinkert, Propaganda und Terror, 258–9.

[42] Die deutsche Wirtschaftspolitik in den besetzten sowjetischen Gebieten 1941–3, ed. Rolf-Dieter Müller (Boppard, 1991), 5. Penter, Kohle für Stalin und Hitler, 189, stresses for the Donbass region the evacuation of plant but warns against overestimating the extent of the evacuation of industrial workers.

[43] On the deaths of Soviet prisoners on the territory of occupied Belorussia, see Gerlach, Kalkulierte Morde, 788–859; on the estimated total deaths of Soviet POWs, 857; on the fate of Soviet POWs in the Donbass region of Ukraine, see Penter, Kohle für Stalin und Hitler, 202–7.

[44] Pohl, Herrschaft der Wehrmacht, 308.

partisan movement gained momentum; German anti-partisan activity with the goal of seizing labour in turn escalated resistance further.[45]

From the outset, recruitment teams struggled to meet demands set by the Reich labour authorities. To take the example of the head of one such team operating in southern Ukraine in 1941/2, one can observe both his rapid resort to intimidation and violence to fill the 'transports', and the unfolding of his bureaucratic rationale that made a virtue out of necessity. This entailed 'selling' the idea of female recruits to the labour administration back home. Having arrived in Uman in southern Ukraine shortly before Christmas 1941 with the mission (as he understood it) to recruit labour for his home region of Bavaria, Graf Kajetan von Spreti reported in February 1942 that he had dispatched his first trainload of Ukrainian civilian workers for Bavaria only after having had the town governor of Uman hang two Jewish women and one Jewish man for allegedly spreading rumours about the fate of workers sent to Germany and causing panic among the deportees' parents.[46] Meanwhile, Spreti was grappling with the absence of male civilians to recruit, having established on his arrival that along with 6,000 Soviet POWs present in his area of operations there were 4,408 civilian workers registered with the local labour office (Arbeitsamt) of whom the overwhelming majority (4,100) were female. Among the women registered, he identified female agricultural workers, including milkmaids, that farms in Bavaria urgently required. Having sought confirmation from the Reich Labour Ministry in Berlin[47] and received the go-ahead from the Reichskommissariat Ukraine for the recruitment of female labour, particularly for agriculture,[48] he then sought in the following months to square his 'transports' not just with a series of upward revisions of the total target but also with a stream of contradictory orders from Bavaria:

> First of all it was only men to be sent, because it had not yet been clarified how women were to be deployed . . . then I received a telephone message from the Bavarian regional labour office on 20 February 1942 that suddenly 2,000 female workers were needed as soon as possible. I received a further message on 23 February ordering the dispatch

---

[45] *Ibid.*, 316; Baum, '"Fangaktion"', 302; for the atrocities involved in the seizure of labour deportees in the course of 'anti-partisan' operations in Belorussia, see Gerlach, *Kalkulierte Morde*, 996–1007.

[46] Reichskommission Uman an den RAM z.Hd Min. Rat Lesch [*sic*], Berlin, betr. Einsatz von Sowjetrussen, Berichterstatter Graf Spreti, 16 Feb. 1942, Staatsarchiv (StA) München, Arbeitsämter Freising, 762. On Spreti's recruitment operations, see also Elsbeth Bösl, Nicole Kramer and Stephanie Linsinger, *Die vielen Gesichter der Zwangsarbeit. 'Ausländereinsatz' im Landkreis München 1939–1945* (Munich, 2004), 40–1.

[47] Graf Spreti, Uman, an den Reichsarbeitsminister betr. Einsatz sowjetrussischer Kriegsgefangener, 24 Dec. 1941, StA München, Arbeitsämter Freising, 762.

[48] Der Reichskommissar für die Ukraine, i.v.v. Wedelstaedt, Landeshauptmann, an Reichskommissar beim Gebietskommissar / Arbeitseinsatz, Uman, 28 Dec. 1941, StA München, Arbeitsämter Freising, 762.

of 5,000 workers for the spring planting, predominantly female. Then I received the order that transports from 18 April onwards were to comprise *only* women. This was then corrected on 26 April to the effect that it was now also possible to deploy male agricultural workers. It will be evident that this sort of management makes the task here much more difficult.[49]

Spreti's correspondence with the Bavarian regional labour office also made it clear how young the recruits were: of the 900 that had by March 1942 been sent to work in Bavaria, most were aged between 16 and 20, had not previously been employed and had been taken out of schools or other institutions.[50]

In the subsequent months, it became a routine assumption among labour officials that the transports of civilian deportees from the occupied eastern territories would include substantial numbers of mainly young women: indeed, propaganda designed to combat increasingly well-informed antipathy towards the prospect of working in Germany came to address young women specifically.[51] Meanwhile, Sauckel had in his first programmatic announcement on 20 April 1942 not only signalled his overall plans for 'a gigantic new deployment' of workers of both sexes from the age of 15, but also an eye-catching programme specifically to recruit Soviet women to work in Germany. Referring to a special mission from Hitler, Sauckel announced his goal of recruiting '400,000 – 500,000 strong and healthy girls' from the occupied eastern territories to work as servants in urban and rural households in Germany.[52] This announcement was coupled with a reassurance to those German women who had not yet been drawn into the workforce that, on Hitler's orders, the supreme importance of the health of German women and mothers took precedence over any plans for conscripting women for work in war production.[53]

By late 1942, with the trawls for deportees increasingly scouring an already emptied reservoir, female labour was still presented as a relatively promising target for combing out and delivering to the Reich.[54] That said, it was soon evident, for instance, that Sauckel's push to recruit hundreds of thousands of domestic servants was unrealistic: it was reported from

[49]Werbekommission Uman, Reg. Rat. Graf Spreti, Kiew, an den GBA, Berlin, betr. Erfahrungsbericht der Werbekommission Uman, 10 July 1942, StA München, Arbeitsämter Freising, 762.

[50]Präsident Landesarbeitsamt Bayern an den Reichsarbeitsminister betr. Einsatz von russischen Zivilarbeitern, 21 Mar. 1942, StA München, Arbeitsämter Freising, 762.

[51]Quinkert, *Propaganda und Terror*, 263–4.

[52]Der Beauftragte für den Vierjahresplan/GBA, Das Programm des Arbeitseinsatzes, 20 Apr. 1942, StA München, Arbeitsämter Freising, 757.

[53]*Ibid.*

[54]Chef des Wirtschaftsstabs Ost an den Inspekteur der Wi in Kaukausus, Don/Donez, Mitte, Nord betr. Arbeitseinsatz, hier: Anwerbung von russischen Arbeitskräften für das Reich, 19 Oct. 1942, BA Berlin, R3901, 20270.

Belorussia in January 1943 that against a target of 30,000 domestic servants, by November 1942 only a few hundred had been secured.[55] By the spring of 1943, regulations regarding recruitment from the occupied Soviet territories were changed again, allowing whole families to be brought to Germany as long as half the persons in the family were aged 10 or over, and on the other hand putting in place measures to seize entire cohorts of a particular age.[56]

Meanwhile, the notion that the forced deportation of young women was a particular outrage was proving to be a rich seam for Soviet counter-propaganda.[57] This did not go unnoticed, and in March 1943 a complaint from the German army leadership reached the labour authorities claiming that the deportation and exploitation of young Russian women in the Reich and the dismal spectacle of returnees from Germany (including pregnant women and mothers with newborns transported in unheated wagons without food) was a propaganda disaster for the German authorities in the occupied east.[58] This elicited the following observation from Walter Letsch, a civil servant from the Reich Labour Ministry now seconded to Sauckel's Plenipotentiary of Labour apparatus: 'The mass recruitment and deployment of young Russian women and girls in the Reich', he noted, 'is necessary for reasons that are decisive for the outcome of the war. It is indispensable.' Moreover, he commented, 'eastern workers' were no longer for the time being brought back home from the Reich, and pregnant women were not going to be brought back in future at all. To that extent, the 'difficulties' alluded to would not recur and therefore, he concluded, 'no action is necessary'('zu veranlassen ist daher nichts').[59]

An endlessly flexible resource?

Farm work was one key destination for female forced labourers from Poland in the early stages of the war and initially for 'Ostarbeiterinnen' as well. With a long-term shortage of labour in agriculture caused by rural–urban migration now made more acute by the wartime conscription of farm labourers and farmers themselves, the trope of the 'overburdened German farmer's wife' was coupled with larger alarmist messages about

[55] Auszugsweise Abschrift aus 'Meldungen aus den besetzten Ostgebieten', Nr. 38, Arbeitereinsatzlage, 22 Jan. 1943, BA Berlin, R3901, 20271.

[56] Fernschreiben an Graf Spreti von Beauftragt. GBA, RKU Rowno, 3 Apr. 1943; Aktennotiz Graf Spreti, 8 Apr. 1943, StA München, Arbeitsämter Freising, 757.

[57] Quinkert, *Propaganda und Terror*, 264.

[58] OKH betr. Angaben sowjetischer Agenten und Kriegsgefangener zur politischen Lage in den besetzten russ. Gebieten, 6 Mar. 1943, BA Berlin, 20273.

[59] GBA, Vermerk Dr. Letsch betr. Angaben sowjetischer Agenten und Kriegsgefangener zur politischen Lage in den besetzten russ. Gebieten, 10 May 1943, BA Berlin, R3901, 20273.

the whole future of German 'blood' and 'soil'.[60] While such arguments were used to push German youngsters into harvest help and forms of 'service' on the land, after the defeat of Poland the channelling of Polish workers – who as migrant seasonal workers were long established as a source of agricultural labour on eastern German estates – on to farms in the Greater German Reich appeared to offer a less piecemeal answer.[61] Polish women sent to work in the Reich between 1939 and 1941 had been predominantly placed on farms, and when Soviet women started arriving in early 1942, they too were initially directed primarily into agriculture. A study of agricultural employment in wartime Lower Austria ('Gau Oberdonau') shows the numbers of 'Ostarbeiterinnen' employed after 1942 as agricultural workers in 'Gau Oberdonau' as being on a par with male 'eastern workers' and by May 1944 coming to equal the number of Polish women employed in agriculture there.[62] Farm work, it seems, corresponded to sexist and racist assumptions on the part of the labour administration about the place of female 'Slavs' at the bottom of the wartime labour hierarchy, but also their supposed fitness and willingness to take on long hours and hard, dirty work.[63] At the same time, the labour administration also saw female workers from eastern Europe as a particularly manoeuvrable mass: labour offices were more prone to switching them than their male compatriots from jobs in industry into short-time harvest work such as sugarbeet and potato harvesting.[64]

After 1942, the initial concentration of foreign labour in agriculture gave way to a broader deployment across economic sectors: Soviet workers, both male and female, were increasingly channelled into industrial jobs. The capacity of 'Ostarbeiterinnen' for work in industry was commented on by German observers and labour experts from a variety of perspectives. Some saw the deployment of women in Soviet industry as a factor that could now benefit the German war economy. The German Labour Front (Deutsche Arbeitsfront or DAF) issued a report in May 1943 praising women workers from the occupied Soviet territories for their levels of education and intellectual adaptability. Comparing them with German women workers, the DAF declared that 'the *Ostarbeiterin* shows a certain dexterity and capacity to adapt to factory work here', and noted that it was 'not uncommon' for women in the Soviet Union to learn a 'masculine' manual trade that equipped them with a basic

[60]Daniela Münkel, *Nationalsozialistische Agrarpolitik und Bauernalltag* (Frankfurt am Main, 1996), 392–403, 439–51; Ela Hornung, Ernst Langthaler and Sabine Schweitzer, *Zwangsarbeit in der Landwirtschaft in Niederösterreich und dem nördlichen Burgenland* (Munich, 2004), 107–14.

[61] Herbert, *Fremdarbeiter*, 67–88.

[62]Hornung, Langthaler and Schweitzer, *Zwangsarbeit*, 126–7.

[63]*Ibid.*, 121–2.

[64]*Ibid.*, 129.

technical training.[65] Sauckel himself had cruder notions, which could be read as a colonialist and racist view of robust but primitive natives, of why 'Ostarbeiterinnen' should be set to work in German industry. These stemmed not least from Sauckel's obsession with the physical condition of the women he observed on his May 1942 visit to occupied Ukraine: in the words of his report, 'Wherever one goes one is struck by the rude health (*strotzende Gesundheit*) of the women.'[66] This fixed idea underlay Sauckel's blustering insistence on the dichotomy between the 'valuable' but allegedly more fragile German woman worker and the endurance of the female 'eastern worker'. The 'health' of 'Russian women' that rendered them a potential substitute for male labour again featured in his speech at a meeting of labour administrators in Weimar in January 1943:

> As long as I can get them from you I will put Russian women to work at machines . . . Everything that lives over there in Soviet Russia is healthy. I will put these Russian women to work in their hundreds and thousands. They will work for us. They can hold out for 10 hours and can do every sort of man's work.[67]

The deployment of 'Ostarbeiterinnen' in industry in the Reich over the last three years of the war ranged from work as semi-skilled operatives to heavy unskilled labour. In the chain of substitutions and reorganisations taking place as skilled men were called up, Soviet women were both replacing men and substituting for women; however, they tended to be *compared* to German women. A study undertaken by Krupp comparing the work performance of Germans and foreigners of different nationality showed 'Ostarbeiterinnen' performing strikingly well against the comparator group of German women workers.[68] Many employers spotted this and in the light of such experiences specifically demanded more 'Ostarbeiterinnen', particularly where they could be slotted into reorganised and standardised production processes requiring semi-skilled rather than skilled workers.[69] German and Austrian women were a much less elastic reserve of labour: foreign women were both cheaper and more

---

[65] Arbeitswissenschaftliches Institut der Deutschen Arbeitsfront (ed.), Arbeitseinsatz der Ostarbeiter in Deutschland. Vorläufiger Bericht zur Untersuchung des Arbeitswissenschaftlichen Instituts über Arbeitseignung und Leistungsfähigkeit der Ostarbeiter, Berlin, Mai 1943.

[66] Bericht des Gauleiters Sauckel über seine Reise in die Sowjet-Ukraine in seiner Eigenschaft als Generalbevollmächtigter für den Arbeitseinsatz [Mai 1942], BA Berlin, R43 II, 652.

[67] Totaler Arbeitseinsatz für den Krieg. Mobilisierung der europäischen Leistungsreserven. Programmatische Rede des Generalbevollmächtigten für den Arbeitseinsatz, Gauleiter und Reichsstatthalter Fritz Sauckel auf der ersten Tagung der Arbeitseinsatzstäbe am 6. Januar 1943 in Weimar, cited in Renate Meyer-Braun, 'Die haben uns angestarrt wie im Zoo' – Frauenarbeit auf Bremer Großwerften. Vortrag, Universität Bremen, 6 Feb. 2002 (manuscript).

[68] Herbert, *Fremdarbeiter*, 207.

[69] *Ibid.*, 278–81.

flexibly deployable.[70] The protective legislation in force for German and Austrian women workers concerning working hours, which had been initially loosened at the very start of the war, but then restored, did not apply to foreign women workers.[71] Where foreign women workers were put onto semi-skilled and unskilled production-line jobs, some limited scope opened up for employers to devise part-time shifts for German women. These were seen as an incentive, particularly after the decree of 27 January 1943 compelling hitherto non-employed German women aged 17–45 to register for war work, for German women to take up and remain in industrial work and as a way of combating absenteeism.[72] Alternatively, production was reorganised so as to give 'Ostarbeiterinnen' heavier and more hazardous work, with German women shifted to lighter tasks.[73] In this way, German women workers were given an improved position in the hierarchy of the wartime workforce, with new categories defined by race and nationality extending the hierarchy downwards below them.[74]

The labour administration was engaged in many respects in a 'race to the bottom' in the way it sought to turn foreign female labour into 'pure' labour, boundlessly deployable. The new Maternity Protection Law of May 1942 and the 'housework day' introduced by the Labour Ministry in October 1943 were attempts to manage, rationalise and reconcile the multiple roles of German working women as mothers, in the household and in production.[75] These measures were simultaneously designed to differentiate the female workforce further along lines of race and nationality. Foreign women were excluded from such measures: they were denied family life and deprived of basic elements of privacy. Their bodies were exposed to scrutiny and inspection from the moment of deportation to repeated inspections in their barracks accommodation.[76] They were exposed to sexual exploitation and could be punished for

[70] Tim Kirk, *Nazism and the Working Class in Austria* (Cambridge, 1996), 81–4.

[71] Dörte Winkler, *Frauenarbeit im 'Dritten Reich'* (Hamburg, 1977), 90–1, 154–6.

[72] On the decree of 27 Jan. 1943, see *ibid.*, 134–41. Women with two children under 14 or one child below school age were exempted from the compulsion to register.

[73] Dietrich Eichholtz, *Geschichte der deutschen Kriegswirtschaft 1939–1945*, III: *1943–1945* (Berlin, 1996), 281.

[74] Tilla Siegel, 'Die doppelte Rationalisierung des "Ausländereinsatzes" bei Siemens', *Internationale Wissenschaftliche Korrespondenz zur Geschichte der deutschen Arbeiterbewegung*, 27, 1 (1991), 12–24.

[75] On the Maternity Protection Law, see Carola Sachse, *Siemens, der Nationalsozialismus und die moderne Familie: Eine Untersuchung zur sozialen Rationalisierung in Deutschland im 20. Jahrhundert* (Hamburg, 1990), 47–53; on the introduction of the 'housework day', see Carola Sachse, *Der Hausarbeitstag: Gerechtigkeit und Gleichberechtigung in Ost und West 1939–1994* (Göttingen, 2002), 35–47.

[76] Bernhild Vogel, 'Kollektive Resignation und individuelle Revolte – "Kinderlose" Mütter in den Zwangsarbeitslagern', in *Frauen gegen die Diktatur: Widerstand und Verfolgung im nationalsozialistischen Deutschland*, ed. Christl Wickert (Berlin, 1995), 172–81; Frankenberger, *Wir waren wie Vieh*, 26–7; Hauch, 'Zwangsarbeiterinnen und ihre Kinder', 369–70.

sex with Germans, even where evidence suggested this was coerced.[77] With regard to control over reproduction, eastern European women were systematically disadvantaged compared to other foreigners. Reversing the original policy of re-deporting pregnant workers from the Reich back to their homelands, a change that took place at the end of 1942, Sauckel's labour apparatus left a loophole allowing 'western' women workers to continue to travel back to their country of origin, while this was ruled out for Polish women and 'Ostarbeiterinnen'.[78] In a mercilessly anti-natalist reversal of the enhanced 'maternity protection' granted to German women workers, abortions for 'Ostarbeiterinnen' and for Poles were decriminalised: this led in practice to forced abortions.[79] If the women concerned did go ahead and give birth, they were often compelled to leave their children in crèches and 'homes' in which many died from neglect and malnutrition; meanwhile, the mothers were to return to work as soon as possible, with the concession – at least on paper – that they might be put on 'other work' such as clearing-up tasks before returning to their earlier jobs.[80]

There are indications that employers and labour officials alike adapted readily on the whole to a regime of exploiting eastern European women workers, in the process rolling back gender-based rules and safety precautions. Sent as a supply of labour to the Fürstlich-Plessische Bergwerke in Upper Silesia at the beginning of January 1943, Ukrainian women were hired out to building subcontractors involved in constructing new mine buildings,[81] while others worked alongside German women in tasks above ground. Here, the Upper Silesian mine authorities sent in March 1943 instructions to the management of individual coal mines in the region with regard to the campaign to involve more women in working in the Upper Silesian coalfields. The circular specified that coal mines must apply strict rules to the deployment of women and assign them only to jobs they were genuinely capable of. Such jobs were absolutely to exclude work at the pit bank (*Hängebank*). However, the instructions continued, 'insofar as foreign women are available, they can be assigned to

[77] Frankenberger, *Wir waren wie Vieh*, 49.

[78] Der Beauftragte für den Vierjahresplan/Der GBA, Merkblatt über gesundheitliche Maßnahmen bei Ostarbeitern, 30 Dec. 1942, StA München, Arbeitsämter Freising, 757.

[79] Gabriele Czarnowski, 'Vom "reichen Material . . . einer wissenschaftlichen Arbeitsstätte": Zum Problem missbräuchlicher medizinischer Praktiken an der Grazer Universitäts-Frauenklinik in der Zeit des Nationalsozialismus', in *NS-Wissenschaft als Vernichtungsinstrument. Rassenhygiene, Zwangssterilisation, Menschenversuche und NS-Euthanasie in der Steiermark*, ed. Wolfgang Freidl and Werner Sauer (Vienna, 2004), 225–73, esp. 239–52; Hauch, 'Zwangsarbeiterinnen und ihre Kinder', 422–4.

[80] Vogel, 'Kollektive Resignation'.

[81] Fürstengrube Kattowitz, Rundschreiben Nr. 15 betr. Ostarbeitereinsatz, 16 Feb. 1943, BA Berlin, R9363, 6.

the more difficult jobs'.[82] At the same time, underlining the way in which female labour was regarded as conveniently flexible, mine managers used 'eastern women' ('Ostfrauen') as a handy source of domestic help in their private households, deploying them out of hours cleaning windows or cleaning up after the decorator.[83]

Not all firms reacted the same way to being supplied with female workers. Some companies complained at being sent women when they had requested foreign men, and requested them to be swapped. Rebutting such complaints, the labour administration noted that there was nothing to be done about the high proportion of women and youngsters under 18 among the 'Ostarbeiter' transports: there was no prospect of swapping contingents of 'eastern workers' on the basis of age or physical capacity and it was up to the firms to reorganise production to ensure an 'optimal deployment' of the workers they had been sent.[84] When an aircraft factory complained that the 'Ostarbeiterinnen' it had been sent were not strong enough for the work, a scribbled exchange on the correspondence between the labour officials included the comment that 'The labour office in Saxony has no men to send, and anyway, the female *Ostarbeiter* are stronger than the men.'[85]

Some taboos about deploying foreign women did remain in force. Whereas Ukrainian women constituted 28.5 per cent of the workforce in the coal mines of the Donbass in German-occupied Ukraine in July 1943, working underground as well as in jobs on the surface, all women were banned from working underground in coal mines in the Reich itself.[86] This ban, declared a representative of the DAF, was based on the conviction that women could not be contemplated undertaking the 'singularly masculine' job of miners at the coalface even during wartime: this ban on working below ground applied to foreign women workers as

---

[82]Claassen, Geschäftsführung, Bezirksgruppe Steinkohlenbergbau Oberschlesien der Wirtschaftsgruppe Bergbau, an die Hauptverwaltungen der Steinkohlengruben, betr. Verstärkter Fraueneinsatz im oberschlesischen Steinkohlenbergbau, 10 Mar. 1943, BA Berlin, R9363, 2.

[83]Kassenabzugsbeleg, Fürstlich Bergwerks-AG Sekretariat, 22 Mar. 1943, BA Berlin, R9363, 6.

[84]GBA, MR Dr. Letsch, MR Dr. Petzold betr. Arbeitseinsatz von Ostarbeitern in Deutschland, an das Reichsministerium für Volksaufklärung und Propaganda, 8 Oct. 1942, BA Berlin, R3901, 20270.

[85]GBA an den Präsidenten des Landesarbeitsamtes Sachsen, Dresden, 10 Sept. 1942, BA Berlin, R3901, 20269.

[86]Penter, *Kohle für Stalin und Hitler*, 216–17; Hans-Christoph Seidel, '"Ein buntes Völkergemisch hat eine Wanderung durch unsere Gruben gemacht": Ausländereinsatz und Zwangsarbeit im Ruhrbergbau 1940–1945', in *Zwangsarbeit im Bergwerk: Der Arbeitseinsatz im Kohlenbergbau des Deutschen Reiches und der besetzten Gebiete im Ersten und Zweiten Weltkrieg*, ed. Klaus Tenfelde and Hans-Christoph Seidel (Essen, 2005), I, 75–159, here 87.

well.[87] In this case at least, the gender of the foreign women workers was regarded as decisive. Issues about the permeability or impermeability of boundaries demarcating men's and women's work where foreign women workers were concerned also arose in shipbuilding. In the Bremen shipbuilding yards, as Renate Meyer-Braun has shown, German women, mostly female relatives of the male employees, had taken on jobs in production from the start of the war. However, it was the deployment of 'Ostarbeiterinnen' as welders that opened up the question of the taboo about women working on board the ships under construction. For the local labour office and the factory inspections officer, with the prospect of eastern European women welders working alongside men in the conditions on board ship that were particularly hard to oversee, the gender of the 'Ostarbeiterinnen' suddenly appeared relevant: the women came into view as women not as workers requiring protection but as a potential moral threat, an 'immoral' presence in a hard-to-supervise work situation.[88]

In a further instance, this time in munitions production, questions of health and safety were brought into play in a discussion involving the deployment of 'Ostarbeiterinnen'. In an argument in 1942 between the regional labour office in Pomerania and the Air Ministry it was argued that 'Ostarbeiterinnen' should replace German women producing grenades in a munitions plant: the German women, it was proposed, should be 'released' due to the dangerous gases to which they were exposed. The labour officials involved in the dispute took the view that 'Ostarbeiterinnen' with their supposedly more robust constitutions should indeed be employed rather than German women. However, rather strikingly, perhaps in a residue of earlier assumptions, the deputy director of the Pomeranian regional labour office made the point that the plant should invest in better ventilation, 'since after all even *Ostarbeiterinnen* should as far as possible be guaranteed some measure of health protection'.[89]

'Ostarbeiterinnen' as domestic helps

On the face of it, Sauckel's 1942 campaign to recruit young Ukrainian women to work as servants in German households flew in the face of administrative and economic logic. Leading civil servants in the Reich

---

[87] Ernst Stein, 'Schaffende Frauen in Bergwerksbetrieben', *Der Vierjahresplan*, 5, 16 (Nov. 1941), 859–61.

[88] Meyer-Braun, 'Die haben uns angestarrt wie im Zoo'.

[89] Präsident des Landesarbeitsamtes Pommern an den GBA, betr. Einsatz ausländischer Arbeitskräfte in der Lufthauptmunitionsanstalt Speck, 13 Aug. 1942; Dr. jur. W. Holtz, Direktor, Länd. Stellv. des Präsidenten des Landesarbeitsamtes Pommern, an Präs. Professor Jung, 18 Aug. 1942, BA Berlin, R3901, 20270.

Labour Ministry projected an image of the labour administration across the territories under Nazi rule as dedicated to optimising production for the war effort.[90] Its purpose was to make the supply of labour from across Europe flow correctly, guided by objective analyses of shortfalls and the possibilities of substitution; it was characterised by a technocratic logic of initiative, improvisation, flexibility and problem-solving.[91] This logic of transparency and 'flow' was in tension with the fixed idea on the part of Hitler and Sauckel that the resources of the German household and the German housewife must be preserved and enhanced even in the midst of a wartime labour crisis. Sauckel's announcement in April 1942 that up to half a million domestic helps were to be brought from the occupied Soviet territories to relieve the burden on German housewives was a spectacular manifestation of this thinking. In the view of Edward Homze, '[a]t at time when Germany was fighting most of the world and German industry was desperately short of labor, Hitler was, in the best tradition of Viennese courtliness, worrying about the additional burden the war had placed on the German Hausfrau'.[92] For Ulrich Herbert, there was more than a whiff of colonialism about a policy that conjured up a notion of German privilege and comfort resting on the labour of conquered peoples.[93] Yet the pledge to provide domestic help en masse was also bound up with the maintenance of conventional gender roles and ideas of the traditional 'home': the gender polarity supposedly inherent to German identity and distinguishing it from 'lower' peoples was part of the 'normality' that was to be upheld and disseminated in the face of a mass influx of foreigners into the Reich. This at least is one reading of Sauckel's April 1942 programme, where the announcement about 'hauswirtschaftliche Ostarbeiterinnen' as part of his gigantic new deployment of labour from the conquered Soviet territories was coupled, as we have seen – along with fulsome praise for the efforts of German women already in the labour force – with the pledge to stave off the conscription of women who were not yet employed.[94]

Allowing labour resources to vanish into the realm of private consumption thus had a political if not economic logic. Recruiting foreign servants no doubt also made sense to German middle-class housewives, given that ever fewer German girls and women wanted to accept the low

[90] Syrup, 'Probleme des Arbeitseinsatzes'; Walther Stothfang, 'Totaler Krieg – totaler Arbeitseinsatz', *Der Vierjahresplan*, 7, 3 (Mar. 1943), 98–9.

[91] Walther Stothfang, 'Bilanz des Arbeitseinsatzes', *Der Vierjahresplan*, 7, 10 (Oct. 1943), 355.

[92] Homze, *Foreign Labor*, 141.

[93] Herbert, *Fremdarbeiter*, 177.

[94] Der Beauftragte für den Vierjahresplan/GBA, Das Programm des Arbeitseinsatzes, 20 Apr. 1942, StA München, Arbeitsämter Freising, 757.

wages and long hours of domestic service when other jobs beckoned.[95] A perception of the 'Ostarbeiterin' as a 'natural' servant also took root within the armed forces stationed in the occupied eastern territories.[96] Army units secured local women to work in their canteens, and officers started to recruit women for their own households as well, bringing them back to Germany when they went on home leave. In September 1942, once the Wehrmacht's conquest of a further swathe of Soviet territories gave Sauckel access to new supplies of labour, a meeting was held to confirm that the recruitment of domestic servants would now begin in earnest. It was noted at that meeting that the 'self-service' actions by members of the Wehrmacht were to be confirmed and legalised retrospectively.[97] By November 1942, however, the practice was seemingly getting out of hand and a ban was imposed on such 'private' recruitment.[98]

Nevertheless, there was a countervailing logic as well. Given the rules and regulations regarding the surveillance and physical segregation of Polish and Soviet workers, their stigmatisation through the P and OST badges and the insistence on maintaining social and sexual boundaries between them and Germans, placing Soviet women as domestic servants in German homes was problematic, all the more so given Nazi views of the German home reproducing Germanness through the intimacy of domestic life.[99] One answer, signalled in the decree that implemented the recruitment campaign, was to play down the problem of racial difference by selecting candidates who would 'resemble Germans as closely as possible'.[100] This peculiar strand of thinking seemingly went back to Sauckel's idiosyncratic impressions of Ukraine picked up during his May 1942 visit, when he spotted among the population 'numerous racially good, healthy and even Nordic looking people, particularly among the

---

[95] Ingrid Wittmann, '"Echte Weiblichkeit ist ein Dienen": Die Hausgehilfin in der Weimarer Republik und im Nationalsozialismus', in *Mutterkreuz und Arbeitsbuch. Zur Geschichte der Frauen in der Weimarer Republik und im Nationalsozialismus*, ed. Frauengruppe Faschismusforschung (Frankfurt am Main, 1977), 15–48; Mareike Witkowski, 'In untergeordneter Stellung: Hausgehilfinnen im Nationalsozialismus', in *Ungleichheiten im 'Dritten Reich': Semantiken, Praktiken, Erfahrungen*, ed. Nicole Kramer and Armin Nolzen (Göttingen, 2012), 155–75.

[96] On soldiers' typical view of Soviet women simply as kitchen helps in their units, see 'Die Stellung der Frau in Sowjet-Russland', Bericht der Propagandaabteilung des Luftflottenkommandos 4 vom Dezember 1943, BA Berlin, R6, 191.

[97] Aktenvermerk über eine Sitzung beim GBA über den Abtransport von 400 000 – 500 000 ukrainischer Frauen nach Deutschland für hauswirtschaftliche Arbeiten, 4 Sept. 1942, in *Wehrmachtsverbrechen: Dokumente aus sowjetischen Archiven* (Cologne, 1997), 208.

[98] Hauch, 'Zwangsarbeiterinnen und ihre Kinder', 370.

[99] On domestic ideology and German national identity, see Nancy Reagin, *Sweeping the German Nation: Domesticity and National Identity in Germany, 1870–1945* (New York, 2006).

[100] 8 Sept. 1942, Sonderaktion des GBA zur Hereinholung von Ostarbeiterinnen zugunsten kinderreicher städtischer und ländlicher Haushaltungen, *Reichsarbeitsblatt*, Teil I, 1942, Nr. 27, 411.

women'.[101] In theory, domestic helps were to be selected and 'racially screened' before dispatch to Germany, but oral testimonies suggest that private employers simply picked out their candidates from a line-up of recently recruited young Soviet women at the local labour office, leaving the rest to be assigned to other jobs.[102]

The other approach used by the labour administration to square the circle of bringing an alien 'Ostarbeiterin' into the heart of the German home was the attempt to lay down regulations for how private homes employing such domestic helps were to be organised.[103] Regulations specified that an 'Ostarbeiterin' working as a domestic servant could not share her quarters with a German servant.[104] She was to carry out domestic tasks without being in close contact with the family or becoming involved in the care and education of children.[105] Her employers, meanwhile, were advised to educate their servant 'in German order and housekeeping' and to refrain from discussing 'war-related difficulties and worries' in front of her.[106] These elaborate instructions represented a bureaucratic operation on the part of the labour administration to preserve a sense of proper racial order and hierarchy. At the same time, they embodied a striking paradox in the way they sought to counter the very privacy and individuality that was the essence of domestic ideology, and seemed symbolically to drag the home into the realm of the regulated economy and the official gaze.

The first transport of domestic helps from Ukraine departed from Stalino (Donetzk) in September 1942.[107] Households seeking an 'Ostarbeiterin' as a domestic servant had to apply to their local labour office and have their political reliability checked by a Party functionary.[108] Those whose applications were approved were summoned to select 'their'

[101] Bericht des Gauleiters Sauckel, BA Berlin, R43 II, 652.

[102] *Verschleppt und vergessen: Schicksale jugendlicher 'OstarbeiterInnen' von der Krim im Zweiten Weltkrieg und danach*, ed. Susanne Kraatz (Heidelberg, 1995), 89; see also Annekatrein Mendel, *Zwangsarbeit im Kinderzimmer. 'Ostarbeiterinnen' in deutschen Familien von 1939 bis 1945. Gespräche mit Polinnen und Deutschen* (Frankfurt am Main, 1994).

[103] Merkblatt für Hausfrauen über die Beschäftigung hauswirtschaftlicher Ostarbeiter-innen in städtischen und ländlichen Haushaltungen, *Reichsarbeitsblatt*, Teil I, 1942, Nr. 27, 413–15.

[104] *Ibid.*, 414.

[105] 8 Sept. 1942, Sonderaktion des GBA zur Hereinholung von Ostarbeiterinnen zugunsten kinderreicher städtischer und ländlicher Haushaltungen, *Reichsarbeitsblatt*, Teil I, 1942, Nr. 27, 412.

[106] Merkblatt für Hausfrauen über die Beschäftigung hauswirtschaftlicher Ostarbeiter-innen in städtischen und ländlichen Haushaltungen, 413.

[107] Generalmajor Hans Nagel, Abschlussbericht des Wirtschaftsstabes Ost, in *Die deutsche Wirtschaftspolitik*, ed. Rolf-Dieter Müller, 322.

[108] Sonderaktion des GBA zur Hereinholung von Ostarbeiterinnen, *Reichsarbeitsblatt*, Teil I, 1942, Nr. 27, 410–12.

domestic servant at the local labour office.[109] From then on, employers seem to have regarded themselves as in a position to treat their servants as they pleased. At any rate, a security service (SD) report in January 1943 suggested both the satisfaction of housewives at having a servant whom they could order around at will, and their lack of regard for regulations about separation and social distance. Beyond recommending that Nazi women's organisations should be dispatched to inspect and admonish the wayward housewives, however, the report suggested little by way of remedial action: the reach of the regime in this case was inevitably limited.[110]

Conclusion

'In labour deployment there is no such thing as impossible', declared Fritz Sauckel in a typically grand verbal gesture made at the end of October 1942 in a circular to officials of the labour administration in the Reich and in the occupied territories.[111] It corresponded to the self-image of the senior officials in the labour administration that their efforts, constituting a many-faceted 'kaleidoscope'[112] of initiatives and devices to achieve their targets, should be seen in terms of technocratic solutions to gigantic tasks and challenges. For all the euphemistic visions of balancing forces within a 'new European order', the movement of labour across the continent under Nazi control was anything but a smooth flow of surpluses shifted to areas of shortage, but involved coercion on a grand scale by officials in the field and the snatching up of 'pools' created by ethno-racial displacement, enforced food shortages and flight/evacuation as front lines shifted. If Soviet propaganda chose to focus particularly on the fate of young women dragged to Germany and subjected to abuse, the bureaucratic response was to hold the line. If the forcible recruitment of young women from the occupied Soviet territories was not primarily motivated by an anti-natalist vision of decimating the Slavic peoples through attacking their reproductive potential, the actions taken by the labour administration to secure at any price the labour of women who became pregnant, including forced abortions, could make it effectively part of such a strategy.

[109] Mendel, *Zwangsarbeit im Kinderzimmer*, 165.

[110] *Meldungen aus dem Reich*, 349, 11 Jan. 1943. See also Herbert, *Fremdarbeiter*, 176; Witkowski, 'In untergeordneter Stellung', 169.

[111] Beauftragter für den Vierjahresplan an alle Beamten und Angestellten der Arbeitseinsatz- und Treuhänderbehörden im Grossdeutschen Reich, in allen angegliederten und besetzten Gebieten und im befreundeten Ausland, 30 Oct. 1942, StA München, Arbeitsämter Freising, 757.

[112] Stothfang, 'Totaler Krieg', 98.

Coming back to the quotation and the question posed at the start, the instruction to recruit 'primarily women' can be seen partly as a simple reflection of the availability of women and absence of men in occupied Ukraine and Belorussia. It does not, despite some accounts, seem to be the case that transports from the occupied eastern territories were carefully put together to ensure a 'parity of the sexes'. Any sense of labour contingents being straightforwardly 'ordered' with a pre-set composition regarding skill, age or gender is belied by the shortages on the ground and the hostility to recruitment that soon set in. It seems, rather – taking the example of Graf Spreti in the Ukraine – that recruiters in the field had scope for pushing their own recruitment solutions upon their 'home' areas.

Up to a point – for instance in the case of the campaign to secure domestic servants – women in the occupied Soviet territories were recruited specifically as women for 'female' tasks. However, they were also recruited as a generic supply to fill gaps in the labour force regardless of gender. If employers requested skilled male labour and there was none available, the labour administrators sought to manage expectations but also promoted Soviet women as a substitute. Tamara Frankenberger has suggested that the 'Ostarbeiterin' was in many respects *the* embodiment of an ideal worker: cheap, flexible, compliant, not subject to restrictive protective regulations and without family ties. Within the logic of 'flow' and repeated substitutions and relocations in the latter years of the war, they could appear as a supply of 'pure' labour deployable anywhere. The awkward fact of their pregnancies, which emerged as an issue already in the summer of 1942, merely prompted swift and often brutal intervention. In some cases, their previous experience and training within the Soviet economy gave them an additional advantage; more generally, their gender and the supposedly natural affinity with menial and dirty work made it appear that they could be summoned to undertake – for instance – cleaning or clearing-up work after hours. From the point of view of employers, who had welcomed the Nazi destruction of trade unions that restored what was characterised as managers' right to manage, the advent of such a labour supply might seem like a welcome return to a much earlier era. There remains, however, more to be done to assess the exact limits of what work the labour administration and employers deemed acceptable for 'Ostarbeiterinnen' to do and where remaining inhibitions or taboos, at least relating to work within the Reich, still prevailed.

Finally, the deployment of 'Ostarbeiterinnen' needs to be seen in relation to Nazi gender ideology, wartime policies towards German women, and the maintenance of racial hierarchies and gender polarities within and outside the workplace. The extension downwards of the labour hierarchy to create new groups at the bottom (Poles, Soviet workers, Jews) in effect enhanced the position of German women workers who would otherwise have been on the lowest rung in terms of pay and status. The availability of workers to take on the hardest jobs potentially modified the working hours and conditions of German women. This can be seen as a rationalising strategy to induce women to juggle housework and paid work on the basis of much-vaunted protective policies and the de-privileging of others. Meanwhile, the pledge (largely unfulfilled in practice) that hard-pressed housewives and mothers of large families could acquire an 'Ostarbeiterin' as a servant was rooted in a notion of gender polarity and traditional family structures as a distinguishing marker and privilege of Germans as the ruling class of Europe. It also suggested the maintenance of a sense of 'normality' in the domestic sphere at a time when for many the comforts and routines of home were undermined by wartime conditions. The uninhibited grab for 'alien' women as servants again partly suggests a throwback to an earlier age when households could treat servants entirely as they pleased – but also a sense that these women were a novel resource absorbing the strains on Germans in wartime, part of the perks of empire brought into the German home.

Transactions of the RHS 26 (2016), pp. 175–196 © Royal Historical Society 2016
doi:10.1017/S0080440116000104

THE GRAIL OF ORIGINAL MEANING: USES OF THE PAST IN AMERICAN CONSTITUTIONAL THEORY*

Prothero Lecture

By Colin Kidd

READ 1 JULY 2015

ABSTRACT. Originalist jurisprudence, which enjoins a faithful adherence to the values enshrined in the late eighteenth-century Constitution, has become a prominent feature of contemporary American conservatism. Recovering the original meaning of the Constitution is far from straightforward, and raises major issues of historical interpretation. How far do the assumed historical underpinnings of originalist interpretation mesh with the findings of academic historians? To what extent has the conservative invocation of the Founding Fathers obscured a lost American Enlightenment? Nor is 'tradition' in American Constitutional law an unproblematic matter. How far does a desire to restore the original meaning of the Constitution ignore the role of 'stare decisis' (precedent) in America's common law heritage? It transpires, moreover, that the various schemes of historical interpretation in American Constitutional jurisprudence do not map easily onto a simple liberal–conservative divide.

Originalism has been a controversial presence in American Constitutional law since the 1980s. Reacting against the liberal 'living Constitution' jurisprudence of the Supreme Court during the Warren and Burger courts, conservatives urged fidelity to the original principles which had animated the Constitution in the later eighteenth century. According to conservatives, the Court's ultra-liberal decisions during the 1960s and 1970s had signified a double betrayal: both the overturning of enduring moral values in the name of fashionable progressive ideas, and a rejection of Constitutional authority, indeed of the very idea of the rule of law. Originalism offered itself as an obvious way of correcting the folly and perfidy of judges. An insistence on the original meaning of the Constitution provided an attractively compelling method for frustrating the agenda of a liberalism which seemed arbitrary, rootless and impulsive. However, notwithstanding this claimed contrast between unwarranted liberal innovation and originalism's deep anchorage in

* I should like to thank John Hudson for remarks on an earlier draft of this piece.

late eighteenth-century American history, a self-conscious originalism was not – contrary to superficial appearances – a natural outgrowth from preexisting tradition. Rather, it was more closely analogous to 'invented tradition',[1] and displayed ostentatiously exaggerated respect for the eighteenth-century Founding.

The culture wars were part of a wider realignment in American politics. In particular, divisions over abortion, sexuality, race, militarism, crime and counter-cultural deviance contributed to the decline of the party system inherited from the New Deal era, when a Democratic coalition consisting of a southern regional bloc and northern blue-collar interests confronted a privileged but far from illiberal Republican party. During the latter part of the twentieth century, moral and cultural issues led to a redrawing of the social and regional maps of American politics. The irrepressible dynamism of popular evangelicalism – alongside American Catholicism – did much to invigorate the anti-counter-culture of the New Right. Moreover, radical reform lacked a democratic mandate, and was associated rather with an interventionist federal judiciary which, in the eyes of its critics, used a rights agenda to trump local majorities. Not only did the decision in *Roe* v. *Wade* (1973) effectively legalise abortion during the first two trimesters of a pregnancy, but it seemed to mark the culmination of a series of usurpations – so its critics reckoned – by the Court of the terrain of legislatures. *Engel* v. *Vitale* (1962) controversially outlawed school prayer, while *Abington* v. *Schempp* (1963) excluded Bible-reading from the classroom, and eventually the Lemon Test, introduced in *Lemon* v. *Kurtzman* (1971), effectively prohibited not only laws which gave support to religion, but also the excessive 'entanglement' of state and church. Furthermore, a series of decisions – in *Mapp* v. *Ohio* (1961), *Gideon* v. *Wainwright* (1963), *Miranda* v. *Arizona* (1966) – seemed to side with the rights of criminal defendants against the forces of law and order. *Furman* v. *Georgia* (1972) placed a moratorium on capital punishment as an unConstitutional infringement of the Eighth Amendment's ban on 'cruel and unusual punishment'. Less immediately explosive, *Griswold* v. *Connecticut* (1965), which overturned a state law banning contraceptives, discovered a controversial zone of 'privacy' within the 'penumbras' of the Bill of Rights.[2] Concerns about the undemocratic manner in which change had occurred compounded alarms over the character of the changes themselves. It was bad enough, as it seemed to conservatives, that liberal elites were using the Bill of Rights to ride roughshod over public opinion. But what if the liberal judiciary's invocation of the Constitution was utterly spurious? What if abortion, say, or sexual privacy, were not historically encompassed within the heritage of American liberties? What

---

[1] *The Invention of Tradition*, ed. E. Hobsbawm and T. Ranger (Cambridge, 1983).
[2] 381 US 479 (1965).

if the Founders were not unduly worried, say, about the death penalty? The ferocity of the anti-counter-cultural reaction in America owes much to the feeling that a liberal judiciary had duped the general public. Understandably, given the totemic importance of the Constitution and Bill of Rights, eighteenth-century history has become a theatre of the culture wars.

This is further compounded by the reverential attitude of many Americans, Democrats as well as Republicans, towards the Founding Fathers of the nation and the institutions they created. The wisdom of the Founding Fathers is a largely unquestioned axiom of American two-party politics. To question the glorious perfection of the Constitution, to pinpoint blemishes here and there in its design, is bad form, a breach of a commonly understood and shared etiquette. Needless to say, this attitude does not prevail in all quarters of American life. Most obviously, ideological critiques have come from Marxists,[3] African-Americans,[4] feminists and from radical legal realists in the Critical Legal Studies movement,[5] who located manifest flaws in American institutions, and from a few outspoken jurists and political scientists who have drawn attention to the undemocratic features of the Constitution.[6] Nevertheless, these groups, though vociferous within the academy, are marginal to mainstream opinion, where the Founders retain a quasi-religious status. As the sociologist Robert Bellah has shown, the cult of the Founders is part of America's 'civil religion', a form of ancestor worship which in a secular state substitutes for a more conventional kind of established church.[7] Indicative of the demigod-like esteem in which the Founders are held is *What Would the Founders Do?* (2006) by Richard Brookhiser, a senior editor at the ultra-conservative *National Review*, which applied late eighteenth-century wisdom to modern-day problems of which the Founders could never have dreamt. What, a straight-faced Brookhiser asked, would the Founders say about stem-cell research? How would the

---

[3] Cf. M. Horwitz, *The Transformation of American Law, 1780–1860* (Cambridge, MA, 1977).

[4] Cf. R. Perlstein, *The Invisible Bridge: The Fall of Nixon and the Rise of Reagan* (New York, 2014), 262–3, for Congresswoman Barbara Jordan's famous speech to the House Judiciary Committee during Watergate: 'But when [the Constitution] was completed on the seventeenth of September in 1787, I was not included in that "We, the people."' . . . I felt somehow for many years that George Washington and Alexander Hamilton just left me out by mistake.' Yet, even this critical preamble notwithstanding, Jordan's speech went on to celebrate the Constitution.

[5] M. Tushnet, 'Critical Legal Studies and Constitutional Law', *Stanford Law Review*, 36 (1984), 623–47.

[6] R. A. Dahl, *How Democratic Is the American Constitution?* (New Haven, 2002); Sanford Levinson, *Our Undemocratic Constitution* (Oxford and New York, 2006).

[7] R. Bellah, 'Civil Religion in America', originally published in *Daedalus* (Winter, 1967), reprinted in *American Civil Religion*, ed. R. E. Richey and D. G. Jones (New York, 1974), 21–44.

Founders have fought the war on drugs? What would the Founders do about weapons of mass destruction?[8]

The cult of the Founders frustrates dispassionate analysis of the Constitution. It means that the Constitution is regarded as enjoying sacrosanct status, akin more to the Ten Commandments than to a set of explicitly amendable rules for self-government. Certainly, it seems clear from Article V of the Constitution that the Founders never intended the Constitution – which *they* recognised as a product of political compromise – to be set in aspic. As Madison himself wrote in *Federalist* no. 37, 'a faultless plan was not to be expected'.[9] Yet the Founders were not to know that the United States would grow to a scale which made the Article V amendment process – with its requirements of two-thirds super-majorities in both houses of Congress (or a national convention requested by two-thirds of the States) and ratification in three-quarters of the States – so hard to accomplish. The difficulty of amending the Constitution only serves to reinforce the notion that the handiwork of the all-wise Founding Fathers was to be preserved largely unchanged forever.[10]

Originalism had its beginnings in Richard Nixon's pledge during his 1968 campaign to appoint only strict constructionists to the Court. Today, academic jurists stress that strict construction – a method for interpreting any text – and the original intention behind the text are not synonymous; nevertheless, in the crude hurly-burly of political campaigning Nixon's commitments prefigured the later turn to originalism proper. Nixon had grave difficulty finding professionally credible jurists who dissented from the idea of the 'living constitution'. His first nominees to the Supreme Court – Clement Haynsworth and G. Harrold Carswell – were rejected by the Senate. While Nixon did secure the appointment of William Rehnquist to the Court, his other successful nominees included Harry Blackmun, the author of the ultra-liberal decision in *Roe* v. *Wade*. There were further wry incongruities, for the principal pioneer of an originalist approach in legal history during the 1970s was a convinced opponent of Nixon. Raoul Berger (1901–2000) had made his name as an uncompromising opponent of Nixon's exaggerated claims of Executive Privilege during the Watergate crisis,[11] but became an unlikely standard-bearer for an originalist interpretation of the Fourteenth Amendment of 1868 with his controversial book, *Government by Judiciary* (1977). Berger has been labelled a conservative, but his jurisprudence was *sui generis* and defied partisan categories. The early glimmerings of originalism

---

[8] R. Brookhiser, *What Would the Founders Do? Our Questions, their Answers* (New York, 2006).
[9] *The Federalist*, ed. T. Ball (Cambridge, 2003), 169.
[10] By contrast, see D. Lazare, *The Frozen Republic: How the Constitution Is Paralyzing Democracy* (New York, 1996).
[11] R. Berger, *Executive Privilege: A Constitutional Myth* (Cambridge, MA, 1974).

Berger inspired in the late 1970s immediately provoked a major academic counterblast from Paul Brest, a proponent of Critical Legal Studies:[12] a sophisticated critique of originalism's claims which *preceded* the full-fledged emergence of an originalist jurisprudence in conservative circles.[13]

For it was only during the 1980s that the perceived disjunction between the wisdom of the eighteenth-century Founders and the reckless irresponsibility of the Warren and Burger Courts provoked a more decisive conservative turn to originalism. In 1982, Steve Calabresi founded the Federalist Society. Calabresi, then a law student at Yale, later a law professor at Northwestern University, began the Federalist Society along with some fellow law students. Although the Society emerged out of disenchantment with the ultra-liberal consensus of the professoriate, it was not narrowly ideological and promoted open debate. Indeed, Calabresi was himself a Reagan Democrat. Nevertheless, conservative originalism – though not a straitjacket of orthodoxy – was the dominant motif of the Federalist Society. Chapters rapidly sprang up at other law schools, and eventually by 2001 there were chapters at over 200 law schools. Meanwhile, there were also around 30,000 lawyers enrolled in professional chapters.[14]

In 1985, Edwin Meese III (b. 1931), Ronald Reagan's new attorney-general, issued an originalist counter-blast to the liberal judiciary. In a speech to the American Bar Association he proclaimed his – and the administration's – adherence to a 'jurisprudence of original intention'. Meese specifically complained about the 'misuse of history' implicated in an 'activist jurisprudence' which imported its own whims into the Constitution. What was the point of the Constitution, he argued, if it were traduced by self-indulgent judges whose 'chameleon jurisprudence' meant its 'changing color and form in each era'.[15] Meese soon found himself in a spat with Justice William Brennan (1906–97), the leading liberal on the Supreme Court, though Brennan was ironically – like Earl Warren himself – the appointee of a Republican president, Eisenhower. In response to Meese, Brennan invoked the 'transformative purpose' of a text characterised by 'majestic generalities and ennobling pronouncements'. Only originalists could be so obtuse as to construe the Constitution so narrowly as to overlook 'the Constitutional vision of human dignity' embodied in the Bill of Rights. Brennan also pointed to the intractable difficulties which inhered in a jurisprudence of 'original intention'. Was

[12] L. Kalman, *The Strange Career of Legal Liberalism* (New Haven, 1996), 109.

[13] P. Brest, 'The Misconceived Quest for Original Understanding', *Boston University Law Review*, 60 (1980), 204–38.

[14] S. Teles, *The Rise of the Conservative Legal Movement* (Princeton, 2008), 135–80.

[15] E. Meese III, 'Interpreting the Constitution', in *Interpreting the Constitution: The Debate over Original Intent*, ed. J. Rakove (Boston, MA, 1990), 13–21, esp. 17, 20.

any coherent intention to be found in 'a jointly drafted document drawing its authority from a general assent of the States'? The apparent 'self-effacing deference' of originalists to the Founders was, Brennan reckoned, an arbitrary and presumptuous 'arrogance cloaked as humility'.[16]

Matters came to a head in the summer of 1987 – the bicentennial of the Constitution – when Ronald Reagan nominated a notorious originalist, Robert Bork (1927–2012), for the seat vacated by Justice Lewis Powell, the 'swing' justice on the Supreme Court. The major concern of Bork's mentor at Yale, Alexander Bickel (1924–74), had been the injudicious overreach he observed in the decisions of the Warren Court. In his influential book *The Least Dangerous Branch* (1962), Bickel framed the central problem in contemporary Constitutional theory, 'the counter-majoritarian difficulty'. The Court's powers of judicial review – its capacity to strike down unConstitutional laws made by the duly elected legislative branches at the state and federal level – needed to be exercised sparingly, for fear of raising issues of legitimacy. The Court's role, as Bickel saw it, was to complement – and sometimes correct – majoritarian democracy, but without cocking a snook at democratic standards.[17] Bork elaborated Bickel's misgivings into a form of originalism which liberals found threatening. Was Bork, they alleged, going to turn back the clock, curtailing recently won sexual freedoms and rights of expression? It so happened that Bork, as solicitor-general under Nixon in 1973, had, at a moment of dire crisis in the Department of Justice, executed Nixon's order to fire Archibald Cox, the special prosecutor in the Watergate affair, who was pursuing Nixon relentlessly for access to presidential tapes.[18] A bogeyman to liberals, though an eminently qualified jurist of great intellectual distinction, Bork was rejected by 58 votes to 42 in the Senate.[19] Reagan then nominated Douglas Ginsburg (b. 1946), another originalist, who took the view that the original Constitution had been in abeyance since the Court's acceptance of the New Deal from 1937–8 onwards, what Ginsburg later referred to as the 'Constitution-in-exile'.[20] However, Ginsburg ran into difficulties when it came to light that he had dabbled in marijuana while a junior faculty member at Harvard, and his nomination was withdrawn. Eventually, a more liberal non-originalist conservative, Anthony Kennedy, was successfully confirmed in the seat vacated by Powell.

[16] W. J. Brennan Jr, 'The Constitution of the United States: Contemporary Ratification', in *Interpreting*, ed. Rakove, 23–34, at 23, 25, 28, 31.

[17] A. Bickel, *The Least Dangerous Branch: The Supreme Court at the Bar of Politics* (1962; 2nd edn, New Haven, 1986).

[18] S. Kutler, *The Wars of Watergate* (1990; New York, 1992), 407.

[19] For Bork's post-mortem on the affair and its wider juridical significance, see R. Bork, *The Tempting of America: The Political Seduction of the Law* (New York, 1990).

[20] D. Ginsburg, 'Delegation Running Riot', *Regulation*, 1 (1995), 83–7, at 84.

Notwithstanding this setback, an originalist phalanx was already forming on the Court. Rehnquist had been elevated to chief justice in 1986, and in the same year another originalist, Antonin Scalia (1936–2016), was easily appointed to the Supreme Court, confirmed – strange as it might now seem given his later reputation as an originalist bruiser – by a vote of 98–0 in the Senate. More controversially, in 1991, Clarence Thomas (b. 1948) – nominated by George Bush Snr – joined this ultra-conservative grouping on the Court.

Nevertheless, there is no single agreed originalist method of reading the Constitution, whether in the law schools or among originalist justices on the Court. Originalism contains many mansions, and the quest for original meaning is not as straightforward as Meese and others have tended to assume. Although originalists tend to promote their brand of interpretation as the only honest method of approaching the Constitution – simple common sense in fact – originalism, when examined more closely, turns out to be composed of various overlapping, but distinct and potentially competitive, strategies. According to Lawrence Solum, originalism has 'evolved' into 'a family of related theories'.[21]

What, then, are the main varieties of originalism? At the outset, it is important to note that although originalism is often referred to as 'original intent', original intent turns out to be only one genre among several different types of originalist interpretation. The focus of original intent is on the intentions of the Founding generation which lie behind the words of the Constitution. What did the Framers intend by the words and phrases they used? Needless to say, the objective of original intent is far from scientific, but relies on the other hand on what historians would recognise as the historical imagination, the ability to reconstruct the mental world of the late eighteenth century. Though it helps here to ransack eighteenth-century dictionaries, philology in itself is insufficient, and needs to be supplemented, it is recognised, by a wider appreciation of social forms and practices. Dennis Goldford describes this version – focused on the original intent of the Framers – as 'hard' originalism, to be distinguished from a 'soft' originalism, based on the accepted meanings of the Constitution understood by its ratifiers in the state ratifying conventions and its wider public meaning in contemporary discourse.[22] Soft originalists tend to rely on the text of the Constitution itself rather than on the intentions which lay behind it. Yet textualism itself is far from straightforward and encompasses several different approaches to the Constitution. The most obvious kind of textualism is 'clause-bound' analysis, which takes each particular clause on its own. However, a 'structuralist' variant of textualism argues that

---

[21] L. Solum and R. Bennett, *Constitutional Originalism: A Debate* (Ithaca, NY, 2011), 2.
[22] D. Goldford, *The American Constitution and the Debate over Originalism* (Cambridge, 2005), 9.

individual clauses need to be considered in relation to the text of the Constitution as a whole. Potential inconsistencies or ambiguities between clauses can then be clarified with respect to the overall architecture of the Constitution. 'Purposive' textualism, on the other hand, considers the text in terms of the noble aspirations which it enshrines.[23]

Clarence Thomas is the only Supreme Court justice to employ a jurisprudence of original intent, though Ralph Rossum has demonstrated that, strictly speaking, original intent forms only one pillar of Thomas's compound doctrine which Rossum terms 'original general meaning', drawn from original intent, as well as the original understanding and public meaning of the text.[24] Thomas's originalist immersion in the Founding era verges on the bizarre; not only spectacularly erudite, but also at times gruesome and ghoulish. For instance, in *Baze* v. *Rees* (2008), the Supreme Court upheld Kentucky's procedures for administration of lethal injections, and rejected complaints that it violated the Eighth Amendment's ban on 'cruel and unusual punishments'. Thomas's concurring opinion in Baze drew on a wide variety of sources, including modern historical scholarship, to clarify what the Eighth Amendment had proscribed. Some procedures were recognised as 'intensifying' a death sentence, including gibbeting, dissection, burning at the stake, embowelling, beheading and quartering, which constituted, Thomas reckoned, 'aggravated forms of capital punishment'. Thomas also ransacked contemporary dictionaries – including those of Samuel Johnson and Noah Webster – to capture the 'ordinary meaning' back then of the word 'cruel'. What was forbidden was 'intentional infliction of gratuitous pain'. The notion that execution needed somehow to be 'anesthetised' to be Constitutional found no warrant in Thomas's jurisprudence of original understanding.[25]

Although Antonin Scalia was Justice Thomas's closest ally on the Supreme Court over the past twenty years, he expressed a kind of head-shaking contempt for the futility of Thomas's misguided originalism. In Scalia's view, the attempt to recover original intent was doomed to failure and, worse, to a kind of subjectivity of the sort it attempts to evade. The only sure ground, Scalia reckoned, is the text of the Constitution itself. Its general acceptance in the ratification process suggests that it embodied a set of widely shared meanings (whatever the intentions of the Framers). This is the logic behind the jurisprudence of original meaning,

[23] For the varieties of textualism, see J. O'Neill, *Originalism in American Law and Politics* (Baltimore, 2005), 4–5.

[24] R. A. Rossum, *Understanding Clarence Thomas: The Jurisprudence of Constitutional Restoration* (Lawrence, KS, 2014), esp. 12–15.

[25] 553 US 35 (2008).

which soon supplanted original intent as the core doctrine of conservative originalism.[26]

For all his notorious bombast, Scalia – unlike Thomas – recognised that there are other claims of tradition besides the original Constitution. Traditions collide, and *stare decisis* – the authority of precedent in case law – presents a rival source of historic legitimacy. Thomas, on the other hand, appears unconstrained by precedent when he perceives that existing traditions of judicial interpretation have betrayed the original intention behind the Constitution. Willingness of this sort to overturn well-established precedent for the sake of original meaning verges on a kind of judicial activism, arguably a variant of the phenomenon which it criticises. Scalia's originalism was, he conceded, necessarily limited by his lawyerly respect for *stare decisis*. 'In its undiluted form', Scalia acknowledged, originalism is a 'medicine that seems too strong to swallow'.[27] Scalia was far from alone in this deference to extra-originalist continuity. In his closing statement to the Senate Judiciary Committee, Bork made clear that *stare decisis* inevitably imposed limitations on what an originalist jurisprudence might reasonably hope to achieve. Bork recognised 'a number of important precedents that are today so woven into the fabric of our system that to change or alter them would be, in my view, unthinkable'.[28] Yet, one should not exaggerate Scalia's pragmatism. Even the ultra-conservative Justice Samuel Alito has playfully mocked the anachronistic excesses inherent in a jurisprudence of original meaning. During oral discussion of *Schwarzenegger* (later *Brown*) v. *Entertainment Merchants Association*, which dealt with violence in video games, Alito unhelpfully summarised what he took to be Scalia's line of questioning: 'Well, I think what Justice Scalia wants to know is what James Madison thought about video games. Did he enjoy them?'[29]

The division between Thomas and Scalia exemplifies the main axis of division within conservative originalism, but it does not exhaust the range of purported originalisms. Indeed, the prominent jurist and philosopher, Ronald Dworkin, tried to navigate by means of an originalist method to a liberal destination. Dworkin drew a sharp distinction between his own scheme of 'semantic originalism' (in effect a brand of purposive textualism, in which the text embodied 'abstract moral standards'), which he contrasted with 'expectation originalism', the notion that the text possessed merely the precise legal force that its Framers expected it

---

[26] For the evolution of Scalia's jurisprudence of original meaning and its insistent distance from the originalism of Bork and Thomas, see B. A. Murphy, *Scalia: A Court of one* (New York, 2014), esp. 111–12, 126, 143, 153, 164, 246–7, 369.

[27] A. Scalia, 'Originalism: The Lesser Evil', *University of Cincinnati Law Review*, 57 (1989), 849–65, at 861.

[28] *The Bork Hearings*, ed. R. E. Shaffer (Princeton, 2005), 161.

[29] www.supremecourt.gov/oral_arguments/argument_transcripts/08–1448.pdf (at 17).

to have.[30] Moral philosophy has, of course, moved on since the late eighteenth century; therefore, a recalibration of the ethical aspirations of the Founders – say, for example, about the changing connotations of the 'cruel and unusual punishments' unspecified, perhaps deliberately, in the Eighth Amendment – meshed easily with the original motivating principles behind the Constitution. On the other hand, Dworkin's critics deny that this pseudo-originalist outlook bore any fidelity to the Constitution.[31] An alternative attempt to square the originalist circle on liberal terms is Jack Balkin's refusal to accept the premise that originalism and the 'living Constitution' are intrinsically incompatible. Instead, Balkin has espoused a hybrid 'living originalism', which depends on a recognition of the enduring structures of the Constitution – what he calls 'framework originalism' – complemented by an openness to evolving ethical standards.[32]

More commonly, however, liberal jurists have confronted originalism head on, explaining why, in their view, it rests on marshy foundations. Few were as alert to the historical dimension as Brest. Non-originalist 'translation' of the Founders' intentions, he insisted, was a necessary part of Constitutional interpretation; otherwise Congress would not be able to 'regulate any item of commerce or any mode of transportation that did not exist in in 1789; the First Amendment would not protect any means of communication not then known'. Moreover, he was sufficiently aware of the way historians operated to perceive that strict intentionalism – contrary to the expectations of originalist jurists, who aimed at settled meaning – threatened to inject instability into the law. Historians discover new documents, and reinterpret otherwise familiar sources. Moreover, 'we have witnessed enough dramatic revisions of social and political history', Brest warned, 'to be sure that the past itself is not about to stand still'.[33]

Historians have been less prominent in the wars over originalism, with the major exception of Jack Rakove, who outlined the 'perils of originalism' in his Pulitzer Prize-winning book *Original Meanings: Politics and Ideas in the Making of the Constitution* (1996).[34] Indeed, it was Rakove who coined the phrase 'the Holy Grail of original meaning'

---

[30] R. Dworkin, *Freedom's Law: The Moral Reading of the American Constitution* (Oxford, 1996); R. Dworkin, 'Comment', at 119–26, in A. Scalia, *A Matter of Interpretation: Federal Courts and the Law*, ed. A. Gutman (Princeton, 1997); R. Dworkin, *Justice in Robes* (Cambridge, MA, 2006), 29–30, 117–39.

[31] K. E. Whittington, 'Dworkin's "Originalism": The Role of Intentions in Constitutional interpretation', *Review of Politics*, 62 (2000), 197–229.

[32] J. Balkin, *Living Originalism* (Cambridge, MA, 2012).

[33] Brest, 'Misconceived', 221, 231.

[34] J. Rakove, *Original Meanings: Politics and Ideas in the Making of the Constitution* (1996; New York, 1997), 3.

to capture the unattainability of the objective originalists pursued.[35] The originalist enterprise is doomed to failure – intellectual failure at least – Rakove reckoned, because it seeks to find 'determinate meanings' at a moment of Constitution-making which was 'dynamic and creative, and thus uncertain'. Contested ambiguity cannot be reliably transmuted into fixed meaning. That kind of alchemy is beyond even the powers of Constitutional jurists. This is because, according to Rakove, the politics of Constitution-making and then ratification produced a 'range of understandings' which amounted to 'rather less than a consensus'. Indeed, Rakove calculates that there were approximately 2,000 protagonists who participated in the various conventions that first framed, then ratified, the Constitution. Divining a single original intent or even a shared understanding amongst this varied cast is not so much fraught with difficulty, as it is an outright chimera.[36]

However, jurists themselves come to adopt a more historically sensitive approach to the Constitution, and two of the most subversively anti-originalist reinterpretations of American Constitutional history have come from the Yale Law School, from Bruce Ackerman (b. 1943) and Akhil Reed Amar (b. 1958). Ackerman undermines the claim of originalism by unmasking the Constitution itself as an unConstitutional usurpation on the previous constitution – the Articles of Confederation, which preceded it.[37] The Founders' achievement, he insists, very persuasively, rested on 'flagrant illegalities'.[38] The sole purpose of the Convention was 'revising' the Articles of Confederation, under whose rules any changes required unanimity of agreement. A new Constitution was not part of the Convention's remit, and what actually transpired at Philadelphia was an 'illegal initiative'. According to Ackerman, what the draft Constitution at Philadelphia amounted to was 'ten delegations [i.e. those present *throughout* the Convention] urging nine states to bolt a solemn agreement ratified by all thirteen'.[39] But somehow a 'bandwagon dynamic' took over, and the Founders forged a new and binding Constitution from their blatant disregard of the old one.[40] His colleague Amar rejects Ackerman's reading of the original unConstitutional deviance which lurks behind the Constitution of 1787. Instead, Amar emphasises that the Articles of Confederation had not established a new Constitutional order among the

---

[35] *Ibid.*, 10.
[36] *Ibid.*, 6, 8, 10.
[37] B. Ackerman, *We the People*, I: *Foundations* (Cambridge, MA, 1991).
[38] B. Ackerman, 'Our Unconventional Founding', *University of Chicago Law Review*, 62 (1995), 475–573, at 476.
[39] *Ibid.*, 481.
[40] *Ibid.*, 568.

thirteen states. The Articles, according to Amar, amounted to no more than a treaty.[41]

Nevertheless, the Founding was not the only unConstitutional moment in Ackerman's twin-track interpretation of American history.[42] The Constitution, Ackerman argues, was not binding at all times and in all circumstances. The Constitution provided a compelling framework for law and governance, except at moments of crisis, when the United States experienced what Ackerman terms, somewhat euphemistically, 'unconventional innovation and democratic renewal'.[43] In other words, at certain times, politicians – in the name of 'the people' – rode roughshod over the rules prescribed in the Constitution. Apart from the Founding itself, the other two examples of such crises in American history were 'the unconventional ratification'[44] of the post-Civil War Amendments, or 'amendment-simulacra',[45] in the late 1860s, and the implementation of the New Deal in the 1930s. However, Ackerman insists, neither moment of crisis amounted to a revolution. On each occasion, reformers 'broke the rules without seeking to destroy the entire institutional framework'.[46] At a time of crisis, there was a reversion to popular sovereignty to refit and stabilise the ship of state. However, Ackerman's thesis made Constitutional theory a much more treacherous business than originalists imagined. Far from being an uninterrupted story of Constitutional continuity, America's Constitutional heritage was one of punctuated equilibrium.

Amar is the polar twin of Clarence Thomas, an anti-originalist, but just as concerned to recover the authenticity of late eighteenth-century jurisprudence and keenly aware of the wider ideological significance of seemingly antiquarian truffle-hunting. Amar's historical researches turn the Constitution, and especially the Bill of Rights, inside out. Amar presents a defamiliarised Bill of Rights, which was not a guarantee of 'rights' as we currently understand them. Rather, the modern emphasis on rights has caused jurists to overlook the majoritarian character of the Bill of Rights, which was initially composed of twelve, not ten, items. Once the Bill of Rights is viewed in its entirety, including its first two unsuccessful items (concerning the size of electoral districts

[41] A. R. Amar, 'Of Sovereignty and Federalism', *Yale Law Journal*, 96 (1987), 1425–520, at 1446–8; A. R. Amar, 'Philadelphia Revisited: Amending the Constitution outside Article V', *University of Chicago Law Review*, 55 (1988), 1043–104, at 1048; A. R. Amar, 'The Consent of the Governed: Constitutional Amendment outside Article V', *Columbia Law Review*, 94 (1994), 457–508, at 462–9, 489, 507.

[42] See B. Ackerman, *We the People*, II: *Transformations* (Cambridge, MA, 1998).

[43] Ackerman, 'Unconventional', 573.

[44] *Ibid.*, 571.

[45] Ackerman, *We the People*, I, 51.

[46] *Ibid.*, 569.

and congressional remuneration), and the so-called First Amendment is relegated to third place in the initial ensemble, it comes more clearly into focus as a quasi-governmental blueprint outlining the infrastructural underpinnings of republican self-rule. In other words, the document – contrary to received assumptions – is largely about governmental structures, not about individual rights as such. In Amar's interpretation, the Bill of Rights, as initially conceived, provided guarantees for intermediary institutions in the individual states – such as churches, militias and juries – which contributed to the inculcation of civic virtue and the formation of good republican citizens.[47]

Here, Amar's work intersected with another trend in liberal jurisprudence, the recovery of classical republicanism. By a curious coincidence, conservative originalists were not the only group to turn during the 1980s towards the restoration of eighteenth-century values. So too did an emerging movement among liberal Constitutional theorists, most prominent among them Cass Sunstein (b. 1954) and Frank Michelman (b. 1936), who used the recent historiography of late eighteenth-century America to launch what has been termed a 'republican revival'.[48] This phenomenon is one which historians acquainted with the celebrated works of Bernard Bailyn (b. 1922),[49] Gordon Wood (b. 1933)[50] and John Pocock (b. 1924)[51] might expect to find familiar.[52] However, they would be wrong. The republicanism of the jurists bears strangely little resemblance to the republican themes analysed in the historiography. Whereas Bailyn, Wood and Pocock emphasised the place of participatory virtue and fear of corruption in the agenda of classical republicanism, its supposed revivalists invoke deliberation, equality and popular majoritarian sovereignty as its principal characteristics. There is, moreover, a further ironic dissonance. The historical recovery of republicanism was an outgrowth of the contextualist revolution in the

---

[47] A. R. Amar, *The Bill of Rights* (New Haven, 1998).

[48] Both contributed to the special issue of the *Yale Law Journal* on republican theory: C. Sunstein, 'Beyond the Republican Revival', *Yale Law Journal*, 97 (1988), 1539; F. Michelman, 'Law's Republic', *Yale Law Journal*, 97 (1988), 1493.

[49] B. Bailyn, *The Ideological Origins of the American Revolution* (Cambridge, MA, 1967); B. Bailyn, *The Origins of American Politics* (New York, 1968).

[50] G. Wood, *The Creation of the American Republic 1776–1787* (1969, New York, 1972).

[51] J. G. A. Pocock, *The Machiavellian Moment* (Princeton, 1975).

[52] See, amidst a vast literature, R. Shalhope, 'Toward a Republican Synthesis: The Emergence of an Understanding of Classical Republicanism in American Historiography', *William and Mary Quarterly*, 3rd ser., 29 (1972), 49–80; R. Shalhope, 'Republicanism and Early American Historiography', *William and Mary Quarterly*, 3rd ser. 39 (1982), 334–56; L. Banning, *The Jeffersonian Persuasion* (Ithaca, NY, 1978); D. McCoy, *The Elusive Republic* (Chapel Hill, 1980).

history of political thought.[53] What mattered to contextualists was the precise idioms of debate in a specific time and place. The past was a foreign country; and there was no expectation that the arguments of the nowadays obscure eighteenth-century pamphleteers discussed by Bailyn and Wood would find any purchase in the present. In the event, the republicanism which Sunstein and the revivalists used to refurbish late twentieth-century liberalism had been burnished beyond recognition.

Understandably, observers questioned the ideological coherence of the republican revival. According to the intellectual historian Daniel Rodgers, republicanism became during the 1980s a kind of 'short-hand for everything liberalism was not'.[54] Among the most acute critics of the republican revival was Richard Fallon of Harvard Law School. Fallon recognised that the restoration of an eighteenth-century classical republican ideology was not 'practicable'. What had once been possible in the 'context of relatively small homogenous communities' was a most unlikely candidate for revival in the radically different 'social conditions' of the late twentieth century. Therefore, what was on offer was a 'watery version' of the original, 'reformulated' to take account of modern needs and expectations. In particular, the revivalists aimed to restore republican ideals without sacrificing recently won freedoms such as the right to privacy; a blatant contradiction, according to Fallon, for the classical republican emphasis on the virtues of the citizenry seemed all too compatible with legislation on morals.[55]

There was, however, one aspect of the Constitution where eighteenth-century perspectives did indeed clarify matters, namely the Second Amendment, whose strange, convoluted clauses were – until recent decades – considered by jurists an 'embarrassing'[56] and anachronistic hangover from the eighteenth century: 'A well-regulated militia, being necessary to the security of a free state, the right of the people to keep and bear arms, shall not be infringed.' The insights of classical republican historiography on the educative role of militia service and the dangers of standing armies helped to parse the meaning of the Second Amendment – but only within the law schools.[57] For classical republicanism has left scarcely a mark on the wider public debate – dominated by the National

---

[53] Cf. Q. Skinner, 'Meaning and Understanding in the History of Ideas', *History and Theory*, 8 (1969), 3–53.

[54] D. Rodgers, 'Republicanism: The Career of a Concept', *Journal of American History*, 79 (1992), 11–38, at 33.

[55] R. Fallon, 'What Is Republicanism, and Is it Worth Reviving?', *Harvard Law Review*, 102 (1988–9), 1695–735, esp. at 1699, 1723, 1733–4.

[56] Cf. the rehabilitation from condescension in S. Levinson, 'The Embarrassing Second Amendment', *Yale Law Journal*, 99 (1989), 637–59.

[57] D. Williams, *The Mythic Meanings of the Second Amendment* (New Haven, 2003); S. Cornell, *A Well-Regulated Militia* (New York, 2006).

Rifle Association, hunters and proponents of gun control – or on the courts, where a narrow fixation on the right of *individuals* to bear arms inhibits a more sensitive appreciation of the Second Amendment as a republican heirloom.

Tensions of this sort between academia and the courts are inevitable. Even where the judiciary – as in the case of Thomas – is up to speed with historical scholarship, history is pressed into the service of judicial decision-making. In the courts, the aimless reconstruction of context and curiosity-driven research yield – understandably enough – to the imperatives of legal reasoning. Many leading jurists are, in fact, sheepishly conscious of the danger of lapsing into what is termed 'law office history', an accurate if pejorative label which serves to distinguish the disinterested salvage of the past, replete with all its messy contradictions and complexities, from historical research as a tool of advocacy.[58] Jurists are sensitised to the difference between lawyers' history and historians' history, though in practice they resort to the former.[59]

Nevertheless, it matters enormously how the past is framed; and here there is a significant disjunction between academic history and the perception of the late eighteenth century in the public realm. In the latter, the conservative cult of the Founders tends to obscure the phenomenon of the American Enlightenment – well established in the academic literature – from which the Constitution emerged. Historians recognise that the idea of a complex Constitutional mechanism was the greatest achievement of an American Enlightenment which amplified and extended the early Enlightenment quarrel of the Ancients and the Moderns. The Founders were Moderns, conscious that modernity possessed certain insights unavailable to the Ancients. The Constitution – indebted to the mechanistic science pioneered in the seventeenth century – was conceived as a machinery of checks, balances and separated powers which far surpassed the wisdom enshrined in the traditional Aristotelian conception of politics.[60] Moreover, while conservatives fondly assume that the Founders were devout Protestant patriarchs, academic research suggests that Deism and other forms of anti-Trinitarian heterodoxy were influential in the worldview of the late eighteenth-century political elite.[61] Here, differences of register have substantive real-world consequences in

---

[58] Cf. A. H. Kelly, 'Clio and the Court: An Illicit Love Affair', *Supreme Court Review* (1965), 119–58.

[59] Cf. N. M. Richards, 'Clio and the Court: A Reassessment of the Supreme Court's Uses of History', *Journal of Law and Politics*, 13 (1997), 809–77; M. S. Flaherty, 'History "Lite" in Modern American Constitutionalism', *Columbia Law Review*, 95 (1995), 523–90; Kalman, *Strange Career*.

[60] D. Wootton, 'Introduction', in *The Essential Federalist and Anti-Federalist Papers*, ed. D. Wootton (Indianapolis, 2003).

[61] D. L. Holmes, *The Faiths of the Founding Fathers* (Oxford, 2006).

Constitutional law. During the 1980s, liberal separatists and conservative non-preferentialists debated the original definition of what the late eighteenth century understood by the term 'establishment of religion'[62] banned – or seemingly banned – in the First Amendment of the Bill of Rights. Did the Founders mean to prohibit all forms of state-sponsored religious organisation[63] or only forms where one denomination enjoyed special privileges? In other words, as some historically sophisticated conservatives maintained, was it possible to have a system of non-preferential state support for religion in general which would not amount to what the Founders would have called an 'establishment'?[64]

However, we should not be too quick to enlist the enlightened Founders on the liberal side in the culture wars. The American Enlightenment – as it has been reconstructed since the pioneering work of Henry May in the 1970s[65] – was, it seems, a multi-vocal conversation in which the most sceptical and radical voices were largely drowned out by the cautious and far from subversive incrementalism of a dominant Moderate-Didactic Enlightenment, which attempted to reconcile reason and biblical revelation under the auspices of an updated rational Christianity. The concept of Enlightenment is itself a snare for the unwary,[66] and category errors are to be found at work on both sides of the liberal–conservative divide.

Indeed, it should be clear by now that conservatism does not map easily onto originalism. Just as originalism is not a single phenomenon, but, as we have seen, stands shorthand for a variety of originalist perspectives, so too American conservatism is a very broad church, with a considerable amount of bickering in the aisles. There is no consensus among conservatives about the basic contours of America's Constitutional history. Different groups of conservatives advance strongly divergent schemes of periodisation and invoke strikingly different usable pasts.

Libertarian originalists do not regard the overreach of the Warren and Burger Courts as the major wrong-turning in American jurisprudence; they locate it earlier in the abandonment of strict laissez-faire doctrine – what is sometimes described as Lochnerism[67] – on the New Deal Court from *West Coast Hotels* v. *Parrish* (1937) onwards and enshrined in the

---

[62]Cf. C. Kidd, 'Civil Theology and Church Establishments in Revolutionary America', *Historical Journal*, 42 (1999), 1007–26; V. Munoz, *God and the Founders* (Cambridge, 2009).

[63]Cf. L. W. Levy, *The Establishment Clause: Religion and the First Amendment* (New York, 1986).

[64]Cf. T. J. Curry, *The First Freedoms: Church and State in America to the Passage of the First Amendment* (Oxford, 1986); G. V. Bradley, *Church–State Relationships in America* (Westport, CT, 1987).

[65]H. F. May, *The Enlightenment in America* (New York, 1976). See also R. A. Ferguson, *The American Enlightenment 1750–1820* (Cambridge, MA, 1997).

[66]Cf. R. Darnton, *George Washington's False Teeth* (New York, 2003).

[67]Cf. *New York* v. *Lochner* 198 US 45 (1905).

celebrated footnote to the Carolene Products decision of 1938, which set out the standards of scrutiny for judicial review of legislation.[68] The post-Carolene situation is described by leading libertarian conservatives as the era of 'the Lost Constitution'[69] or 'the Constitution in Exile',[70] and they promote a radical restorationist approach to the law. Randy Barnett (b. 1952) has attacked Scalia's concessions to the demands of *stare decisis*, for 'invoking the precedents established by the dead hand of nonoriginalist justices'.[71] Libertarians have little truck with the social conservatism of Thomas and Scalia, which is indebted to Catholic natural law standards. The libertarian end of the conservative movement favours – with seeming ideological promiscuity – abortion rights, drug use, guns and unrestricted property rights. Libertarians locate these freedoms in the rarely invoked Ninth Amendment: 'The enumeration, in the Constitution, of certain rights, shall not be construed to deny or disparage others retained by the people.' Whereas for Bork the Ninth Amendment was an 'ink blot' whose imprecision left it void of legal meaning,[72] for Barnett, it signified a general presumption of liberty behind the law, though one which the Court had quietly suppressed. According to Barnett, this is one of the seemingly obvious roads not taken in American jurisprudence.[73] In particular, the 'privileges and immunities' clause of the Fourteenth Amendment ('The citizens of each State shall be entitled to all privileges and immunities of citizens of the several States') was immediately gutted by the Supreme Court's narrow ruling on its scope in the Slaughterhouse cases (1873). One of the principal reasons why the liberal Court was tempted into an activist and sometimes, undeniably, arbitrary jurisprudence was the early neutering of 'privileges and immunities'. The Ninth Amendment and the 'privileges and immunities' clause were the dogs that did not bark in American legal history. Had they been implemented by the Courts as their Framers had wanted, contended the ultra-originalist Barnett, then some of the central tensions in American jurisprudence would have been resolved without resort to judicial sleight of hand or accompanied by the howls of outrage from the social conservatives he regards as faux-originalists. However, by a further ironic twist, Thomas – from a markedly

---

[68] *US* v. *Carolene Products* 304 US 144 (1938). Henceforth, the Court would defer to the legislative branch, but would apply stricter standards of scrutiny to legislation which appeared to violate Constitutional prohibitions, to distort the political process or to discriminate against minorities.

[69] R. Barnett, *Restoring the Lost Constitution: The Presumption of Liberty* (Princeton, 2004).

[70] A. Napolitano, *The Constitution in Exile* (Nashville, 2006).

[71] R. Barnett, 'Scalia's Infidelity: A Critique of "Faint-Hearted" Originalism', *University of Cincinnati Law Review*, 75 (2006), 7–24, at 13.

[72] *Bork Hearings*, ed. Shaffer, 106.

[73] See e.g. Barnett, *Restoring*; R. Barnett, 'The Ninth Amendment: It Means What it Says', *Texas Law Review*, 85 (2006), 1–85.

different ideological position – now shares Barnett's desire to revivify 'privileges and immunities'.[74]

There are other unexpected wrinkles in the fabric of conservative originalism. Significantly, the famous speech delivered by Attorney-General Meese announcing the arrival of a 'jurisprudence of original intention' was drafted by his chief speechwriter, later an eminent scholar, Gary McDowell,[75] who belonged to the influential Straussian wing of the conservative movement. However, there is an incongruity here, for the Straussians[76] – followers of the German émigré philosopher Leo Strauss (1899–1973) – tend to regard the Founding era with an awkward ambivalence singularly at odds with the conventional flag-waving norms of mainstream conservatism. The Straussians are proudly elitist, prizing their unconventionality and their privileged access to a strain of occult wisdom which their guru transmitted to his disciples over two decades at the University of Chicago between 1949 and 1969, and was then passed from these disciples to subsequent generations of initiates. Straussian conservatives have tied themselves in knots over the years trying to reconcile American patriotism with a fastidious disdain for what – following the insights of Strauss – they identify as the base philosophy of the Founders. Instead, the Straussians champion the high aspirations of the Ancients, and contend that philosophy took a wrong turning during the early modern era when it was perverted by the interest-based ethic of Machiavelli and Hobbes, ignoble philosophers who pandered to the lowest common denominator in humankind. It was, nevertheless, this soiled strain of early modern philosophy which, they contend, left its mark on the Framers' system of Constitutional machinery.[77]

Martin Diamond (1919–77), a former socialist turned Straussian, found certain aspects of the Founding dispiriting. During the early modern era, the ancient notion of an all-encompassing 'polity' or 'regime' had given way to the diminished concept of 'government', to a politics of limited aspirations. Disappointingly, liberalism and modern republicanism were not 'the means by which men ascend to a nobler life'; rather, they were 'simply instrumentalities which solve Hobbesean problems'. The

---

[74] See *McDonald* v. *City of Chicago* 561 US 742 (2010).

[75] McDowell had previously proposed procedural solutions to tackle the problem of judicial overreach: see G. McDowell, 'A Modest Remedy for Judicial Activism', *Public Interest*, 67 (Spring 1982), 3–20.

[76] For the Straussians, see – variously and subjectively – S. Drury, *Leo Strauss and the American Right* (New York, 1997); A. Norton, *Leo Strauss and the Politics of American Empire* (New Haven, 2004); M. Burnyeat, 'Sphinx without a Secret', *New York Review of Books* (30 May 1985), 30–6; C. and M. Zuckert, *The Truth about Leo Strauss* (Chicago, 2006).

[77] K. L. Deutsch, 'Leo Strauss, the Straussians and the American Regime', in *Leo Strauss, the Straussians and the American Regime*, ed. K. L. Deutsch and John A. Murley (Lanham, MD, 1999), 51–67. Cf. P. Rahe, *Republics Ancient and Modern: Classical Republicanism and the American Revolution* (Chapel Hill, 1982).

Constitution and the *Federalist* were almost 'wholly silent' on 'the ends of government'. Whereas the Ancients had 'ranked highly, as objects of government, the nurturing of a particular religion, education, military courage, civic-spiritedness' and so forth, the American Founders made no 'special provision for excellence'. Had the Founders, perhaps, traded high ideals for mere political stability, a government of 'narrow ends'? Indeed, Diamond asked the very Straussian question: 'how might Aristotle rank America?' Diamond answered – with at least a hint of regret – that 'the new political science gave a primacy to the efficiency of means rather than to the nobility of ends'. The Constitution had nothing to do with 'ethical character formation'. Rather, 'the American political system was deliberately tilted to resist, so to speak, the upward gravitational pull of politics toward the grand, dramatic, character-ennobling but society-wracking opinions about justice and virtue'. Nevertheless, Diamond was able to contort his arguments into a far-from-resounding encomium upon the 'solid but low foundation of American life' in the Constitution.[78]

A more direct and less nuanced version of Diamond's complaint appears in the work of the conservative political commentator George F. Will (b. 1941), who popularised the Straussian critique of the Founders and the government they had created. Will castigated Reaganite conservatism as a variant of 'the liberal-democratic political impulse that was born with Machiavelli and Hobbes'. From these early modern bogeymen – the authors of 'the great redefinition' – there derived the modern political enterprise, a dismal project whose 'inadequacy' Will found 'glaring'. Now, instead of an Aristotelean conservatism founded upon the principle of 'what ought to be', there prevailed a scheme of politics which lowered human aspirations. It was a cause of lamentation that the 'Founding philosophy' of the United States stated 'clearly and often, that public-spiritedness is unnatural'. In the Constitution and the *Federalist* the ideal of living 'optimally' had been suborned, replaced with the banal goal of 'regularity'. According to Will, true conservatism followed the lofty normative prescriptions of the Ancients, not the Moderns' descriptive accounts of the lowest common denominators in human nature.[79]

The Straussians have also played a major role in the rehabilitation of the opponents of the Constitution, the Anti-Federalists of 1787–91. Where previously Anti-Federalism had been written off as a kind of naysaying negativity without much substantive ideological content of its

[78] M. Diamond, 'Ethics and Politics: The American Way', in *The Moral Foundations of the American Republic*, ed. R. H. Horwitz, 3rd edn (Charlottesville, 1986), 75–108, at 81, 92, 95; M. Diamond, 'Democracy and the *Federalist*', *American Political Science Review*, 53 (1959), 52–68, at 62, 64, 66; M. Diamond, 'The Separation of Powers and the Mixed Regime' and 'The American Idea of Equality', both in *As Far as Republican Principles Will Admit: Essays by Martin Diamond*, ed. W. Schambra (Washington DC, 1992), 63, 249.

[79] G. F. Will, *Statecraft as Soulcraft* (1984), 23–4, 40–1, 159.

own, the insight of the Straussians brought into focus the *positive* message of the Anti-Federalists. In particular, Straussians recognised that Anti-Federalists articulated a version of the ancient vision of politics as a nursery of virtue and excellence. The central figure in the excavation and recovery of Anti-Federalist ideology was Herbert Storing (1928–77), a Straussian at the University of Chicago.[80] Storing published a pioneering monograph which mapped the ideological contours of Anti-Federalism and also anthologised Anti-Federalist writings.[81] The linkage between the Anti-Federalist espousal of ancient values and the true meaning of the Anti-Federalist-inspired Bill of Rights can be glimpsed in the career of Walter Berns (1919–2015), an originalist, but of a distinctively Straussian cast. Berns favoured, for example, a reading of the establishment clause of the First Amendment which permitted support for religion in the States on a non-preferentialist basis. Surely, Berns reasoned, the Bill of Rights was not intended to restrict the operation of institutions which nourished civic virtue?[82]

The ambiguous status of the Constitution gave rise to an intra-Straussian civil war. While Diamond stood representative of the critical reading of the Constitution, Harry V. Jaffa (1918–2015) insisted that it was mistaken to decouple the Declaration of Independence from the Constitution, and contended that this double-bottomed version of the Founding embodied a high ethical purpose.[83] However, Jaffa was at the patriotic extreme of the Straussian movement, and others questioned his reading of the Founding. Thomas Pangle, for instance, dismissed Jaffa as a vulgar myth-maker whose crude patriotism, which rested on 'thin poetry and compromised scholarship', betrayed the Straussian inheritance.[84]

Superficially, there seems to be some congruence between the Straussian depiction of the Founders – the Anti-Federalists at least – and the historical recovery of classical republicanism. Ralph Lerner, a prominent disciple of Strauss, tellingly described the Supreme Court of the Founding era as 'a republican schoolmaster'. The federal judiciary played the part of 'statesmen-teachers' and 'Platonic Guardians', educating the citizenry in the values requisite for the support of republican

---

[80]M. Dry, 'Herbert Storing: The American Founding and the American Regime', in *Leo Strauss*, ed. Deutsch and Murley, 305–28.

[81] H. Storing, *What the Antifederalists Were For* (Chicago, 1981); *The Complete Anti-Federalist*, ed. H. Storing (7 vols., Chicago, 1981).

[82] W. Berns, *Freedom, Virtue and the First Amendment* (Baton Rouge, 1957); W. Berns, 'Religion and the Founding Principle', in *The Moral Foundations of the American Republic*, ed. R. H. Horwitz, 3rd edn (Charlottesville, 1986), 204–29.

[83]H. V. Jaffa, 'In Defense of Political Philosophy', *National Review* (22 Jan. 1982), 36–44, at 41; H. V. Jaffa, *Original Intent and the Framers of the Constitution* (Washington DC, 1994).

[84]T. Pangle, 'Patriotism American Style', *National Review* (29 Nov. 1985), 30–4, at 32.

self-government. Lerner was characteristically – for a Straussian – grudging in his attitude towards the Federalists: 'how did the Framers expect to sustain and perpetuate a republican regime? The manner in which the Federalists addressed themselves to this question leaves much to be desired.' There was a glaring 'insufficiency' in 'muted' and 'incomplete' Federalist responses to Anti-Federalist charges about how republican virtue might be sustained.[85] However, any notional affinity between the Straussians and the republican turn in historiography turns out to be a mirage. The Straussians were critical of the attempts of historians to ground republican ideology in social context;[86] Gordon Wood, for example, was pigeonholed among the category of 'quasi-Beardians'.[87] On the other hand, Wood castigated the Straussians as 'sanctimonious' textual exegetes and quasi-priestly 'fundamentalists' who knew nothing of proper, context-oriented historical scholarship.[88]

Quirks and tensions of this sort provide merely a prologue to the complex relations between history and originalism. For the Founding era is but one in a succession of receding pasts which inform American Constitutional theory. In the centuries before the Constitution lie the vicissitudes of the English constitution and common law stretching back to Magna Carta, whose memorial at Runnymede was erected by the American Bar Association. Other layers sit between the late eighteenth century and today's topsoil. Arguably, the immediate post-Civil War era of the mid-1860s, not the late eighteenth-century Founding, provides the hinge on which most of modern Constitutional jurisprudence turns, including its most vexing issues, such as substantive due process and the question of whether the Fourteenth Amendment incorporates the Bill of Rights.[89] However, those are matters for another occasion.

The historical distortions which underpin originalism, and the misunderstandings to which it gives rise, present academic historians with major dilemmas. How far should historians divest themselves of their right – perhaps duty – to address the civic needs of the present? On the other hand, to what extent is the historical critique of originalist conclusions inflected by ideological as much as by methodological concerns, and as

[85] R. Lerner, 'The Supreme Court as Republican Schoolmaster', *Supreme Court Review* (1967), 127–80, at 128–9, 156, 159–60.

[86] T. Pangle, *The Spirit of Modern Republicanism* (Chicago, 1988), 36.

[87] M. Zuckert, 'Redefining the Founding: Martin Diamond, Leo Strauss and the American Regime', in *Leo Strauss*, ed. Deutsch and Murley, 235–51, at 242. Charles Beard (1874–1948) had argued in *An Economic Interpretation of the Constitution* (New York, 1913) that the Constitution was a ploy to secure the property of financial-mercantile-creditor elites at the expense of indebted agrarian interests.

[88] G. Wood, 'The Fundamentalists and the Constitution', *New York Review of Books* (18 Feb. 1988), 33–40.

[89] See amidst another vast literature, W. E. Nelson, *The Fourteenth Amendment: From Political Principle to Judicial Doctrine* (Cambridge, MA, 1998).

such to betray the ethos of the academy? Yet disinterested curiosity-driven history does suggest a tantalising third-way alternative to the crudely reductive ideologies of the culture wars, for the conservative enlightenment of late eighteenth-century America is not easily aligned with the values today of either Right or Left. Alas, sophisticated uncertainty of this sort lacks an audience outside the academy; and even those jurists most alert to the dangers of 'law office history' seek decisive answers to real-world legal problems, not a mess of caveats.[90]

[90] Cf. L.W. Levy, 'History and Original Intent', in L. W. Levy, *Original Intent and the Framers' Constitution* (Chicago, 1988), 313.